ME

BY BRENDA UELAND

IF YOU WANT TO WRITE

ME

BRENDA UELAND
from a drawing by Frances Cranmer Greenman

BRENDA UELAND

Me

THE SCHUBERT CLUB
ST. PAUL

Editorial Committee: Bruce Carlson and Tom Tredway

MANUFACTURED IN THE UNITED STATES OF AMERICA

Printed by

North Central Publishing Company, St. Paul, Minnesota

ISBN 0-912373-01-6

CONTENTS

I. CHILDHOOD   3

1

Why I write the book. My grandfather, the farmer-statesman in Norway. My young father digs ditches and becomes an American lawyer. My mother.

2

A child running on a porch. Kindergarten in our house. The hired girls in the attic. The seven children. Driving downtown. Minnesota morning, 1898.

3

Mother's ideas on health. Sunday dinner. Trains are romantic in the Middle West. Our attic and the tank room. Elsa and I wear knee pants. My fight with Sigurd. Miss Linquist and the ghost in our attic.

4

The two forces in me, to be fierce and to be gentle. Disappointed in Christmas presents. My best friend and adventures in the swamp. My lying. Family picnics and being ashamed of them all.

5

Sex attitudes then. My father's law partner is John Lind. High school. Blanche Lane, even fatter, becomes my friend. I am forced to go to dancing school.

Contents

II, HIGH SCHOOL 67

My parents' social life; parties with much culture and no alcohol. "Peer Gynt" comes to town. Shocked at what Lucile tells me about marriage. A nice English teacher. Religion in our house; Torvald asks: "Is God a bird?" My lying again. A music teacher who fed me.

III. COLLEGE 83

1

I go east to college and am shocked to find that I am a card. The money emotions in our family. Father resists automobiles. How my mother contended for her children. A queer adolescent depression.

2

Wells College is remote and safe and not near enough to the trade-unions. I go to Barnard; good professors and bad colds. Richmond Hill Settlement House and a little whiff of Bohemianism.

3

Summer at home. Francesca. On the Minneapolis Tribune; *I begin to walk nine miles a day. Mrs. George Edgar Vincent and Dr. Owre. In love with a city editor with arm garters. The ghost in our attic.*

IV. GREENWICH VILLAGE 121

1

I save three hundred dollars and go to Europe. I persuade poor Father to let me study art. Walking to Columbia every day or across Brooklyn Bridge. The helplessness of the tal-

Contents

ented young. I cut my hair off. Young men are now really attracted to me; I feel wonderfully charming.

2

Father comes to New York and shows his ignorance about Art. Hopelessly in love with a married man. Meriam Cooper, a Southern gentleman.

3

Working for Bruce Barton on Every Week. *An anxious life. Getting married and the War. What the various Uelands felt about the War.*

V. MARRIAGE 173

1

To Philadelphia and I am supported like a regular everyday wife. Some things that were wrong with our marriage. Alone in New York again. I become a little fast. John Reed; Biff.

2

To Cambridge. I am afraid of domesticity, until I sell a story. On East 58th Street. Minneapolis conversation. Regretfully having a baby. I become maternal now and from this time forward will always be kind.

VI. WORK 201

1

Marital misery. To my surprise people are glad when I want a divorce. I become extraordinary, for a short time. Mr. John N. Wheeler. Reading Tolstoy on the train.

2

A staff writer on Liberty *and why I can never ask for good salary. Tomola. The last assignment. Free-lancing and a slump of the Will. The divorce.*

Contents

3

In Stamford; I think Will and physical condition are the panacea. My mother's visit. Her death. My inner struggle; whether to be good or to be remarkable. It may be all right to discipline yourself, but never a child.

4

Fridtjof Nansen.

VII. HOME AGAIN 250

1

The Depression drives me into retreat. My golden Julie with her wonderful frivolity. My work dwindles; financial help takes all the gumption out of me. More Minneapolis talk.

2

Francesca shows me something about music and God. Rolf and painting. Julie becomes sick.

3

Julie is very sick. I like to think I have a mystical experience. Father on religion; his loneliness. At the University. Dr. David Swenson and Plato. My father's death.

4

On learning not to scold people. All mothers should try to be some fun. Working in the garden. Twenty below zero. A hot summer and the house is full of pianos; Seroff.

VIII. THE PRESENT 322

1

I have to say some things above love. Gaby wants to talk to me about it. My symbolic dream: William Blake talks to me in the thunder.

Contents

2

A writing class; the pupils teach me many things. Walking; I find that physical condition is not the panacea, but the Imagination. Am I too much like my Uncle Fred? I look forward to everything, including eternity. I shall always be growing better.

ME

I. CHILDHOOD

1.

Why I write the book. My grandfather, the farmer-statesman in Norway. My young father digs ditches and becomes an American lawyer. My mother.

IT IS NEARLY TEN O'CLOCK IN THE MORNING, AND IT IS JULY 6th, 1938, and I sit here in my square room with green wall-paper. It looks north through a very large square McKinley period window. I look down on our front lawn spreading broad and green to the wooded bank, and there a thicket of criss-cross sumach rises, and above that a high leafy wall of elm trees and box elders. Below is the narrow, dark, smooth boulevard and Lake Calhoun.

It is now, at this moment, a heavy, damp, gray summer day. Yesterday it was blazing—bright and beautiful. Last night there was a wonderful storm. A terrible chariot went bumping over the clouds from St. Paul and back again to Minneapolis. It was as though someone were throwing tanks of water at the corners of the roof and down the gutters.

So here I am, trying to tell the story of myself. I quietly ask, pray, at intervals, to be truthful, simple, and not to put on airs. I ask that it come out transparently, from my true self; that it may be useful to people in some way, throw light on things for them. I ask at least to be interesting and to go straight to the point and that I resist looking up genea-logical facts about my grandfather, who was a Norwegian statesman, and about my mother and father, who were es-pecially fine, clear, high-minded people. For in writing one's life, the first impulse is to read letters and look into albums

3

and not go right to the point, which is: what do I remember and what do I think? This research is really a dawdling and an ambush so that months can be spent in libraries. I have the impulse, but now I curtail it.

Why do I write my autobiography? Two friends thought it was a good idea, and one of them was a publisher. But I find myself afraid to start (we are always afraid to start something that we want to make very good, true, and serious), and when people say: "What are you writing now?" there is a momentary obstruction in my throat and it is hard to get it out: "My autobiography."

Why do I feel apologetic and hang-dog about it? I suppose it is because we are afraid of having people think we think we are important. But we *are* all important, I tell myself. Well, then, it is because I am afraid of making my life sound fancier, nobler, than it is. Or less so, which is just as bad. But then I say to myself consolingly:

"At least I come from a family of such honest, unpretentious people."

My brother Rolf, for example. He is so morbidly afraid of saying what he does not feel that he hardly says anything at all. Why, one night they were speaking of the dedication of books and silent Rolf began to insist that even that harmless practice was a hypocritical and silly thing to do.

"I might," he said, "put a person's name on the page of a book customarily used for dedications. But if so, why not state the facts: i.e., 'I am putting the name of Selma Peterson on this, 1. Because it may give her some slight pleasure to get the publicity. 2. Because of a few cups of coffee she gave me while writing it.'"

So whenever I am anxious about my flamboyance and tendency to show off, I say to myself: "Remember you are related to Rolf. Be more like that. Then it will be all right."

Now the interesting thing about my life is my inner life, and the obscure, unknown, noble, witty, angelic people in it—

my family and my friends. I have seen and known a few famous people. But I never paid much close attention to these, or liked them a thousandth as well as my friends, who have never been heard of.

It was Gertrude Hodson who first said that I should write the book.

"Why, Gertrude," I said (because she is one of those people who make me feel like joking), "there is nothing especially interesting in my life. There are no 'memoirs' in it. I never was an ambassador or a courtesan. I never knew Ellen Terry or Max Beerbohm or Wild Bill Hickock. Yes, I knew Theodore Dreiser once. But I never took the trouble to listen to him or to ask any questions. Why, the most dramatic thing I could put in the book would be to tell of that never-to-be-forgotten day when Gertrude Hodson, swimming before our house in Lake Calhoun, switched from dog-fashion to the breast stroke."

But my inner life, like everybody's in the world, is interesting. I have much to say about that. I have many thoughts about how I and others might become better and happier; about how it feels to be a woman and the limitations of that (which are most of them our own making and not imposed on us, as the old-fashioned, aggrieved feminists like to think); and about what women might become, and how, when they see this light and act upon it, in one generation the world will be filled with the most wonderful children.

But there is this dilemma about the book. I have been divorced and have had a very unconventional life. I have had several love affairs. Now since it is my inward life that is interesting, these experiences have affected me very much and should be told. And I will not write any lies in the book (consciously), or make myself out to be other than I am. But I will not injure anyone by exposing him, since this is an unfair and unchivalrous thing to do.

Well, now my life. Now I begin.

I am forty-six years old. I will be forty-seven in October. The word sounds old. Some women may shudder to say it and once in a while even I have the faintest echo of a shudder in myself. For example, I read in the newspaper: "Woman hurt in auto accident. Mrs. Gus Johnson of St. Paul, 34," ...

"Poor thing!" I think in passing, and see her middle-aged figure and gold inlays in front, and eye-glasses. And then I think with a tiny surprise: "But look. Here I am, or think I am, clear, nimble, bouncey, young and romantic, and I am even twelve years older!"

But I don't seem to be really depressed by it. As I write this, between sentences I thoughtfully brush my hair so that it is all standing on end. It is black and not gray at all. When I look in the glass it seems to me I do not look middle-aged, but quite young and handsome, though I may be editing my looks; that is, looking in the glass I may instantaneously see something that is not there.

But I certainly feel physically young, easy, and tireless. Presently I will go for a six-mile walk (wishing that I had time to go twenty), and then I will swim for a half-mile in the lake, when it is like yellow glass in the late afternoon.

I am wearing, now, faded-blue tight denim trousers and very thick-soled brogues and a yellow cotton shirt which is tied under the collar by a green silk handkerchief with white stars on it.

I was born in this white wooden house on a lake forty-six years ago. What is Time? What has elapsed between that Then and this Now (myself in denim trousers at this typewriter)? Only Time, a nothing, comes between me and my young and comely parents of that day. Wipe out Time and in the next room I am being born. It was my mother's room and it has a Franklin stove in it and a bay of windows toward the east. She was thirty. (I can see how she *looked* at thirty, because she was all her life very clear, smooth, and beautiful.

But I cannot imagine her ever *feeling* thirty, that uneasy, mistake-making, wrong-track unphilosophical age.)

My father was thirty-eight. I am sure he paced because he always did during hard lawsuits. Dr. Tom Roberts, with his blond walrus mustache, was a fine ornithologist and our family doctor, and he said when I appeared: "This one has very dark plumage."

There were already three little girls in the house, Anne, Elsa, and Dorothy, and so they were momentarily disappointed in me because by that time they thought a boy would be an interesting change.

Mother used to say that it was the most beautiful, gemlike, radiant October day that she had ever seen. I liked to think that this was so, because I like weather so much, all kinds of it, and especially in Minnesota, where the light can be so pure that the grass is emerald and the lake sapphire and the red sumach like ruby glass. And whenever my mother said it was a beautiful day when I was born, I would secretly say to myself: "Why, of course it was. Because I myself have such a warm, generous, radiant, jolly nature. October people are all that way. There is blood in their faces and green hazel in their eyes, and their black hair flourishes." This sounds like self-love, and so it is. There has always been a great deal of it in me, especially when I was younger.

But now, without fumbling in the files, I will tell what I remember about my parents. You will see how little I know about them, and that inaccurately. Or rather I know *all* about them, but no facts.

My father came from Norway to Minnesota when he was eighteen, and his father was Ole Gabriel Ueland, a poor farmer and a great Norwegian statesman at the same time. His meager rocky farm was high in the barren mountains above the North Sea.

Ole Gabriel Ueland had great native ability and hardly any schooling. A story says that, when a youth, he went to the parson to be examined for his qualifications to teach. "Can you read?" asked the parson. "Yes, I can even read a book I never saw before." I know vaguely that he had so much curiosity about mathematics that he worked and puzzled at it himself—at algebra and solid geometry. And he was so interested in astronomy that without help, as a boy, he made astronomical maps and a wooden solar system to make the universe clear to himself. "Walking with him on starlight nights," Father said, "he would point out and explain planets, stars, and constellations."

Now this seems wonderful to me. The drive that sends a person, now and then, beyond what is convenient and dutiful. How amazing! How rare! Yes, that is being a sky rocket. Every night of my life I look at the stars with aesthetic joy and intellectual guilt, for I do not know one from the other and have no clear conception of where the moon is in relation to the sun. I know just enough to make others, in social conversation, feel that I know something about it and they do not. Yes, I admire Ole Gabriel Ueland.

The Ueland farm was in the heights that run parallel to the seacoast. The mountains were so close to the farm buildings that they served as pastures and my father, as a boy, herded sheep and goats on these mountains, and on clear days he could see a narrow strip, deeper blue than the sky, and knew it was the North Sea stretching over to Scotland, with no skerry or island to shelter the rocky coast.

Ole Gabriel Ueland was the leader of the Norwegian parliament for about forty years. I think that what he did was to get the franchise for the farmers of Norway. Before him, only a few of the official class could vote. Once someone said to Oscar I of Sweden that, as the king of two countries, he must be overburdened with work, and he smiled and said: "Oh, not at all. Norway is governed by a Klokker, and in Sweden I have so many great nobles to manage affairs." A

Klokker is the leader of the singing in a country church choir. Ole Gabriel Ueland was one of these.

His picture is now in this room, and he has small intelligent eyes set deep, and broad cheekbones, a fringe of light whiskers framing his lower face, and dark hair that lies in smooth slabs and twists into his ears. He has a big nose: "the Ueland nose," my brothers, who all have it, call it ruefully. And Father too was humorously troubled by his nose, which he thought was unusually big and square. (I am the only one in the family with a sharper nose, though I admire the Ueland nose and prefer it.)

After Ole Gabriel Ueland's death, Björnsen wrote a poem about him, and the manuscript is framed in the library downstairs, and we are very proud of it. Except Rolf and Sigurd, who never show pride, but substitute humorous disdain instead.

Well, when Ole Gabriel died in 1870, my father was eighteen, and everything abruptly changed for him. A farmer in Houston County in Minnesota returned on a visit to Norway. He infected half the population with what was called "the American fever." My father caught it in its most virulent form. "No more amusement of any kind, only brooding on how to get away to America. It was like a desperate case of homesickness reversed."

I have always remembered how my father said that. It is such a sharp description of the feeling. From that phrase I know how it was with him—the longing, the longing, the insatiable chest-filling longing! a vacuum, an emptiness pressing on the heart. I have it too, at least once in every two days, for something, I know not what.

Father argued, importuned, nagged at his mother to let him go. At last, on his solemn promise to be back within five years, she consented. She stocked him with new clothes, a feather quilt and with a little money in addition to the ninety-three dollars inherited from his father. "I started, equipped as well as the boy of the tale, who left his home for adventures with 'horse, hound and a hundred dollars.'"

He came on a sailing ship with thirty others. Then west by train. "We saw mountains which must have been the Alleghenies and felt much depressed. Was that America? Had we been fooled? We expected to see flat ground with no timber or boulders to clear. When we came far enough to see that kind of country, our spirits rose again."

My darling father! I shiver now; there is a chill through jaws and flanks when I think of him again so minutely. Love, sadness, pride: there is much emotion in me about him.

"My fellow travelers," he has written, "took tickets for Houston, Minnesota, all apparently heading for the place of that farmer whom they had seen in Norway. Seeing this, I took a ticket to the next station beyond, Rushford. It took some little courage to cut loose from all I knew, and plunge into the unknown, rather than crowd myself on somebody's hospitality. I was the youngest of the lot, only eighteen, and it was so far, so far from home!"

That is how he has written it, with an exclamation point after "home." And as I read it, some spring is released so that I swallow, and incipient tears make my eyeballs ache. Why? Sorrow, admiration, I suppose. To go on alone and a little farther than the others, that was like him. Not to stay cozy and warm in the midst of one's crowd, the herd, but to go on beyond, if only just a little. Oh, I admire that very much. I wish I could do that. I never have. I wish I would do it sometime before I die.

There is a small framed photograph of Father, and it hangs in the upstairs hall. This is a shabby, high-ceilinged room full of light from three gigantic windows toward the south. There is a blackboard along one wall, built in as in a schoolroom, with a railing for erasers. Mother had this put in when we were very small, to draw on.

But Father's picture. He is eighteen in it, "a newcomer."

He wears a dark sailorlike jacket and a white shirt with a loose bow tie under his defiant and jaunty chin. The waistcoat buttons shine like metal. He has thick, longish, chestnut-blond hair, brushed fiercely back from his splendid forehead, and he has the blond Mongolian look of Scandinavians, for his light eyes are slanted up by his ruddy cheekbones. His nose is blunt, square, and large, but there is clear-cut carving around the nostrils. And then his mouth: it is a wide, horizontal mouth with a beautiful line where the lips meet and curl scornfully back. Michelangelo never carved a more beautiful mouth.

His personality shows so well in this photograph: so resilient, truculent, and dauntless. Such style, such swing. Such a vigorous brain and spirit. Compact as a thunderbolt. He would work so fiercely and with such a rush at any problem that presented itself. If only I could fight that way, boldly and fiercely but with such good nature, without one whit of malice or ill will. Only the gods can contend that way.

Yes, I love my father. If you keep reading this book you will see that I never got to know him well and was always afraid of him and uneasy with him because he had not one trace of that sympathetic imagination (like my mother's and most women's) which makes one able to stand in other people's shoes and see just how they feel. So I never really enjoyed being with him. That is, I never felt free with him, self-forgetful, jokey.

Father, young and alone in Minnesota, worked on farms. He worked in Minneapolis digging the Washington Avenue sewer, the first in the city, with a pick and shovel. The wages were $1.75 a day, a top-notch price for common labor. In a little second-story room he lived with two Norwegians, a cabinetmaker and a sailor, thus reducing the cost of living from $4.00 to about $1.50 a week. "That was all nice and satisfactory," he said, "except sleeping three in a bed."

Poor Father. This was his first Christmas Eve in America:

"It was not so pleasant as those I was used to at home in Norway. The roommate and I tried to do something (the sailor had left the city) to celebrate, so we bought some alcohol punch. Neither of us over-indulged, but for some reason he turned awfully sick and vomited and vomited on the floor. It made a terrible stench in that close little room, impossible to stand, so it was either clean up after him or leave the room. I chose to leave and having no place to go, walked up and down Washington Avenue for hours, then back to look for a change in conditions; finding none, then went out again; this again and again nearly all night. Walking up and down the street in the bitter cold I thought of Christmas nights at home in Norway, how the floors had been scrubbed clean; the wood blazing in the fireplace; the house lighted up with five-pronged candles with a little powder in the crutch for explosion to delight the children; all members of the family in clean holiday clothes; the smelling and tasting of the cooking in the kitchen for the great evening meal; the table spread with the best food we ever tasted, and foaming home-brewed beer passing around in Father's silver tankard. I felt homesick that night."

For five years he worked as a day laborer and on farms. At night he studied law. In the sixth year, May, 1877, he was admitted to the bar. He could write this letter to his mother, whom he never saw again:

You will see ... that I have successfully passed the examination. Only five passed, four Americans and I. I think I got through the best of the five. And so I have reached that far.

I have written you before that I earned enough to pay my expenses. To be entirely candid, I have been compelled to practice the strictest economy possible. I have not told you that before because I knew it would take but little to make you worry on my account. Now when I expect to earn more, I will admit that my money affairs are not in good condition. I have however due me sufficient to pay all I owe (which isn't much) so the worst is only that my clothes are threadbare and shabby. That will also soon be "all right" as the Americans say.

A little later he was taken into a young people's literary society of an American church, where he became acquainted with a girl of fifteen, "the prettiest there and probably in the whole city."

"But," Father would say, "she was not only considered by *me* to be the prettiest girl in the city. She just *was* the prettiest, that was all there was to it." Ten years later they were married.

People, strangers, still come up and speak to me about my mother, with love in their faces and a certain look. They seem to feel sorrowfully that I may be very fine, but I will never, never be as wonderful as she was. Do they do that about other mothers? I suppose so. Still, there was something special about her.

A little photograph of mother at fifteen also hangs in the upstairs hall, where the yellow sunlight falls through the banisters and is shattered on the floor and blazes in white highlights on the railings. She has black hair, smoothed back from a noble, childlike, beautiful face. She has pansy-black eyes full of great but unpressing intelligence. My eyes, for instance: I feel there is intelligence in them but also a kind of striving, a kind of glare.

Mother was an American. Her name was Clara Hampson. She was beautiful, and her beauty lasted all her life. She had the most perfectly carved, aquiline nose I have ever seen. But women with beautiful faces often have commonplace or weak or lumpy bodies. But hers was graceful and fine, and all the details were perfect, such as the elbows, wrists and knees, and the way they bent and were wrought. A German countess once gave her some hereditary lace sleeves because her hands alone deserved them. She had lovely feet, solid and smooth, like those of the Diocletian Venus. (She would never wear corsets or high heels.) As long as she lived, her texture, her color, were pellucid and clear, fresh and comely. She never had any of that muddiness or opaqueness which is the only ugly thing about age.

Her father had died at thirty-three, his health broken by the Civil War. His sickly, dispirited young widow, with my mother and her brother Fred, came from Akron, Ohio, to Minneapolis. They lived some place "over a hardware store" and were very poor. My mother was gay, though, and popular, and talented at plastering scrolls of curls on her forehead. At fifteen she was teaching in the Emerson School.

That was characteristic of her, not to mind being poor. With no family backing, she always seemed to be serenely gay, as a little girl, and ever afterwards. She never had any social inhibitions (like me) or any diffidence, never any of that thing that makes most of us stiffen ever so faintly when we meet strangers—afraid of people richer than ourselves, afraid of those who might bore us. She was really remarkable—so transparent, so flawlessly open and interested and tender to all.

One thing seems curious. She seems to have been socially acceptable from the first to prosperous and fashionable people, in spite of the hardware store and an ailing unknown young mother from Ohio. Perhaps it was because the city was smaller and it was nearer to pioneer times.

When Father and Mother were married, they lived first on Fifteenth Avenue South in a narrow brick Gothic house with wooden lace on the eaves and a purple and green stained glass in the windows. It is still there, though that part of town is decayed and rotting now. First Anne was born and then Elsa, and they remember living there: the gum that old Mr. Holtzermann gave them when they walked together over into his garden. And when they walked together over to Dr. Bendeke's house, they remembered the huge stuffed deer's head and Francesca practicing on her violin.

Then in 1890 my father built this large, square, wooden house on the south shore of Lake Calhoun, where I live. At that time it was far out in the country, five miles from the courthouse. A pretty narrow boulevard came around the lake with scallops of clipped willow trees all along it. We had five acres. And across Richfield Road, which led the hayracks and the milk wagons to the far country, to Edina and Eden Prairie and beyond, there were woods.

2.

A child running on a porch. Kindergarten in our house. The hired girls in the attic. The seven children. Driving downtown. Minnesota morning, 1898.

THIS IS MY FIRST MEMORY:

It is a summer day. The long front porch crosses the front of the house and then swings in a curve to the east. There are white balustrades and slender wooden pillars with carved capitals. They alternate, a square Corinthian column and then a slim round Doric one. The porch is of painted wood and sounds hollowly as you run up and down it. And there is something about running along and around the corner and back again that is like the pleasure of running on the deck of a vast, wooden, feeble ship.

I am running up and down our long porch with a child of my own age, in pointless joyousness.

As I run I see my reflection in the windows. Black mirrors, they make. I am a tiny child, perhaps three, in a thin white dress-up dress. It makes a white transparent lawn pyramid to the knees. I have a round head of short black hair. The other child is in white too, and we are friends and chase each other and it is very exciting, pounding along the reverberating wooden porch.

I have a thin gold chain around my neck and there is a

tiny gold heart on it. Perhaps this is the day I lost the gold heart in the slot in the lock of the folding doors to the dining room. These are double folding doors, as high as the ceiling, of oak and paneled. There is a little slot under the latch. I had the tiny gold heart pinched in my thumb and forefinger and I dropped it and lost it forever in the lock of the door.

So this is the first day that I remember, and it is festive and joyful. But there is also a shock and pain in it because I lost that little gold heart. I suppose it is still there. For years afterwards, I would think with a kind of awe: it must be still there!

The next memory. I am in my mother's room in our big baby carriage. But I am in it for fun and am not the current baby in the family. That is, there was a regular baby for it, who I think was Arnulf.

There are no baby carriages like it now. It was a big wicker basket on four large wooden wheels which were not wire but had light wooden spokes and fellies and a round hub. I sat in the carriage and manipulated it by reaching over the edges of the basket and turning the wheels by hand. I had wheeled myself before my mother's mahogany dressing table, which came from England and has a large standing oval mirror on it.

From the baby carriage I looked into the mirror. I can see what I saw then plainly. I had short ruffling black hair cut roundly like a little boy's and dark eyes and tiny square teeth. And I felt disappointed about my looks. I thought that in a way perhaps I was good-looking (and with a kind of hope, I looked at myself and away and back again), but my kind of looks did not please me, was hardly to my taste at all. My taste has changed since then. For I think now, from the photographs, that I was a very handsome, a beautiful, burning, straight-nosed, black-eyed child.

The memory is here cut off. I have a faint ghost of a feeling that my mother told me gently to be careful not to bump into the dressing table too hard. But I cannot be sure. My mother uttered remarkably few dont's to her seven children. I can remember being told "don't" only once and that was when, absent-mindedly fiddling, I had knocked over a glass dish on the sideboard for the fourth or fifth time. Mother had asked me pleasantly to be careful about it. At last she said, with real vexation in her voice, "No. You must not do that." It was such an extraordinary thing that it stood out unpleasantly.

But to return to looks: I have always been so interested in beauty or the lack of it. My mother, I heard everybody say, was beautiful. I could see it when I grew up but not as a child. I wished that she looked more like Mrs. Hush, and was ashamed of her when she came to school to visit. Now if only she looked like Mrs. Hush, who had a snub nose and freckles! And Margaret Hush, her daughter, was in the schoolroom with me and was dappled with freckles like a trout, and I thought she was perfectly beautiful and kept my eyes playing lovingly over her merry face in long gazes. My standards were my own in a queer insistent way.

Another aesthetic conviction was the importance of oval fingernails. All people's fingernails got my scrutiny, the first thing. (My own were rather square.) Then there was at about the same time my passionate admiration for flat ears, for fierce athletic ears, tiger-cub ears. Mine did not satisfy me. They were fairly flat but the lobe of the left one was a sixteenth of an inch too narrow.

Mother was one of the first to become interested in kindergartens and to promote them. So we had a kindergarten in our house downstairs in the high sitting room where the rectangular shafts of sunlight made such a bright morning coziness and the dust motes whirled in them like microscopic stars.

I remember my first day at kindergarten. Jamie Johns was there, who seemed much older and very imposing, like a university man comparatively. He might have been bearded, in view of my respect for him.

The teacher asked me to lead the line of marching children, and whatever I did the others would do. All I could think of was to pound one fist on the other; this seemed silly and embarrassing, and though I was awed to see that all the others in the line did it, still, it seemed an asinine thing and I felt ashamed of it, and sheepish that I could think of nothing more interesting or with more variety to it. Jamie Johns thought it was sappy and burlesqued it. Yet all the time there was a feeling of pleasure and power that I led and they did as I ordered.

Kindergarten was a lovely thing. Everything. The long low tables with inch-squares marked on them. The galumphing games on the shiny floor, like drop-the-handkerchief. That game song where you put the right name in every time, such as: "While Eddie will show us just what to do." The pretty flute-voiced teacher and the young lady at the upright piano.

In the latter half we went to the tables. We strung colored beads. We sewed with pretty wool on cards. We cut out colored paper and pasted it. What wonderful creative absorption! What comfort and fun! That absorbed, hushed, happy feeling, infinitely slow and leisurely, without egotism and fear of failure. After a lifetime of anxiety and strain I have found that that is the way to work at everything.

Later I went to kindergarten at another house in Linden Hills. It was a half-mile walk. I remember that once I was late and had the inner guilt, turmoil and anxiety—*Angst-weh,* I called it afterwards when I was in New York, when I was married or in love, or in general trouble. "Anxious-woe" is the translation, a perfect word for it. Another word my husband invented was "the floops"; for it is as though a dreadful skittering feeling passed in scalloping waves across the chest. Helen Baxter calls it "butterflies in the stomach." That is a good expression for it too.

Well, I have often thought how *angstweh,* the floops—that feeling we experience when we find there is no money in the bank, when we have to look for work, or get a divorce, or have failed horribly in something—that feeling is never worse than the day you were late for kindergarten. I extract a little courage out of this thought.

Another good idea of my mother's was the blackboard she had built in along the wall of the upstairs hall. It was like a real school blackboard with its long rail for chalk and erasers. And she made drawings on it, first for Anne and Elsa, which they copied. And as the younger children came along and copied the older ones, all got to be exceptionally good draftsmen, I think. Rolf at seven could draw a train coming around a corner toward the spectator in perfect perspective. Or when Torvald was a little boy of four, long before he went to school, he would call downstairs:

"How do you spell hooken?"

"Hooken, dear?"

"Yes. Hooken ladder."

We had changing enthusiasms in our drawings. Sometimes it was Indians, then ships, then ice boats, then Santa Claus and reindeer. I always drew knights, soldiers, and horses. Never ladies and fancy clothes.

But now I must tell how life was in our house. We went to bed with candles, and then there were lamps. In the sitting room, for reading, there was a round globe like a pink moon. Later there was gas and the wonderful innovation of gas mantles and their blazing light.

There were two hired girls in the house, and they slept in a plastered bedroom on the third floor, in thin iron bedsteads with brass knobs. The rest of the third floor was an attic, a forest of raw two-by-fours and a hot smell.

Upstairs in the white barn the hired man slept above the

carriage room in a bedroom that was plastered and painted but a little smelly like himself. He could hear Lady Mane, our horse, stamping below and the cow munching and fragrantly breathing, and the chickens in the vile-smelling whitewashed basement letting out now and then a sweet musical caw in their sleep.

The first two hired girls I remember were Emily and Betty, and they could not seem more dear, important and distinguished to me, if they had been Lord Asquith and Abraham Lincoln. Emily was tall, thin, aristocratic and nobly wise and she married the gardener of Jim Hill in St. Paul. Betty was Scandinavian with lashless dark blue eyes and apt to have damp little cold sores in the corners of her mouth—a damp skin too, and moist hands. But she moved fast and was a wonderful unsmiling cut-up and joker. That running up and down the back stairs and springing out to say "Boo!" so that your heart split, and catching you by the ankle in the dark. Oh, my!

As for the children in the family, first there was Anne, pretty and brown-eyed and fiery. Then Elsa, tall and looking like a blond boy-angel, slowly striding and thoughtful. Then myself. Then four boys: Sigurd, Arnulf, Rolf and Torvald. In a large family the older children snub the next younger one and ditch him and run out of his life as much as possible. So I did not see much of Anne and Elsa. Between Elsa and me there had been Dorothy, who died at two, just after my birth. And I used to think about her and study her picture—such a clear golden child—because she would have been my natural partner, my ally, I used to think regretfully.

Dorothy's death was due to some unexpected freak of pneumonia, and it apparently had a terrible effect on my parents. They could not bring themselves ever to speak of it, ever to say her name. Just once Mother talked of it thirty years later. She said she had worked diligently with Anne and Elsa, kept notebooks on them and written down all they said, and used all her imagination to interest them and lead them out. She was apparently setting out to be the best, most thorough, wise mother and teacher in the world. But Dorothy's death disheartened her. She let up on her resolutions when I came, she said, and neglected me perhaps.

As for Father, when he was seventy years old, once I was good-naturedly arguing with him because he was objecting to Mother's working so hard at the State Capitol for child labor and other reforms, and I was defending her work (as I should have), for his objections were, in a way, a kind of masculine jealousy. Finally I happened to say: "But you should not have had so many children." His expression changed immediately to a vanishing flash of anguish, and he said: "Our only regret is that we lost one." Only once in many years did one see his face open that way and show his soul. And so I saw then that either my parents had very deep feelings about children, or it must be inconceivably terrible to lose a child.

Since I had not Dorothy, I was disdainfully compelled to play with Sigurd, who was younger than I. He was blond, looked Norwegian, a funny little boy with green eyes and long tangling eyelashes and a hole of a dimple in one cheek when he smiled. He was easy to tease because of this dimple. He used to tie rags on his shoes and say he was a soldier. Sometimes he would pose before the mirror with his chin thrust forward. He thought it receded and did not look fighty enough.

And pressing along right after Sigurd in the family came Arnulf, slim and frail, with long silken pale hair and large dark eyes, very beautiful and wan. Mother had a theory that baldness came from very short hair; so our boys had a thick, longish thatch of it until years of accumulated indignation won them a trip to the barber. Contrariwise, the girl children, like myself, had for a long time short, shingled hair.

It took quite a long time to name us, and in the interval Father would suggest horrible things like "Ole" and "Knute" and "Dagfinn." Sigurd was "Boy" until Arnulf was born and they were forced to give him something distinguishing. As for Arnulf, when they told him at last that "Arnulf" was his name, he said: "No, I want it to be Albert." He accepted it, however, when they told him that Arnulf meant "eagle-wolf."

Anne and Elsa ate downstairs at "the big table" in the evening, that is, in the dining room with Father and Mother, or I should say Papa and Mama, for it was not until we were eighteen or twenty that we all changed, rather solemnly and prissily, to "Mother and Father."

Sigurd and Arnulf and I had to eat in the upstairs hall at a square kindergarten table. We had very weak cocoa and bread with butter and thin jelly on it. As time went on I, and Sigurd too, felt very much aggrieved that we had to eat upstairs. How about Anne and Elsa? we cried nasally. It wasn't fair! "Well, Elsa ate at the big table when she was eight, and I am seven and three-quarters." I finally went on a kind of hunger strike and got promoted to the big table.

Mother was very calm and dear. She had a lovely friendly matter-of-fact voice when she talked. She called me "B'enna" affectionately. There was not much patting or hugging or kissing—oh, sometimes a slanting kiss toward the cheek— and I was glad of it and had no wish for it. In fact we would all have felt embarrassment. Father, for example, wanted to hug us sometimes and would humorously make us "rub noses" with him, and he called me "Poompy"; I had a vague idea that I was a pet of his. But this rubbing noses and his hugs were an embarrassing ordeal and I did not like them, though I tried to be polite about it.

But Mother's tranquillity, her calmness! I remember other grown-up ladies speaking of it with admiration. When a child fell down, Mother made no special rush and showed no agitation or anxiety. "Well, dear, too bad. Oh, dear, did it hurt?" Still there was nothing of that loathsome willed detachment of the psychologist. No, it was warm and really sympathetic.

Now, in 1938, I think of myself as liking wild freedom and recklessness in children. But here I live alone in this large house and have blessèd silence and emptiness all day long. Well, Mother had it full of children, her own and all the others. She loved her house and the few good pieces of furniture and the paintings on the wall and her grandfather's gilt mirror. Yet we played hockey downstairs in our long paneled hall, our principal living room. The goal was at each end. We took up the rugs. There were perhaps ten or twelve children, and we all had sticks and a puck and we played fiercely all afternoon. I cannot remember being told that we should not, or even that "today is not the day for it."

There were occasional punishments. They were very simple and effective, but nobody seemed to feel very badly. The punishment was to go to the bathroom and lock ourselves in for a little while.

To make dinner endurable, we were supposed not to sing or to clatter spoons and forks while eating, or waiting for dessert, or to balance them on water glasses and so on. If a spoon clattered to the table three or four times, we had to "leave the table until dessert." Mother did not put in her voice an inflection of crossness or annoyance. Sometimes it was a little firm, but usually it was just conversational. There was no dreadful calmness and self control in it. She just told us what we should do.

Perhaps the best way to show the difference between then and now is to tell of a trip downtown. It was only four miles, but it was a slowly unfolding, fascinating adventure, a journey, a voyage.

There was no boulevard in front then. The lake came just to the edge of our wooded bank, and sometimes in rainy years our green-painted steps led right down into the water. But when we drove downtown, we went down our long dirt driveway to Richfield Road and then turned into the pretty boulevard that led around the lake. Our horse was Lady Mane, such a darling horse, such a person! She was a huge dark bay and she had been in races, I was able to boast. "Yes, sir, Lady could run a mile in a minute or something." And indeed, when trotting along and our carriage came up even with some other equipage, her head would go up and her velvet ears turned back and she so nobly wanted to race, although her steps were getting a little jerky and short.

"Yes," Mother would say on a summer morning, "we will go downtown, dear. You and Sigurd can go."

We were brushed and dressed by Betty. I wore my boy's cap. The hired man hitched up Lady in the barn and I hastened out to help him. Even now I could twist all those straps in their various ways, in the dark. The hired man's name was Gus, but Mother always called him "August." She did not like Gus as a name. It was just as for many years she called Pete, a kind of sinister ruffianly Swede who worked around here, "Mr. Gunderson." I see now that she did it to build up his self-respect, not because she objected to saying the word "Pete," although that too was hard for her, as it would be hard for her to say "Gosh."

Then Gus—no, I guess then it was Alfred, a big young man with a red face like the Duchess's in "Alice in Wonderland," who was eager to weigh two hundred pounds so that he could be a policeman.

Alfred drove out of the barn with Lady and the carriage. It was a big strong graceful family carriage. There was a whipsocket and a whip in it. There were two adorable, be-gemmed, polished lamps with kerosene in them, to be lighted at night. I can still feel those lamps under my fingers, with a big ruby in each. The top of the carriage was down. On the high front seat Alfred and two small children could sit. On the back seat there was plenty of room for three people.

Mother was all dressed up. But she was always beautifully dressed. I never saw her in anything homely, or in a hurriedly-put-on house-dress. I never saw her in an apron or a casual sweater. No, she always dressed like a lovely dignified lady. She wore now her summer straw hat with a veil floating about it and she wore brightly clean white shoes and a white linen dress with a jacket. The jacket had much elaborate sewn braid and heavy lace on it.

We went out to the carriage. Sigurd with his long blond hair, ruffled blouse and tight knee pants, sat in the back seat with Mother, throwing horse chestnuts. But I sat in front with Alfred. I wanted to see to it that Alfred did not use the whip *as a whip*. It was all right perhaps for him to gently flick the flies off Lady with the whip, but he couldn't flick it *at her*. No, I couldn't stand that. I couldn't stand it even if a hired man spoke gruffly to Lady. No, he must be very polite to her, pleasant-voiced and conciliatory.

We wheeled slowly down the drive. Mother had to tell me again to be careful not to stick my legs out and touch the wheel, because it was not safe. Now there was the boulevard curving all around the lake toward the far-away courthouse tower. We could just barely see the tower, red and dim and four-cornered above the trees. It was a soft, dirt, hoof-thudding boulevard, and between the scallops of willows we could see the still glass lake and smell it.

Now just where the boulevard came to our land and had to turn off toward Lake Harriet, there was the Big Rock—that is, it was about as big as a trunk—and here there was an open sandy beach with yellow sunbeams moving in dancing network under the water.

We would drive Lady and the carriage right into the water, and she would put her head down and dawdlingly drink, or pretend to drink, looking up at the horizon after soaking her nose in it, the water sluicing out around the bit. "Oh, she has had enough. She is just fooling," we would say tenderly, and wheel in the water (look! it comes way up to the hubs!) and drive out and on our way again.

And so we trotted noiselessly along the boulevard and after

what seemed like a long, long dreamy time we came to the
Iron Bridge. Actually it was about three blocks from home.
And then we would say: "Do you suppose she wants another
drink?", for here there was a horse fountain. I would jump
down and unloose her check-rein. I liked this. I was always
thinking about check-reins and whether they were too tight or
not. We looked at other horses and examined their check-reins
and were distressed about them often.

"Well, that is enough. She is just fooling again," we said,
and on we drove, dreamily clopping along. A bright Minnesota day. There is nothing so beautiful. The air is so clear that
sky and grass and flowers are almost like colored glass, lighted
from behind. Far away the yellow and red wheels of carriages
flashed blazing white lights from their spokes. When the carriage spokes flashed white that was always a sign of a bright,
joyful, jolly summer day.

Mother went shopping in Goodfellow's Drygoods Store
and at The Glass Block. It was an intermittently heart-sink-
ing experience, because I would look around and she would
be lost among all the people. Or Sigurd would be lost. But
then I saw her again. I liked the baskets that ran overhead
on whirring wires and came to a clicking stop at the cash
girl's high desk.

Then we drove over to Hennepin Avenue. There was no
pavement there, though it was the center of town, but just a
broad dirty road with deep bumps and pits in it. We went to
Mr. Dassett the Meat Man's and to Mr. H. A. Child the
Groceryman's.

Mother bought many things to which we paid no attention.
And also she got crackers, which we ate in the carriage on the
long drive home. As she did not believe in shortening, in lard,
the crackers we ate on the way home were water crackers, thin,
round, water crackers perforated with many pinpricks; or
Educator crackers, square, hard and tasteless; or Benz crackers as hard as rock. Or else we were allowed to have absurd

inedible things known as "egg biscuits." These were fat with petals and thinly covered with a glazed skin, and inside there was a tasteless dry powder. It is astonishing to think we could get them down, but we ate these by the dozen and thought they were delicious. I was always deeply interested in eating, and presently I began to be a little fat. Francesca has told me since that I was really not fat then, but just sturdy. The genuine fatness did not come until fourteen or so. But they teased me and I was anxious about it inwardly.

Of course the very nicest trips downtown in the carriage were to see circus parades. Then we always hitched Lady blocks away, with her back turned to the parade, "because of the elephants." We lifted out of the carriage the iron weight on its long strap, and snapped it to her bridle, hoping anxiously that she would not turn her head and catch a glimpse over her blinders.

We always contrived to see the parade, if possible, coming and going, cutting across town in nervous excitement to intercept it. I can remember the excitement of hearing Mother read from the morning paper:

"Parade leaves Nicollet and Tenth Street at 10:15, crosses to 5th and then down Hennepin at . . . returning to the circus grounds, etc., etc." These words still shoot excitement into me.

Driving home from the parade, Lady would clop-clop heavily and peacefully along, and going down hill was always fun, for at the bottom of each hill there was over the culvert a bridge of wooden planks. We waited joyfully for the carriage to bounce over these, helping with our united weight. Fun!

3.

*Mother's ideas on health. Sunday dinner. Trains are romantic
in the Middle West. Our attic and the tank room. Elsa and I
wear knee pants. My fight with Sigurd. Miss Lindquist and
the ghost in our attic.*

MY MOTHER HAD MANY HEALTH IDEAS. SHE PUT ME OUT IN
the sun when I was a baby, a startling, unheard of thing, and
I was so darkly sunburned that Mr. Cohen, the joking bald
lawyer who came to Sunday dinner, called me "the Eskimo."
The little boys, as naked as cupids, walked all over the lawn
all day long. Sometimes Rolf carried a tiny pink parasol and
an Easter basket.

And Mother had some ideas about diet, which was extraordinary for that time. She thought that bananas were very
bad, and pie and vinegar. Salad in those days was wet lettuce
on a plate with vinegar and sugar on it, but Mother discarded
this horror for French dressing with lemon. She had us all
eating apples and oranges between meals and all the time.
There were always crates and barrels of them in the cellar.
She thought that tea and coffee were very bad, "a stimulant."
We were not allowed to have either until we were twenty-five,
if she could help it, though we laughed at her and defied her.
"Why, if Mother went down on the Titanic and were the
only one saved, she would say it was because she never had
tea or coffee," we jeered at her affectionately.

She believed that we should all sleep late in the morning
and go to bed early too, if possible. My father, a self-made
immigrant from Norway, would have had us get up early:
work, have character, grit, and all that. She would not have
it. In vacation time she went noiselessly into all our bed-
rooms and drew the shades down so that we would sleep late.
I know that she believed in a long childhood, of play, of

sleep, of freedom. Then we would have more vitality and courage later. I think she was right.

And since there was no tea or coffee, I begin to remember a curious drink that we had, and just the thought of it evokes my whole childhood. It was Postum, boiled Postum poured in a glass with cream and one teaspoonful of sugar. We used to drink the brown, slightly unpleasant liquid, drain it off quickly before the sugar melted in the bottom of the glass. Then with a glorious scoop of the spoon, a scraping, we dolloped it up and swallowed the horrible mess.

At the table the younger children had tin trays under their plates. We were supposed to eat the crusts of our bread, but instead we always circled the crusts under the edges of the tray. When the girl cleared the table, there they were, and once in a while there was mild talk from Mother about eating crusts, and visitors always remarked at this point, how to do so made curly hair. This possibility always interested me.

At dinner on Sunday, Father would carve and with a terrible lack of skill. He was so hurried, so pell-mell, so energetic that he was one of the most awkward men manually, in the world. I believe he once worked as a plumber's apprentice; so we liked to say: "Father was no good as a plumber, so he had to become a lawyer."

He still prided himself on his plumbing though, and when something went wrong in the downstairs lavatory, rushing, he got at it, running to the barn for implements and busily and passionately getting pipes out, or what not. Mother protested, resignedly knowing that he would injure the house in many ways. Just in hurrying through the doors with his tools, or carrying long pieces of torn wood bristling with nails, to the basement, he gouged plaster and tore grooves in the woodwork. He was really like a man in a movie comedy, though perhaps funnier.

Well, at dinner he carved, or mangled, the roast, and served it. It was passed by the second girl all around the long mahogany table. We were all supposed to wait "until Father is served." Otherwise plates came piling back before the poor carver had even begun. It was hard to be the youngest and served last. And once in a while they forgot you entirely, skipped you. For example, I would sit there, not minding particularly, about to speak of it—"Hey, what about me?"— when Mother would see that I was forgotten.

"Why, B'enna! Why, poor little Brenda hasn't been served!" At the kindness and sympathy in her voice, tears would start in my eyes. If only she wouldn't say it I would not be surprised this way into the slow tears. Now this was terribly embarrassing and difficult—tears with everyone present and possibly seeing them, and the skill, the difficulty, of trying to dry them without anyone seeing, of getting a finger up near the eye as a conductor to the accumulated salt water, so that it could run unseen down the hand—before there was a sniffle, or it poured over onto the cheek. But not only I had a hard time with tears at such moments. Even Torvald, the youngest, the pet, the most broad-smiling, jovial little boy— even Toke would be surprised into those damned tears. Sympathy is the devil.

Sigurd had some strange, fascinating, and ominous ideas. He used to say: "If ever you hear an awful yelling out in the woods, then you can know that somebody is being killed by a skunk." A skunk, just from the word, seemed a much more sinister animal to us than a tiger, say.

And sometimes at night we did hear unutterably sad cries, sad lost cries for help: screech owls. And in spring there were loons calling. And on the other side of Lake Calhoun, a mile and a half away, there were train tracks. On summer nights when the lake was still or there was a slight breeze from the north, we could hear for a long time that incredibly beautiful, soft roar of a train, coming from far away. And it softly filled the midsummer night for a long time and at last the train let out its own beautiful, sad, hooting cry. I used to think this was an Indian war cry.

I think trains to us in the Middle West have the nostalgic romantic connotation that ships have to people on the seacoast. For to us it is trains that mean travel, escape, leaving home, sadness, freedom, adventure. They come from the wild plains of Dakota and Montana, and they go on and on and across the world, and you get on one and perhaps you never come back.

Mother used to drive us over by Cedar Lake in the woods, and there, through the oak woods and among the sunny hazel bushes and near the marshes between Cedar Lake and Lake of the Isles, we could watch the engines of the M. and St. L. switching boxcars on a summer day. We ate crackers and watched blissfully and waved at the jolly kind engineers and gazed after the caboose with its pretty windows and red flag. I still like especially railroad tracks swinging through lonely fields and gulleys in the country. I walk along them, and it is very hard for me, now more than ever, when a freight train with flatcars comes larruping slowly along among the green hills of mullein stalks and goldenrod, not to swing onto it and ride at least as far as Milwaukee.

Sigurd used to say that middle western universities should not have crew races. What have crews and rowing to do with us out here on the plains? No, they should have handcar races.

But to get back to some of the scary and wonderfully interesting ideas that Sigurd had. Sigurd used to tell how he and I had an extraordinary and terrible experience. It made such an impression on me that I feel even now that it happened. I can remember it perfectly.

It seems we were up in the attic. I told you how strange and fascinating it was up there: the woods of upright raw two-by-fours and the deep dark corners under the eaves, and the hot smell of unpainted wood, and the ladder that went high up to the loft, and there in the darkness, through the rafters, we could dimly see another eerie ladder that led to the outer roof of the house.

Then there was the tank room; for we had a huge windmill, a beautiful one of bright whitewash and strong square timbers like a ship. The wheel itself was enormous and so high up in the air that to look at it made your stomach drop, and it had paddles and vanes and a great white rudder to keep the wheel turned to the wind. It creaked musically all day long, sometimes in a way to make you feel empty and bored and that there was nothing to do.

The windmill pumped water up to the attic of the house, for here was the tank room. A wonderful horror chamber. You opened a heavy wooden door and there was a pitch black room about twelve feet square. You could stumblingly walk all around the wall of it. And if you stood on tiptoe and looked over the wooden wall, you could see and smell black water. You could breathe on the moist surface and see its ripples. Your voice reverberated. The place was full of ghosts, criminals, ghouls—I have always felt that.

Well, Sigurd remembered when this happened: He and I were playing up in the attic in the dark northeast corner of it, on a lot of old rugs. Suddenly there rose up under us an animal, a skunk, which, carrying us and the rugs, ran once all around the attic, then dumped us and disappeared. I remember it perfectly.

Yes, we had a lovely house, ghoulish in the attic, but pleasant and cheerful downstairs. I think my mother had a fine aesthetic sense, for downstairs it was lovely, so clean, sun-shot, a little bare, with a few fine pieces of furniture. The huge windows were always diamond-clear and open in summer. A great deal of fresh air. The shades were always high up and no scrim curtains kept out the light. The sun poured in on fading rugs and the bare polished floor, and all the sweet air from the lake and the lawn.

We swam in the lake. My mother had some idea that water was weakening; so we were allowed to go in only every other day, and then she kept a clock, and ten or fifteen minutes was the limit. She always went down there to watch us, to count our heads.

Wide, wooden, green-painted steps led down our wooded bank to the lake, and halfway there was "the landing" with seats on either side. Oh, the lovely western sunsets from that landing in the evening! The black tamarack forest pointed up into them. When the lake was yellow glass in the evening, my parents and their friends would row on it. Their voices lifted up so purely and beautifully, mingling from one boat to another, in "Good Night, Ladies." It came over the water with the slow, musical clunk of the oarlocks.

We had Dickens and the Waverley Novels in the library, and Shakespeare and Lamb's Tales and Hawthorne; the Iliad and the Odyssey, and Norwegian fairy stories and Grimm and Andrew Lang. My favorite book was Howard Pyle's "Robin Hood," so much so that I could never bear to read the epilogue where he dies. I once caught a glimpse of the picture of him in bed, dying and drawing his last bow. It cut me to the heart. I could not bear it. I could not bear to look at it. Once Elsa very cruelly insisted on talking about it, reading it aloud.

We forget how sensitive children are to sorrow. I remember Elsa reading aloud to me Hawthorne's "Tanglewood Tales," about Theseus and his father, who, seeing the ship return with black sails (a sad oversight, for Theseus had promised to put up white sails if he was safe and alive) fell into the sea. Why, she had hardly got into one or two pages of the story, and I could not bear it, cried covertly, trying to hide it from her. It was too terrible, too bitter, too frightful, too sad. I can still see that little gold-embossed book in her hand. I got her to stop by some desperate pretext, wondering how she could read along so blandly and interestedly. Perhaps she had crossed that line where stories are just stories and no longer life.

Father read Darwin and Huxley, Matthew Arnold, Emerson, John Fiske, Prescott, Carlyle, Ibsen and Björnson, and Schiller and Goethe and Mark Twain. Mother used to say: "Andreas, you cannot read everything in the world." He came home from his office and was still driven to know everything.

As I said, Anne had Elsa to play with, and Sigurd had Arnulf. But I was rather isolated. This and the affectionate aloofness of my mother, who had too much to do, made me solitary and independent; though now I think all children should have passionate, rollicking love and spoiling from both parents; it makes them flower and grow exuberant and have some richness in them. I was bashful and taciturn with the family but jokey and talkative with outsiders, a cut-up. Though I remember Anne's once saying that I was sulky. It surprised me (though I rather liked the idea) because I never felt sulky inside.

No, I was secretly full of heroic thoughts and imagining myself on a horse at the head of a parade. When I was twelve Mother asked me what I wanted for my birthday. "All I want is a French bayonet," I said, and to my surprise this amused her so much that she laughed.

But this military craving is queer. (I still have it, wear brass buttons on my clothes, sailor pants, and am always vaguely wishing that I were a captain of cavalry in Afghanistan, or could join the navy.) It is queer because I could not hurt anything, abhor hunting, feel uneasy about eating meat, put insects out of doors carefully.

I think it was Mother who taught us all how to be good to animals. There was never a cat-mauling baby in our family. Mother would take the baby's hand and make it smooth the kitten gently in the right direction, saying in an affectionate, tender voice: "Nice kitty, so nice, so dear. Oh, nice kitty."

Well, cats were lovely but horses were a rapture. Darling Lady! how I knew her personality, her soul, and will never forget it. I would pretend that I was her colt and would stay all day in the pasture, much of the time on my hands and knees eating grass.

I suppose this passion for horses had something to do with knightliness, heroics. But I never wanted to be the lady in a life of chivalry, but the very perfect knight himself. At Christmas, year after year, I hoped and asked and implored for a suit of armor at Holtzermann's, the German store—for "knight clothes." They had actually a child's suit of armor standing on a high shelf. Oh, gosh, how I wanted that, ached for it! But I never got it.

Then I dreamed that a beautiful, strong, iron-gray horse without bridle or saddle came and with his teeth lifted me on his back and we galloped off. It was a kind of elopement, and I was radiantly happy. And going to my music lessons, to Mrs. Fahnestock's, carrying a cylindrical leather roll with Schumann and Chopin in it, I would sit in the window of the yellow street car, slouched down, my chin in my hand, and sink into a blissful dream in which I had two ponies, a black one and a white one. And I had a bright red and yellow cart for them, and I dreamed and gloated and saw all the details of their harness, even to the glass buttons or brass stars at their temples. When imagining something particularly happy and wonderful, a lump would come in my throat, a sudden glug of happiness, which it would be hard, for a second, to speak over ... I liked to fix Lady's hair, seeing whether it was more becoming to part her forelock in the middle (I thought she looked wonderfully noble and good that way) or not to part it, just have bangs. And the day that I was seven, the best thing that could happen to anyone happened to me. I got a pony.

Elsa was a kind of boy and I was more so. Mother let us wear knee pants, and we played baseball with the boys in the pasture. Elsa was very good. I was better at football (I was getting a little fat and weight was a help) and made a fine, plunging thunderbolt of a center. A teamster lazily driving up Richfield Road on his creaking wagon (the drowsiness of a slowly, musically creaking hayrack going up the dusty road on a summer afternoon!) was heard to say, seeing Elsa: "Either that is a boy with braids or a girl with pants on." Anne was more of a lady, a duchess even.

My mother was naturally feministic and Father had not come from Norway or read all of Ibsen for nothing. Girls, Mother felt, were just as precious and important as boys. We never felt that girls had to do housework and boys outdoor work. She made no distinction between them in actions, freedom, education, or possibilities. Elsa and I could be presidents and admirals, just as much as Sigurd, if we happened to feel like it.

We were never told to be the least bit modest. Nakedness was all right and fine. My mother wanted us to go barefoot much longer than we wanted to. The girls could hitch up the horse and climb trees and show their underpants as much as they wanted to. She never told us to be careful, cautious, prudent. We never had, thank God, any sense of prudence or contraction in things. We were never warned about "awful men," and told not to go places alone, or in the dark. It is so bad to check children's courage and recklessness, I know that.

Now because of this boy-feeling, this hero feeling, I had high standards about the ability to fight. I had something to maintain there. I seemed never to think girlish timidity or reluctance was justifiable at all. And so there were about three important fights for me; the first one with Skinny Dales, a tall, mean, sickly boy many grades behind in school, who lisped. Once he read a poem and said: "the flowers wivvered away," so that after that we called him "wivvered away," if we dared to.

One winter day I met him on the way to school, with his convoy of little boys. He lifted a mound of fresh snow and cried: "Now I am going to wash her face." I was frightened inside and we grappled. He was very tall and weak and slipped in the snow and I fell on him and pounded him a little bit. This was regarded as a victory on my part. I could see from what Sigurd said that they all thought I was really formidable. I was glad they did, and not so certain about it inwardly.

Then once there was a fight with Gilbert Birchell, who lived in the hollow by the swamp in a log cabin with no mother and a father who "drank" (it was such an ominous and awful word then). We slugged and skirmished on a hillside. He clawed my face and it bled very much, and after this fight I felt proud and arrogant, pleased with the blood. I guess I really won that one.

There was another fight with Leo Bruder, a huge, strong Scandinavian boy with hair like a baby duck's, one of the five tough Bruder boys. Their father kept a pop factory, and their mother was a fierce termagant who chased children and swore. Well, Leo and I fought and hit and I experienced a sinking of the heart as he bounded around. He was so hard, strong and big when I hit him that it hurt my fists. Something happened though, so that we did not finish it and I was not disgraced. I again sailed on a reputation of intrepidity, though in this case too I felt queasy inside and knew the truth.

There were many fights with Sigurd, but one Homeric one. We were walking home on a soft midsummer night from the Lake Harriet band concert. A soprano had been singing a silly song about the goddess Hebe. I absent-mindedly sang a phrase of it, as we walked along. "Quit it," Sigurd said to me. This led to insults and presently a faucet of adrenalin, squirted into my veins and I hit him frightfully hard and he fell to the ground. "Oh, I have killed him!" I thought in fright, and my strength all ebbed. But now, rising and snavelling with rage, he knocked *me* down, in that moment of my pity. And so it went.

It must have lasted a long time, for when I got to my room I was terribly battered. I can still see myself in the glass: bawling, my face blood-covered, swollen with rheum and tears, my chest heaving furiously. Yet it is queer, I gazed at myself with pride, proud of my bloodiness. I cannot tell why.

The long succession of hired girls were all interesting, especially the second girls, who went all over the house, took care of the baby, darned stockings, and had more time to talk. There was Grace, who had worked in an insane asylum. I pumped her by the hour. I seemed to have such an intense interest in people (which later often became an intense interest in myself). "Has your father a mustache, Grace? Did he ever have any middle name? Terence, that's a pretty name. Who was St. Patrick? How does it look in Ireland, Grace? Would you have a yard or a back porch, say? What do they have for breakfast?"

There was that Norwegian Marie with her stories of her hard father; of the ghost she saw in Norway, the dead woman running noiselessly over the snow in her embroidered kerchief and red skirt.

In winter after school I would hitch up Lady to the sleigh and drive Marie and her charge, the baby (I guess it was Rolf then), out to Edina Mills. It was a mile and a half away but it seemed as far as Russia. It was below zero and Lady's coat was uncurried and silky and an inch long, so that she looked like a bear almost. The sleigh bumped along and the bells rang and clods of caked snow flew in our faces. When we turned home at last, I would look back and see the winter sunset through the black bare trees. Sometimes it was lurid red, sometimes gilt and pink. This is always one of my favorite memories, so mournful and beautiful: driving away from a winter sunset.

Then there was Olava, a cook, who said obscene things that I did not understand at once, things that I should ask the hired man, she said. I abhorred Olava; but I did not tell on her. There was Norwegian Hilda, with her mottled ruddy face, wide cheekbones, and a cloud of rough hair. And her figure! I never saw such a beautiful figure. Yes, I really knew what beauty was. There was another Hilda who was quite deaf. She was the one who saw the ghost, the ghost that is up on the third floor. She saw it twice, a woman with a baby. (I wanted so much to have a ghost, to know it was there and in the house.)

And then Miss Lindquist had a fascinating ghost experience. Miss Lindquist was the dressmaker who came to the house for a month at a time and sewed clothes for everybody except Father. She was over six feet tall and had a high sagging roll of pompadour above her high forehead, and pince-nez woggled on her nose, and she wore a Gibson girl blouse, starched and complicated with lace insertion, that seemed to be full of wet wash—something lumpy, her own body or many starched corset covers. Miss Lindquist had an unfortunate adjective when she was fitting us. "Do you want it a little more baggy? ... I see, a little more bag here ... over the bust." It gave just the wrong, the most discouraging mental picture.

Well, the sewing room on the third floor was toward the east. (The attic had now been plastered.) It was late November and six o'clock. Miss Lindquist turned out the gas light and crossed the bare hall to the stairs. In the middle of it, in the blackness, she bumped into an unseen person. Not a word, not a breath, not a step from this unseen one. But Miss Lindquist bumped and bumped again, trying to get around her, and she could tell it was a woman shorter than herself. At last Miss Lindquist got past and downstairs.

And she found that everybody in the house who should have
been there was below: the girls and hired man in the kitchen;
the children and the family all accounted for. Miss Lindquist did not speak of it right then. She did not want to.
It made her so uncomfortable. (And I was so glad to hear
of it.)

And the ghost was seen afterwards by others. I later saw
a ghost in the east room myself, so that now I would not
dare sleep there. Dare! I might dare, but I would not sleep.
I would have that lovely hair-trigger clarity and awareness
of fright.

4.

*The two forces in me, to be fierce and to be gentle. Disap-
pointed in Christmas presents. My best friend and adventures
in the swamp. My lying. Family picnics and being ashamed
of them all.*

ALL MY LIFE I SEEM TO HAVE HAD TWO FORCES WORKING IN
me—pushing me, making me search, search and never rest.
They give me an energy that sets my mind wrangling and
struggling and arguing and discussing things, whenever I
am alone. One energy seems to be the wish to be important
and admired (although this feeling now, in 1938, seems to
be slowly ebbing). The other energy is that I want to *be*
what is admirable inside, whether anyone admires me or not.
And this passion grows as the other one wanes.

These have a kind of rhythm. I sometimes describe it by
saying that for two weeks I seem to be my father and for
two weeks my mother. That is, for two weeks I want to be
bold and remarkable, and this fills me with energy for a while.
But then suddenly, almost in a few minutes, I will think:
"Oh, no, to be good, unselfish is the thing. How obnoxious,
how meaty, empty and egotistical, all that masculine striv-

ing!" And I want to be graceful and tender—even to have ringlets and wear lace blouses—to be a listener, and a fosterer of others and all life.

Well, I remember these feelings of "goodness" rushing into me as a child. I don't think they came often. Perhaps they came years apart. But I would suddenly feel, with an overwhelming happiness and sweetness, that one must be unselfish, and help people and do everything they wanted, and do it without reward. And so I would for a day. I doubt if I did it longer than that.

And once I remember hearing Mother tell how the Quakers in church sat silently and waited for the "inner light." I went downtown to my music lesson that day, a hot bright summer day, looking at everybody on the street car, into every face. Yes, you could see the light in them, and how bright or dim it was. At just one look. In some you knew there was much light. And the light was not necessarily intelligence, because some splendidly mental people did not have it at all, and a Negro or a washwoman had the light in a beautiful white blaze. There was some light in all, but it was often thickly muddied over.

There was another feeling that became an inner spring of much in my life. I disliked feeling lazy. I think this was because I began to associate it with being too fat. At a Christmas Eve party I and the other children were running and sliding into the Oriental rug before the double front doors. Suddenly I felt a strong prancing kind of violent energy, from forcing myself. I felt as strong as a war horse. An intoxicating feeling.

I speak of this because in later life I was to force myself physically often, so as to get a sense of inner drive. But at last I have discovered that if you carry it far it weazens the imagination and spirit. And I often look at those high-pressure business men who drink and smoke very much to feel this inner pressure that is physical and who get so many acts done without thinking whether the acts are good or bad; and I think I know how they feel. But I will probably tell more of this later. Perhaps too much.

I see that Christmas evokes the brightest memories, so I will tell about it.

On the morning of Christmas Eve, the groceryman had brought the tree and Gus made a box for it. We had been stringing popcorn and cranberries for a day or two. And one of the most delightful things was sewing the candy bags out of yellow, red and green tarlatan. I loved doing this because it meant a most wonderful lordly state was to come, i.e., when we could each have a private candy bag and eat as much as we pleased. Think of it, between meals and continuously, walking around and blissful and looking on in contentment (just popping another piece in your mouth) at the holly on the banisters, the mistletoe in the chandelier, the *London Illustrated News* and *Sketch* and all the accumulated Christmas magazines of years, that Mother brought down from the attic.

And there were tremendous doings in the kitchen. You could go out and watch the interesting cleaning of chickens, scrape the cake bowl, and quietly eat long strips of raw cookie dough.

In the morning we trimmed the tree. The beauty and delight of Christmas tree ornaments! But everybody feels that. Mother brought down the boxes from the attic and we found all those nonpareil, exquisitely adorable, lovely baubles: the big, heavy, silver balls, the star for the top, a silver bird with tails of glass wire, a tiny bugle that really blew. Each child looked for his dearest and most precious trinket and put new thread on it and then hung it uneasily and stood back and surveyed it with utter love. And it was on this morning that the lordly candy-eating began.

We trimmed the tree. At noon it was all finished and white

sheets were tacked down all over the library floor. Then Mother pulled out of the walls the large, sliding, paneled oak doors. The library was now sealed off from the rest of downstairs.

Christmas Eve we had a Norwegian supper. There was rolled spiced mutton, Christmas bread with citron in it, brown goat's milk cheese, a cheese in glass which smelled so frightful that only Father of all the grown-ups could taste it. Ludefisk. This is codfish treated in some way so that it has a queer smell that goes sailing through the house. The big people liked it, but the children always came to the table holding their noses: "Ick!" "Icky!" "Ish!" they cried.

"Please, dear, don't. It isn't polite."

But we kept it up all during the meal in a lower key, or by making faces. It was a great satisfaction to show repulsion for ludefisk, for we are always so terribly proud of our dislikes.

After supper the party began. More parents and children came, and mounds of overshoes, leggings and mittens on strings filled the window seats. At last the library doors were opened and there was the tree lit with candles. Then Mother distributed the presents among all the company. But most of our presents we got in the morning. Each child put a chair at the fireplace and pinned a long stout black stocking to the mantelpiece.

Christmas was bliss. But there came the time when it turned to gall, to the bitterest disappointment. When I was a small child, everything seemed so wonderful—those mechanical toys, the jack-in-the-boxes. But at nine or ten, suddenly all presents were just a frightful disappointment, such a blow, so peanutty and measly compared to what I had hoped for.

I began to want something like a diamond ring or a revolver. Instead I seemed to get such awful cheesy things. Once it was a celluloid lobster. My pain and shock at this were beyond description. I went upstairs and cried. Oh, dear, that was a terrible experience. "A pink celluloid lobster! But why? How could Mama? What a cheap, what a meaningless thing! How could she do that to me?"

Once at the Christmas Eve party I got a ring, a cluster of chipped turquoises shaped like a five-petaled flower. I told myself, bracing up my expected agony (it was perhaps the second or third year of bitter Christmasses) that it was a good present, a pretty present. A real ring. "See, I got a ring. Isn't it pretty? Look, it's turquoise!" (though I wanted a diamond ring). But in almost no time I discovered that the gold came off black on my finger. The ring would have been all right, but it was not gold at all; that wire was homely, dark, cheap metal underneath. And later in the evening one of the microscopic blue petals fell out.

The next day it was bright winter and there was deep white snow as always. Diamonds sparkled on it. The high drifts along the driveway had thin eaves with dark caverns under them. We had Christmas dinner, turkey and all that, and then we went over to the woods to slide down hill.

"If only I had got a sled, that would be something like it," I thought. I had sleds enough, but they were just community-owned sleds that cluttered up the barn. They were the very low kind with pointed runners, fine for running with and hurling yourself down on your belly. "But say a flexible flyer. Why couldn't they give me that? Something new and bright and really worth something?"

The youngest Bruder boy came over into the woods and was sliding with us—Hector, an odd-looking blond child of six, in a ragged bundle of clothes.

"What did you get for Christmas, Hector?"

"Oh, some oranges," he said lightly.

Oranges! Oh, poor Hector. Oranges for Christmas! Imagine. That was worse than what happened to me by a million-scillion times. I felt so terribly sorry for him, and for the first time I was able to see a little glimmer of philosophy about Christmas, about presents.

But take the Wetmore girls. They were certainly poorer than we were. We lived in a much bigger house anyway. I went to see them on Christmas Day, and there were their presents laid out on chairs. And so many things! Such a wonderful fancy complexity of presents: handkerchiefs, hair-receivers, baby pins, perfume bottles, a hundred things for each, with cards and names of givers attached and all sorts of fancy painstaking business: towels with initials embroidered on them! Now I certainly did not covet towels or hair-receivers or knitted booties for bed, but I envied the rich boodle, the sum of it, and the excitement and fuss about it.

You see Mother was characteristically sensible and wise. (Sigurd suffered the same way that I did; there was the year he got that acme of dullness, a map of the United States.) There were seven children, and it was hard work and expensive to have them all extravagantly pleased. So she bought a lot of things, and then, the night before Christmas, judiciously divided them fairly and sensibly among us all. Perhaps the map was taken from Sigurd's chair and put on Elsa's. "But no, I guess Elsa had better have the bird book and Sigurd the map." All very sensible.

But it made me many years later anxiously indulgent toward my own child. I cannot bear to have her ever disappointed, and at Christmas I get her five times too much and go into debt for two months. She must be absolutely surfeited. I tell you I cannot bear disappointment in anyone. It is a barbed spear that tears my soul. I cannot endure it. I cannot let them down.

But now that I think of it, I remember that I have let people down very badly two or three times, though not out of niggardliness but my own inadequacy. And at other times my generosity-compulsion has led me into so much trouble.

My best friend was Florence Frane. She was blonde and had an imperious nose with tight nostrils; and a blonde with fierce nostrils and lively, bossy ways—I always love them. Mary Garden is one and Julie Plant, who married Sigurd, was another.

Florence lived in a small stove-heated house beyond Grandpa Chapin's cornfield and the Green, where all the children played in the evening. Mother was always feeling: "Brenda should see other children, the children of our friends." For I was always having a secret impenetrable friendship with the daughter of the policeman or some poor man's child. Mother was not in the least bit snobbish, but it troubled her that I was so laconic at home, parent-shy and aloof. She did not know what I was up to or what thoughts I was sharing with Florence.

We had fun. There was a big boy with a mouthful of large overlapping teeth with green moss on them, named Fred Hanson. Florence and I were walking home from school, and a closed laundry wagon overtook us and passed ahead of us, and on the hanging flap in the back was Fred Hanson. He derisively blew kisses at us.

This was too much. We went searching for him all that afternoon, and in the process, as the search became more dramatic and significant, I became Robin Hood and Florence I persuaded to be Guy of Gisborne. (I remember that, very villainously and deceitfully, I did not tell her that Guy of Gisborne was the villain of the story. I let her think that he was all right.)

We got a pen knife and a notebook and a pencil and wrote notes in it. We went looking for Fred way over by the swamps to the west. Fortieth Street then was a lane. It went through the swamp for a mile. But there were really three swamps, three cowslip-teeming marshes, one after the other. I loved these. Mother used to take us for a walk there on Sunday morning, winding through the wild paths, and once we found some tiger lilies and some lady's-slippers. Between the swamps were knolls of land and oak woods. I loved this west-going road. It ended far away against a farmer's gate on the brow of a hill. What was beyond? To look west at the narrow lane through the marshes made me want to explore west, west, west, beyond the farmer's gate, over the hill, on, on forever.

Well, we walked down into these fascinating marshes and through secret paths in the reeds by Lake Calhoun. It seemed then a jungle, a wilderness, a whole country. And there was a black tamarack forest. You stepped into this dark forest like a cathedral, and fifty feet within it all was darkness and it was as though you were suddenly walled in and forgot which way you had entered.

We searched and searched for Fred. When we did not find him at a certain place, we wrote it in our notebooks. But at last we came to a long narrow dock, one board wide, that went far out into the lake, among the rushes. A sparkling north breeze had come up, so there were bright blue waves and in some parts of the sagging dock the waves leaped over it. Way out at the end of the dock was Fred Hanson, fishing. We went out to him, told him we were after him, showed him the pen knife as some kind of threat, asked him what he had caught. There was a very small perch swimming in the tin can. We made him throw it back in the water and went home feeling exonerated, satisfactorily revenged and satisfied. The rules of chivalry had been successfully carried out.

Florence and I had a game we called "playing dwarf." Again the chief pleasure of it was eating. At her home we sat in a washbasket of laundry in a closet in the kitchen. We sat there and whispered until her mother left the kitchen and then we stole out and took dill pickles and soda crackers. (My mother did not allow us to have either pickles or soda crackers.)

Then we "played dwarf" at our house on cold, dark, winter afternoons. Our basement is large and rambling. There

is one room, "the dark cellar," as dark as a dungeon because
the windows open under the front porch. You can smell the
sour dank earth pressing down through those cobwebbed
murky windows. There were ancient cupboards there with unused jelly glasses in them, or congealed pails of old paint.

The game, in our basement, was exciting because there is
a wide circuit of rooms through which we could run, escape,
feeling ourselves electric with imitation terror. And though
the food at our house was uninteresting, merely apples and
oranges, nothing indigestible, at a gloomy winter five
o'clock, the hired man came down the cellar stairs to stoke
the furnace. It was thrilling to escape from him, to be whis-
pering with beating hearts in the wood room and he ten
feet from us and not knowing it. It was the fine wonderful
excitement a murderer must feel.

We had "The American Boy's Handbook." Elsa knew it
thoroughly and at fourteen, by studying it, made an ice-
boat—not just a junk little thing made of broomsticks and
three girl-skates, but a big one with true runners and a tiller.
The trouble was the ice condition was so uncertain. Some years
there would be smooth ice for only a day, two days, and then
the blizzards came and the ice was two feet beneath the
surface.

But, oh, those days of the year when the ice on the whole
lake was glass! It would be pure bottle-green glass, a foot
thick. The pleasure of making the first white skate-writing
on it! And then that beautiful booming of ice, reverberating
all across the lake, a note like a god's harp-string plucked
and broken.

But to go back to "The American Boy's Handbook." It
showed one how to do all sorts of things, to make telephones
out of tin cans and so on. The diagrams, the physics were too
hard for me and my interest did not pierce them. But one
thing took my eye. It told one how to catch a baby hawk and

bring it up and train it to sit on your wrist like a falcon.

Now this was knightly. This drowned me, swamped me with enthusiasm. Florence Frane and I at once went over to ask Mr. May where we could find a baby hawk; for Mr. May, in his silver-dirty-gray house with rickety porches and geraniums in the window, had a huge glass case full of stuffed birds. He knew all about birds.

"Go over in the tamarack forest," he said. "You'll find hawks' nests there."

And so we went through the marshes with blue flags on either side, jumping sudden ditches and into the dark tamarack cathedral, and its high vaulted ceiling was lifted with a thousand pillars and the floor of it was clean and springy with brown needles.

We looked up for hawks' nests and saw one. It was at the far top, huge like a bushel basket and a big tail of feathers thrust stiffly over the edge. But above it in the blue sky, the father hawk soared. The tree was rough as iron scales, and the first branches were a mile up. The father hawk would doubtless fly at us with his talons. No, we couldn't get the baby hawks. So we thought a baby crow would do.

We walked then a mile or two to a sunny hill with oak trees on it and found a crow's nest. An oak tree is very climbable, better than a tamarack. I got up in it and there were four baby crows in the nest. Florence spread her gingham skirt and I dropped one for her and one for me.

"You know," I said to them at home, "you know," I said to all those I encountered, first the cook and the boys and then Mother and Anne and Elsa, "Florence and I were way out in the woods and some cruel farmer boys had robbed a crow's nest and we begged them not to kill them, but to let us take them home and keep them." The lying in my life interests me. I always felt so pained, so conscience-stricken when I lied, but I always did it so well, so complexly and copiously. The queer part was I usually lied unnecessarily.

Anyway, Florence had her crow and I had mine, and he grew up to be a strange unattractive pet, not at all like a falcon. He would come hopping over the lawn toward one, even when full grown, his red gullet wide open for food.

I went away that summer to Ada, Minnesota, to visit Uncle Fred. When I came back my crow had flown away, they told me, with some others. I had dark suspicions about this. I sometimes would like to feel darkly suspicious, misused, dishonorably treated by my parents. For instance, there was the time Father at last got my consent to sell the pony. I suppose it was because he was a kind of rapscallion of a pony who threw me with remarkable skill, almost every time I rode him. Well, Father said that if he sold the pony, Lady would have a colt probably which would become a big horse and would be really much better than a pony. I consented, and Prince went to a farmer in North Dakota.

But Lady did not have a colt. Never. For years afterwards, whenever I felt angry at Father, obstructed by him in some way, I would think: "Yes, he sold Prince and absolutely broke his promise about getting me a colt instead. If he had only given me the money for Prince; but not even that!" And when, less often, Mother obstructed me in some way I thought darkly about the crow which she *said* had flown off with some wild crows that summer. How convenient! When I was away. Naturally!

People often said sentimentally about us: "My, what a wonderful big family!" And so it was.

But I think that it got to be a discouraging process for Mother. For one day this happened, a painful shock to me: I went into the back hall and Mother was there by the stairs to the third floor and somehow I knew there were actually tears in her eyes, and somehow else I knew (no words were said at all) it was because she was going to have another baby. I could feel the emanation from her of weariness and

discomfort. Baby after baby! Whether this baby was to be
Rolf or Torvald I forget. But I can remember feeling a little
upset when we were going to have Rolf. "Oh, say, six
children!"

There were already two things I was a little ashamed of:
that we were half Norwegian and had so many children in
the family. Two plebeian things. American families with
names like Rand, Elwood, Ridgway, they seemed only to
have one or two children. How fine to be an only child! I
liked to imagine this. Another idea that I nursed pleasantly
was that I was adopted. In the attic there was a large glass-
framed picture, a pencil drawing of a child with dark hair
and a straight-bridged nose, I thought like mine. So I said
to myself: this was me, and I was of noble birth and my
true parents had given me to these rather commonplace
Ueland people to bring up. The revelation would be made
sometime. Anne, Elsa, Sigurd and Arnulf would be staggered.

But when I discovered that, after Rolf, there was going
to be *another* baby (think of it, a seventh child!), I felt
genuine disgust and depression. I did not know how I could
face the world. Babies with their drooling baldness, anyway,
had become thoroughly repulsive to me. Didies, nursing bottles, rubber nipples were nauseating. As for n-rs-ng at the
br—st, it was an obscenity I could not even think about.

It took me a long time to reconcile myself to Torvald's
approaching birth. I had to work on myself. One afternoon
I was looking through the east bay of windows and saw
Rolf out on the lawn, a nobly handsome little boy with bright
hair and a face like a scornful angel. I thought then: "The
new baby might look just like Rolf, only he will have black
hair. How cute. How cute they will be together." I clung to
this thought, trying to get pleasure out of it as if they
were white and black ponies.

I always had this peculiar family shame (which has now

turned to an extraordinary pride). Rolf had it, too. And Anne did, I think. About once a year Father and Mother willed forcibly a family picnic, one of those stubborn conceptions that people get and should never carry out. So we would all have to go on an excursion, perhaps to Lake Minnetonka.

I was writhing with shame and reluctance from beginning to end. They all seemed such bumpkins; it was so terrible to be identified with such a bunch. And the very fact that they wanted to be all together in a noisome mess, and go in this mess to some place where they could be publicly seen—it was very painful. If only there had been *one* outsider along, it would have been bearable—just one respectably attractive stranger to leaven the bunch of familial Uelands.

We took a fast street car to Lake Minnetonka and then a steamboat trip all over the lake. On docks at Excelsior, Deephaven, we saw the Minnetonka people, young men in white ducks, rich people with sail boats, motor boats. And they (I groaned) would see all these Norwegian overbreeding Uelands shambling by with a lunch basket. Horrors, how ishy! Why not just eat peanuts on the boat and be done with it, strew the banana skins around? I was especially ashamed of Father, who curiously was the most transparent, honestly unashamed person I have ever known. Of course, to observers we looked, I am sure, like a pleasant, intelligent, nice-looking family.

Mother writes a letter to Anne about this time:

I took the four boys downtown yesterday for suits, hats, shoes, etc., and people looked at us with pleased and sympathetic smiles. One lady whom I know, asked me in the store if I got them shod in relays, whereupon Sigurd indignantly kicked over the traces and said it was the last time he was coming down with "the whole bunch." I remember once when I was driving in our carry-all with five or six of you, you became conscious of the sensation we were creating and declared that "they would put it in the papers."

5.

Sex attitudes then. My father's law partner is John Lind. High school. Blanche Lane, even fatter, becomes my friend. I am forced to go to dancing school.

I MUST TELL SOMETHING ABOUT SEX ATTITUDES IN MY CHILD-hood. There has been a great change in thirty years. You see, in those days grown-ups made not one single fleeting reference to sex, or talked about the feelings between men and women, about marriage and love and what it is, about prostitution, sexual complexes, and miseries and insanities. Even my open-minded Ibsen-reading mother and father never mentioned these things.

But now I find myself talking with casual freedom about these things to friends, and we say what we think and believe in an off-hand way, whether the children are present or not. Fifteen-year-old Roderick Shearer will be in the room pensively tossing a catcher's mitt while I talk to Henrietta, who is his mother. He is unperturbed and listening to what we say. Perhaps he is not even listening.

"Why, Henrietta," I said. "My heavens, we must be careful because of Roddy. As I was saying about s-e-x." And Roddy is amused, thinks this is fairly funny, and says with mild scorn: "Oh, say. I spose so."

When I was ten, there was talk between Florence Frane and me about "best fellows." ("Red and yellow, kiss your fellow," was the chant.) Her fellow was George Farkell, a boy who had a shock of football hair, for football was coming into style then, and a lot of hair was supposed to protect the head in plunges.

Well, George Farkell was Florence's "fellow," and so she suggested that Arthur Murphy be mine. I was pleased to have one. Arthur lived in a tar-paper shack just to the west of our pasture. His tall, undernourished brother George was the villain of our childhood, the bully, the meany, the sneerer, who attacked us and teased us going to and from school. (There was that winter when he called my tights of black gathered jersey, "looses.")

But Arthur, the younger one, was nice. Yes, Florence agreed, and so did I, that Arthur was my fellow and George was hers. This was mostly an idea, because we hardly ever talked to them. Florence, it is true, once came very near to kissing George behind a door, and she actually thought she might do it sometime. And I tried to imagine myself kissing Arthur. "Would you dare?" "I bet maybe I would."

But one day we did actually all go walking in the marsh, Florence and I together, and George and Arthur sidling along, walking not two-by-two but in a sheepish hodge-podge. We went down Fortieth Street into the marsh where the little road went straight west down into the swamp filled with frog music and cowslips and then over the knolls of oak woods.

George and Arthur were hinting at something. It was a riddle. How they staggered and laughed with fright and embarrassment as we tried to guess it. But we couldn't. When at last they gave the answer haltingly, I was no more enlightened than before.

I went home puzzled. But the next day Florence had got all the significance of the riddle out of them, and told me what it meant, that is, what men and women did that resulted in the birth of children. I was astonished, it seemed so queer —but not shocked or horrified. It was just interesting and I forgot about it. A few years later, however, I experienced for a time a sudden violent interest in sex and for hours I would trace words through the dictionary and encyclopedia, a disappointing and baffling process, because when you finally were about to come to a revelation, you were just referred back to the original word.

Yes, I can see now that I was a neglected child. But the

neglect was not (as many people think) in having so much
freedom, but in not having from my parents or others enough
skillful, generous, exciting attention, for this is the true
discipline for children and leads them into all sorts of discoveries and efforts and enthusiasm. My life has been quite
botched and full of mistakes, but I know so unshakably that
the neglect that gave me *freedom* was good for me.

And such freedom and easiness I had. I never had to
report home after school. I went where I wanted to and
played with whom I pleased and wandered far, far and came
home after dark. There was just one rule: to be home by
half past six; otherwise the hired man would be sent out with
a lantern. I was considered by other children to be just unbelievably free. "No, I don't have to go home after school,"
I can hear myself telling them proudly.

I was inwardly proud of Mother for being so magnanimous
and trusting. There seemed to be two kinds of mothers: the
berating, threatening, loud-voiced mothers of the poorer children, like Mrs. Bruder and Mrs. Murphy, and then there
were the strict, prissy, anxious mothers. Compared to both
kinds, I was so proud of mine. I felt that she was distinguished and intelligent. She emanated goodness, freedom and
praise.

Father became the law partner of John Lind, and we felt
elation at this, because he had been Governor Lind, a Swede,
a much-revered man in Minnesota. One hand had been cut
off in boyhood, in some farm machinery, which made him especially interesting to me—those glimpses of the white stump
just inside his coat sleeve.

Father had a great deal of hearty, faintly jocund vanity,
and when people praised Lind, or anybody very much, he
began to lift his chest and snort humorously through his nostrils. Pish! He had scorn for all politicians, for all that
manipulating and oratory. But much of this was because

Father was contrary. He would spring to the opposite of a
question, and the more lonely it was there the better and
more arrogantly he fought. He was a heckler of Lutherans
and all religious orthodoxy and a critic of that which was
complacent and self-admiring among Norwegians, such as
their fond talk of being "vikings" and so on. I don't think
that Governor Lind was as good a lawyer as Father, either
as a legal scholar or a fighter in court. Later the partnership
broke up.

Father's office was interesting to visit. It was in the New
York Life Insurance building, a narrow red skyscraper of six
stories, with clanging elevators that swung up and down
loosely like iron baskets in a cage. Miss Goldsbury was his
stenographer, and Miss Goldsbury was lovely—pretty, brown-
eyed and kind, and best of all she had the most volatile laugh.
At everything you said, Miss Goldsbury's chin would tuck in,
and out would come this rivulet of liquid rapid gigglings.
It was not a nervous giggle, or perfunctory or mirthless, but
a true one of helpless amusement. This always made me feel
so witty. And it still does. What that giggle must have done
for Father for those forty years! Miss Goldsbury now works
for Sigurd, who became a lawyer, and Sigurd says that when
he goes through the office and feels very dull and lumpish, he
just has to say "Hello, Miss Goosebury," and her shaking
laugh, as she pecks with a forefinger at her typewriter and
gazes down at the roller, makes him feel like Bernard Shaw.

Miss Goldsbury years ago always let me work the stamping
machine and poke at the typewriter and, behold, there was
a B. At the office Father was always hearty and vociferous
and delighted to see us, and if we wanted money, Miss Goldsbury went into the safe and brought out much more than we
needed. At home he was much more absent-minded and dubious and it was hard to ask for money, for he would look at
you a long time unseeingly and then sadly reach in his pocket.

When Governor Lind became Father's partner the event

dragged in its wake an important happening for me. He had a daughter my age, Winifred, and I was invited to stay all night.

Their house, a big red one with a porte-cochère, was way down on Third Avenue in the middle of the city, and after dinner it was eerie and strange to be walking along on a sidewalk downtown, so far, far from home. The streets were not paved but dirt, and a few carriages and buggies went slogging softly up and down. Winifred's sister Jenny was older than Anne even, a tall, smiling, squarely stout girl who wore glasses. She was going to Wells College, but Winifred explained to me that Jenny would stay in college only two years.

"Because, look. If you go four years, why, by the time you graduate, think of it, you are twenty-two!" That is, practically an old maid; yes, dangerously and perhaps hopelessly so.

But I know that, young as I was, I had an honest scorn for this idea, indignant that girls should be considered passé at twenty-two. Think of it, being afraid of being twenty-two for fear someone would not marry you! And what was to be gained by marrying? What was the fun of that? Stuck in a house when you might be learning something and having a lively time. Renouncing your education just to catch some cozy husband. This seemed thoroughly immoral to me even then.

The first day that I went to high school it was midwinter. I walked to the street car which came bounding through the snowy woods—our nice cozy Oak and Harriet street car, with leading citizens of the neighborhood on it, as well as school children. Street cars were socially stimulating places then, like the foyer of an opera. But when I transferred downtown to another car that filled up with girls and boys older than I (they were handsome men, really, in long pants)

I hung on a strap with apprehension in my throat, because the farther downtown one went, the greater the sense of social bashfulness and inadequacy. The children seemed richer and more sophisticated.

I got into one thoroughly frightening class and that was Latin. The teacher was Miss Pratt. Whew! Miss Pratt, with her parallel gray curls and her biting joy in frightening us. To make it worse there were a lot of stylish Douglas School kids there whom I had seen before at an awed distance, and had heard about, girls who wore hats, instead of a stocking cap like me, and tiny kid gloves, not mittens.

"Gallia est omnis divisa in partes tres."

I was so afraid of making a mistake, because of Miss Pratt, that I studied Latin feverishly hard every day. I endlessly repeated each lesson, and each minute point and word in each lesson. I never made a mistake in class, never. And I got a 98 at the end of the term, the highest mark ever gotten perhaps.

But it was the last and only high mark I ever had, and it was the result of fright, and I don't believe in fright or that system of learning and never have. It may be a good thing, but I don't believe in it just the same. It injures people in some place they do not know about.

High school was pleasant enough, though in a queer way each term seemed to be darkened by just one teacher. The other three or four would be all right. But there was always one pill. For example, there was Miss Pitkins, the history teacher, a thin, pert, dressy woman, with little sympathy under her neat clothes. I loved history and read it at home all the time and just for the fun of it, and I could recite the kings of England by heart and still can. And I could draw the statue of William the Conqueror, because of his wonderful horse rampant on his haunches, with hoofs in the air. I can still draw that horse, any time you ask me to. But Miss Pitkins was cruelly difficult to deal with, because every time you recited, by some perversity, she made it seem wrong and foolish and picked out some mistake. To me it was every day an intense anxiety, and after such hard work, there I would get, at the end of the month on my report card, a plus-minus! I never had any true inner lightness about things like this, much as I might pretend to.

How did I look then? I wore a blue serge dress with long sleeves and brass buttons. I suppose Miss Lindquist had made it and during the fittings had sniffed about me interminably asking: "Oh, you want more bag, here?" And Mother would come up to the third floor to see how it was going. "Don't cut off her height you know, Miss Lindquist." And Miss Lindquist fussed about, plucking at the gathers and putting her hand on my backsides, would say: "Now that's better. That takes care of her *here*."

Because now I was really getting too fat; though I was athletic, you understand, and not a pale hypo-thyroid fat girl. But with a kind of helpless horror I saw the scales rise: A hundred and seventeen pounds. A hundred and twenty-three. A hundred and thirty-five pounds! And they went up and up until it was 150 and once even 154, I guess. That, however, was in college. But what made it worse was that now in high school, I was not just a sturdy, running girl, but I began to have a bust which filled me with dismay and true repugnance.

My mother did not wear corsets nor would Elsa. But Elsa was tall and thin, and here I was shorter and fat and woggling. I had to wear them, and brassières. The curtailed action, the disgusting hard-shell matronly appearance, the beetling hips! Oh, I did not like myself at all. And being fat I could not bear my appearance in ladylike clothes, though in heavy jackets and sweaters and several layers of cloth, I was concealed and seemed to have a sturdy compact look that was all right. That is why my mother, always vainly hoping that

I would take more interest in pretty clothes, said a little sadly that I "dressed like a cowboy."

Yes, this being fat was very hard for me. They teased me about it, the boys in the family calling me "the sod-packer," especially when I was diving, though I did not mind the teasing but rather liked it. But I could not bear the fatness. And as I said, it did not get so disgusting to me until I began to have a "bust." It may have been because breasts then, especially if there was the slightest indication that you had two instead of one, instead of a single encased mono-bust, were considered shockingly immodest. I longed to have a broad open chest where the clean shirt or blouse, as on thin boys, hung straight and loose and easy from strong shoulders. I tell this because my struggle against fatness was one of the fierce efforts of my life. They knew very little about diet then. I suppose I was hungry most of the time too, craving soda crackers and chocolate creams particularly.

But my best friend in high school was even fatter than I, and sometimes I wonder if I chose her because she made me seem thinner by comparison, quite slim almost. This was Blanche Lane. Her father had a drugstore opposite the West Hotel, and this meant that we got free ice-cream sodas and also free tickets to the Lyceum Stock Company. We went to the matinées on Thursdays, taking with us a box of Johnson's chocolates sealed in glass paper. The crackling of the paper, the asbestos curtain with its scene of Ancient Pompeii hanging there and to be drawn up soon, the fat chocolates being eaten, the thin orchestra playing, the gilt lumps and plaster festoons and garlands, cupids and tragic masks, the silent thudding of the ushers . . . well, that was a wonderful satisfactory feeling.

Blanche was in love with many actors, especially with Lewis Stone, who had been acting there the summer before, and she told me endless stories of his way of clapping his hand to his sword, his love-making.

I fell in love with the actors too, though I always pretended to be a little jeering about it. On Thursday afternoons, a reception was given on the stage for the audience, and Blanche and I went up, snickering and pushing each other, pretending to make a joke of it, but anxious and romantic inwardly. And we shook hands with them and perhaps got up the nerve to say: "I liked you in the part." And then with a sense of tremendous triumph and achievement we hastened out laughing and went over it again and again and every aspect of it—how we felt, what we might have said, how *he* responded. I had very strong and serious feelings, I know, but I covered them with jokes and a great deal of horseplay.

When I was not with Blanche Lane in those high school times, this is what I did:

We got out of high school at one o'clock. I took a street car home, arriving at nearly two. By that time the family had had lunch. Mother was perhaps at a Peripatetics meeting, reading a paper on Leonardo da Vinci. The little boys had gone back to school. The cook had left the kitchen and it was empty. (Our kitchen has always such a wonderful smell of wooden tables, white oilcloth, fresh bread, of sunlight rising from the scrubbed floor.)

So I got my own lunch, to wit: I cooked a bowl of very rich chocolate, really a sort of liquid fudge, and fried two eggs until they were as hard as greasy leather and then ate them with slabs of white bread and butter. And after that comforting and stimulating fullness, a warmly expanding stomach, I went happily walking up to Linden Hills, to see my friend Elsa Kuhlmann.

At Linden Hills there was a conglomeration of wooden grocery stores, and at Mrs. Prince's candy store, I went in and bought a bagful of waxen chocolate creams, licorice, wine balls, jaw-breakers, little sugar jugs that were full of syrup, and other things. I charged them.

"Charge it," I said grandly to Mrs. Prince, and she did. Once my debt ran up to a dollar and thirteen cents. (My allowance was a dollar a week.) This was an uneasy burden of debt. And just the way I felt about that dollar and thirteen cents is the way I feel now about my bills, a feeling of unmanliness, of not facing things, of silly mystical optimism. I always pay my debts before long, but I always feel a running undercurrent of guilt about them.

After Mrs. Prince's I walked on to Elsa's. The Kuhlmanns were German and Elsa was a nice talkative girl with a wide face and pale braids around her head, and she cheerfully did an amount of housework that was incredible to an American child—the washing, the ironing, the cooking. And Elsa's mother shocked me at first because she looked exactly like our idea of a washwoman, with her hair in that pug. But Mrs. Kuhlmann knew good music and knew all about Goethe and Schiller. She thought Americans had a silly idea of family life, with their hired girls and ragtime, and she would ask me what my mother was doing—a meeting or a committee perhaps? I felt her scorn and did not mind, but I was not on her side. My mother's ideas were best.

I had a fine time those afternoons, eating candy and talking with Elsa. I could make both Elsa and Blanche think I was exceptional, a rascal (once or twice I would smoke a cigarette to prove it). But soon I was going to have a hard time and encounter children who were not in the least impressed by me.

My mother began thinking that I should know some of the children of her nicest friends, cultivated people who lived downtown in red stone houses with porte-cochères. There was to be a dancing school started, and I was to go to it, Mother told me. I think I rather looked forward to it.

But that was a terrible evening. It was downtown in a bleak ballroom of the West Hotel. I wore my eighth grade graduation dress, a thin white dress with much lace insertion in it, and I disliked it and felt stout and dumpy in it. Mother took me down there and we went on the street car. Of course there was nothing so hopelessly plebeian about that, because in those days, men in top hats and ladies in ermine often went to the theater on the street car.

Nobody danced with me, unless led up forcibly by Mrs. Kingly, the teacher, a large colorless woman with huge well-placed feet and a stentorian voice. We stood in a row behind her and copied stiffly and flat-footedly her steps. Then the boys went to one side and the girls to the other, sitting in chairs along the ballroom wall. The whistle blew: "Boys choose partners."

No one chose me. They streamed across to this side and that of me. None looked at me and came straight up. I was left in that row of chairs and perhaps, far along, some other unattractive girl, some uneasy homely child with braces on her teeth. What made it worse was that my mother was there. It always makes it much worse to have your family see things like that.

This dancing school suffering was to last two or three years, and sometimes I think it accounts for a whole train of things in my life, like my bad judgment in marrying and my broken, truncated emotional life thereafter. There may have been a purpose in suffering that way, a final good. The only one I can think of is that because of this book, some parent may forego forcing children.

Mother was so very kind too and not in the least domineering, and I do not know how she could have persisted in doing this to me. She did though. The only explanation I can give is that I just didn't tell her how hard it was for me. I didn't let on. She never knew how I felt.

Dancing school shifted from the West Hotel to another ballroom. And it was some place else the next year. I remember that once a boy actually asked me to dance, but it was little Sammy Sewall and he was a head shorter. I remember that in my anxious fright before dancing school, I would plan, talk to myself in imagination, make up conversations with boys, hoping to charm them. I would say this witty thing and that. It was extraordinary how it never worked, how planned conversation always seemed so extra-false and fell so flat.

There was Louise Lamb, a rather plain girl but, I guess, very rich and with an inner fierceness and dash. I remember her fur-lined carriage slippers; her energetic coldness to me in the dressing room. (The girls put powder on. I have never been able to put powder on. It seemed such dusty foolishness, and what was the point of it? But I envied how they could sit down and dab at it, just the same.) She came in an especially beautiful brougham with spidery wheels, shining horses clattering with their tiny hoofs under the porte-cochère. I came on the street car with our hired girl Marie, carrying my slippers in a bag. I think it was this ride downtown into the dark night, the street car smelling of electricity and lined with bulbs and their fiery filaments—this going to humiliation, to doom, that gave me an uneasiness about night coming on and lights appearing that lasted many, many years. I still have this melancholy. I think it is just habit, going back to that time.

Sometimes when it got too trying I would stay in the dressing room. No, not there, because the social swells were there and chattering happily. So I would go even farther, into the toilet and rest there for a while. I don't think I looked externally pathetic or unhappy. I probably looked solid, scowling and scornful. To thunder with them! But I can't be sure.

There was to be a cotillion, a special party and we were allowed to ask a guest, each. Well, by some unlucky slip of impulsive generosity, I asked Blanche Lane. And Blanche, equally unfortunate and foolish, told her mother I had invited her. And Blanche's mother, to the private and inward horror of us both, insisted that Blanche go.

We did. It was just as bad as always and then doubled in uncomfortableness because nobody danced with Blanche either. Of course not. She was fatter than I. I was extra-humiliated by having as a friend one with such a funny face and a fatty, and moreover my heart absolutely bled for Blanche. But do you know what we did? And there was solace in it, a kind of revenge on our parents. Long before the party was over (we had come alone and I was to stay all night with Blanche) we sneaked away. And what did we do? Oh, the wonderful nerve and gall of it (we thought)! We walked down Hennepin Avenue and there was the Lyceum Theatre. We had no money, only carfare, but somehow we teased our way to free seats in the gallery. The gallery was supposed to be at night full of tough people. Also there was a general feeling in those days that it was very dangerous, bad for "young girls" ("young girls" always meant something special) to be out alone late at night, and worst of all at a theatre.

After the show we went home on the street car. We felt pleased with ourselves and not one bit frightened at being discovered. To hell with parents. We giggled with delight at ourselves on the street car. And when we got to Lanes' house and were getting ready for bed, we locked ourselves in the bathroom and smoked cigarettes. For years I was proud of this escapade. It is fine to be a desperado. Because of my failure at dancing school I took to derision of boys and love and all junk like that. I made Blanche laugh her head off on this subject, and Elsa Kuhlmann.

Once there was a boy in the neighborhood named Harold and I felt presently in a queasy uncomfortable way that Harold "liked" me. Mother one summer day began to talk to me thoughtfully. She said that she thought I should be nicer to boys, encourage them. And in a strange way I was filled with anger that "my own mother should ask me to flirt!" I went down to the lake and in anger and bitterness smoked cigarettes. I was really shocked, nauseated that she should suggest such a thing. Here, I gathered, she warned Anne and Elsa not to sit in hammocks with boys, and yet she would say such a thing to me!

Well, I cannot explain this. Parlor psychologists would say incipient homosexuality, I suppose. But I was affronted, I think, because it was such an unkind reminder of my failure, and perhaps I felt in a way that she was to blame.

II. HIGH SCHOOL

1.

*My parents' social life; parties with much culture and no
alcohol. "Peer Gynt" comes to town. Shocked at what Lucile
tells me about marriage. A nice English teacher. Religion in
our house; Torvald asks: "Is God a bird?" My lying again.
A music teacher who fed me.*

MY PARENTS' SOCIAL LIFE WAS QUITE DIFFERENT FROM OURS
today. First, it was non-alcoholic, and second, it seemed to be
devoted to intellectual things and to culture. In 1905 Mother
wrote to Anne, who had been sent to Wells College in the
East (because she was in love), and told her about a party
Governor and Mrs. Lind gave in their new house:

The house is very handsome. Mr. Bradstreet decorated it.
There was a covered matting to the side door, colored lackeys;
Mr. Dorner and his men served a repast in the dining room.
Chicken salad, sandwiches, coffee and chocolate, then ice cream
and cake, candies and nuts, etc. It was a crush. Too crowded.
Jenny looked nice in a white gown trimmed with real lace.

Yes, elaborate parties were given without any wine or
punch at all. My mother and father were not in the least
prim or intolerant about drinking. There was none of that
obnoxious under-feeling: "This is the way *we* believe in giving parties. Some may serve champagne and brandy, but *we*
do not approve of that sort of thing." No, that thought never
occurred to them. Great pains were taken to have excellent
food and they felt their occasions, with chicken salad and
ice cream, were as lively and gay as any parties could be.
And none of the guests seemed to go about (as we certainly
would now) with pinched expressions and a bored-endurance
look, but all talked gaily and thoughtfully.

This was a curious era in American life, this non-drinking era, and perhaps there was never any other like it. After the roughness and brawling of pioneer life, there appeared suddenly this gentle high-minded social life, the purpose of which was not gossip and flirtation, but loftiness and culture. Don't think I say this as a reproach to our social life now. Not at all. Ours may be more fun, more light-hearted and just as good. But theirs was good too and cannot be jeered at.

Perhaps the feeling of security I had in childhood came from the fact that my parents were always in sensible possession of themselves. But on the other hand, we never saw our parents as equals. There was a wall of reserve between us. Our children now, seeing that we like fun and are weak in a pleasant way—sometimes shouting after cocktails—can feel closer to us and more friendly and even, at times, disciplinarian (which is very good for them; nothing does a child so much good as to give his mother and father a good talking-to). That is why they call us by our first names. There are no uncles and aunts any more, at least not around here. "Hello, Brenda, where are you going?" calls Mark, aged three, who is Rolf's child, as I walk up through the lane.

"Oh, I am just going for a little walk. How are you today?"

"Fine. How are you?"

"Fine. Well, good-by, Mark."

"Good-by, Brenda."

Yes, how lucky and what a blessing it is not to be an Aunt. He could not possibly like me so well then.

But to go back to my parents' evening parties—there was no drinking, but there was lots of culture. Mrs. Frances Squire Potter taught English at the University, an ardent, billowing young widow with a cloud of dark hair and a rich voice like an actress. And with her there was always Miss Peck, who also taught English, I think, but she was stiff, thin and mouse-colored.

Elsa was going to the University (she would not go east

to school for anything. A woman's college, I should say not! She was too democratic for that.)

I spent an evening at Mrs. Potter's [she wrote to Anne]. I can only say with Father that it was decidedly Potteresque. Blanche Booth read the latter half of 'Othello.' Mrs. Potter and Miss Peck sang some of their 16th and 17th century songs, Mrs. Potter accompanying herself with zither and guitar. They told us anecdotes of their English life, served ice cream and cake, and she would end up the evening by reading a criticism of America and Americans by G. Lowes Dickinson. . . .

I think even little English Miss Pepper would admit that Minneapolis was growing to be a cultural center. Mary Shaw in 'Candida' and 'Ghosts'; Mrs. Pat Campbell in some Ibsen and Pinero, Paderewski, Jane Addams, F. Hopkinson Smith—all after vacation.

I am getting tired though of absorbing culture—not that I have any, you understand. But how tiresome and fruitless is this attitude of breathless interest, as you receive beautiful sugar-coated pills of cultuah, which are supposed to give you an appetite for more tablets of similar variety, but which only succeed in dulling the senses, and drowning out any power of original observation or independent reasoning. But my metaphors are getting hysterical; and my longing to get away from this superficial 'cultuah' and teaching in Montana or the Philippines, is slightly giving way before my longing for lunch.

And Mother wrote to Anne how "this promises to be an interesting week on account of 'Peer Gynt.' Mrs. Bright had our reading class at her house, and a few more. Mrs. Bright and Miss Peck played the Dwarf's Dance, and Mrs. Cohen read her paper on Ibsen."

Richard Mansfield was going to play in it. And so all intelligent people reread all of Ibsen and studied and put on their most beautiful empire gowns of yellow velvet with bands of fur trimming, and met and discussed it, and had chicken salad, ice cream and cake.

Mrs. Cohen was very scholarly, a lovely, invalid Jewess whose father had been an Italian rabbi, I think, and her lace peignoir and her frail, learned elegance and her fainting ladylike voice talking sighingly of Fra Filippo Lippi, made her seem to me like one of those great Renaissance ladies. Mother loved Mrs. Cohen and was always anxious about her ill health and would go down to her purple-brown wooden house on Third Avenue and discuss Robert Browning by the hour. I admired Mrs. Cohen, but I was really fond of Mr. Cohen, that round, bald, beaming and really funny lawyer. I will never forget how when I was six he said that sometime he was most "certainly going to give me a pony, with pink pants."

And Father talked about "Peer Gynt" at home, at our dinner table. It was lively, serious talk. It seems that Ibsen first wrote "Brand" to show the cruelty of idealism. Brand sacrifices his wife and child to his uncompromising ideal. When "Brand" appeared, people said: "So *that* is what Ibsen believes—that idealism is all wrong!"

Then Ibsen (Father explained), in answer to this, wrote a play to illustrate the opposite view and this about Peer Gynt, a man without idealism, whose philisophy was "to myself, enough."

I heard my father saying all this many times, to company, during that week, and could not quite understand it: "to myself, enough." I thought about it and listened and searched. And what had happened to Peer Gynt? the progressively weazening process of egotism, until the button-molder comes at last and takes him. And everybody discussed the symbolic meaning of the Great Boyg, the invisible Thing which said to Peer: "Go round about." That meant compromise. The boys and I knew about Peer Gynt from our Norwegian fairy-story book, because he is a folklore hero.

Years afterward I recognized both Brand and Peer Gynt in my inner self, though on a small unheroic scale—egotists both, and full of Will. But there has also been in me something soft and entirely different and it has been trying to expand, and it seems now as though it might supersede and drive out both of them. No, not drive them out, I hope, but reconcile them.

As for the pow-wow about "Peer Gynt" coming, it is inconceivable that such a thing should happen now, no matter what great play or new idea came to town. Perhaps it was because they had more time then. Horses and buggies delayed life so that there was more time to think and be serious and search into things carefully.

Central High School was a gray medieval castle sewn over with firescapes. After a year there, West High School was built, which was nearer our houses. You could walk there around Lake Calhoun and then along Lake of the Isles.

The fall that I went there, Sigurd came to high school. I saw him in moccasins wandering alone in the halls. I thought he was forlorn and had a pang. But I did not dare show it, because it might make him feel worse and certainly would make him mad. That awful feeling we have for brothers, sisters, parents. I suppose it is the germ of maternal feeling.

I began to go with a new girl in Linden Hills. That was Lucile Goodheart. I was flattered that she liked me, because she was three years older at least and oh, beautiful! She had the most beautiful, rich, mantling color and velvet brown eyes with stiff black lashes as on a doll, and her hair was naturally curly and brown, with gold threads winding through it, just to show the curves of it. Her two front teeth overlapped ever so slightly. It made her lips wet and red, and she had a lovely bump on the bridge of her nose and dark mole to throw all her radiance right at you.

What we liked to do in the afternoon was to walk out the car tracks. There were the new cars that went out to Lake Minnetonka. They were yellow street cars like the others, but they went like the wind and you could hear their exciting rail-galloping drone for miles, and their whistle was a peculiar wild scream.

Walking car tracks is fun. You see if you can walk seven rails without falling off and then you get three wishes. In the fall on either side of the tracks was the country, and weeds—the lovely smell of golden rod and purple asters and constellations of daisies and yellow and white clover; the singing of fall insects and the peculiar excitement, tinged with melancholy, that winter is coming and it will get cold and there will be skating. Fringed gentians. "The melancholy days have come, The saddest of the year." There was such a fragrance, such an association in those lines. Perhaps because we read it during the first days of school in September, when the autumn smells arose, and the sadness, and when the first tiny boats of yellow leaves would float on the smooth lake.

Lucile was famously popular with boys. Why, she had been engaged, really, to Hoyt Jackson, a towheaded downtown boy, whose father was a "grain man." They said that Lucile and Hoyt "spooned," that is, sat in a hammock and kissed each other. When I came to know her she no longer went with Hoyt, but there were others and she was very popular.

And one day walking along the tracks, way out beyond Browndale farm, she began telling me what people did when they married. Now this I had learned at nine or ten, but I had apparently sealed it off entirely, made myself forget it utterly. I think I had become romantic, that all sexual concepts had become distilled into romantic ones, as in *Ladies' Home Journal* stories where "he took her in his arms." Because I was horrified and miserable at what Lucile told me.

She told me about her cousin's marriage to a young man. The first night. Her cousin had hated to undress because, naked, she seemed to herself so dumpy. (I knew well how she must feel.) But to her surprise her husband did not mind her dumpiness at all. And Lucile went on glibly telling of it.

I must have experienced real shock and depression about

it, because that evening, even the wedding announcements in the newspaper were unbearable to me and for a long time I did not want to read about them, or engagements. Think of all the people in church, and the minister saying those sanctimonious things, with parents and relatives all simpering, at this horrible and strictly private business.

I think this was back of my feeling that lasted many years, that being "engaged" was disgusting humbug, and so are weddings. If people love each other, all right; but why should they wait for anyone's sanction? Especially when these same grown-ups were so mad, horrified, when boys and girls kissed each other in hammocks. (I had seen at a distance poor Anne's struggles with Father, because of her touching romance with a young man, a kind, laughing athlete with light blowing curls who took me sailing and let me hold the jib, and skimmed all over the lake with me in his racing shell.) Anyone could see that what the grown-ups were interested in was getting the girl safely married and supported, before she had any love affairs, because then she was supposed to be "bad" and no one would marry her at all. (I got this idea, of course, not from my parents, but from current literature.)

For instance, there was general talk like this—it was one of the clichés of the time: a girl should not let a young man kiss her because then he "wouldn't respect her." This made me boil. Who in thunder cared if he respected her or not? If she enjoyed the kissing why shouldn't she do it, in an honest way?

Well, the whole thing was disgusting to me and most of all the weddings.

But I do not feel this way now.

The teacher I liked best in high school was Miss Watts, my English teacher the last year. She looked like a sparrow because of her round eyes and thin lips meeting in a pro-

jecting point, and she had something inside her that made
me feel hopeful and elated. I liked writing themes for her.
I went walking around in an anticipatory dream about some
good story I was going to write for her. I thought about it,
upstairs and down, and walking around, and I looked forward
to the moment when I could really work on it, write it, as
something pleasant and easy like making a new dress. This
feeling of anticipation about any writing left me soon and
stayed away for thirty years. I think it is beginning to come
back, that happy creative absorption that only children have
and that all of us should have all our lives.

Miss Watts told us to write a description. I set to work on
this. What should I describe? Once I had been up at five
o'clock in the morning and had watched dawn from our landing to the lake. I would describe that dawn. That was a true
struggle, with those writhing words: to get on two-dimen-
sional paper in black pencil, shiningly, all that I had seen, the
light in a fawn-colored sky and the morning star. I worked
hard. I think of the Laocoön statue when I recall how I
worked and struggled with words and their arrangement.
And then in class, to my inner joy, Miss Watts read the
description and liked it and it was good.

Then I wrote a story. It began "He was an old man, a
very old man." My esophagus contracts now with disgust at
the obnoxiousness of that story. It seems the old man had seen
better days and was now a derelict whose job it was to clean
out the opera house. He swept up gum and chocolate wrappers
and programs among the dusty ruby-plush seats and the gilt-
encrusted loges. This was during the daytime. But one evening he stayed longer in the opera house than usual. Perhaps
he fell asleep. Anyway, when he came to himself the show
was on and he heard some music and the music awoke memories in his poor old age-corroded soul, and the cover of his
soul came off. That is, the story was about the magical effects

of music, which made him remember the sealed past and know that there is no death.

Well, that was the story. But do you know what they did? For the graduation exercises they made me recite it. Elocution, you know. There was a wan teacher with a dusty mop of wild hair. She was an elocutionist. She trained me in the auditorium. Day after day, I learned my own literary effort by heart and stood there and recited it and Miss Hobbs coached me again and again, with gestures. "He was an old man, a very old man." Gesture. Right arm up. "No, more natural. Like this. Again."

"He was an old man, a very old man."

"Your arm is too stiff. Not this way," and she imitated me ludicrously. "Now. Again." She did it as I should do it, and made her voice quaver.

Graduation night I did that. Before a thousand people. I was in my "graduation dress." Again it was crushed white batiste with insertion; a solid stout bag, I looked like. A girl played wandering Chopin on the piano as I said it. And my parents were some place in the audience. But let me forget it.

Mother wrote to Anne:

Rolf's eighth birthday was on Monday and he got his long-prayed-for automobile and Torvald has automobile privileges when Rolf is at school. Torvald and I were having a little religious conversation and he said: "Is God a bird?"

Torvald was then five. This showed how little religious instruction we had. Father had been brought up in a part of Norway that was noted for its religious melancholy. He revolted against all Lutheranism, all orthodoxy. He felt that it was a blessed rescue from it, I think, when he found Darwin and Huxley and all the English scientists who seemed to puncture religion and put it in limbo forever. And later, with tremendous scholarship, he knew all about the Higher Criticism of the Bible. With this erudition and his sharp intelli-

gence he liked to heckle and confound the Norwegian Lutherans in this country, who believed in verbal inspiration of the
Bible and in Satan and Hell and the Resurrection and the
miracles and all that. He liked to lead some Lutheran minister
into his trap and then spring it: "Well then, how could Moses
have written about his own funeral?"—as he must have,
Father said, and enumerated and pointed out the discoveries
of the Higher Critics and the philologists and the arche-
ologists and the paleontologists.

Well, Father in this criticism of orthodoxy was doing this,
I think: He was persuading himself that the frightening
religious teachings of his childhood were not so, and he was
rescuing other poor Lutherans from a fear of the Devil and
Hell. Darwin and other scholars, those wise, searching, fear-
freed men, proved there was no such thing. From what he
wrote about his childhood I can see that this is so. For when
as a boy he and his brother went up in the mountains to herd
goats, he said:

"The herding was not a hard job, even for boys of ten or
twelve. We had really much fun when the weather was good.
What fancies of adventures into foreign lands did not the
sea and the ships arouse! I recall only one drawback: that
was when toward evening my brother went out of sight to
round up the herd, leaving me alone. Then I would fear the
unusual colors in the sky were signals of the Day of Judgment approaching, as predicted in Matt. 24:39. For the moment it made me very repentant and pious but I was no
sooner well home before I felt as worldly as ever. It was as
though someone in the house could stay the Day of Judgment."

What my mother's religious education was I have no idea.
But both parents seemed to feel that a trace of fear or compulsion, whether of Methodism or Catholicism or any religion, was bad. They became Unitarians, particularly because
the minister was Dr. Simmons, a wonderfully sweet-natured

man and a remarkable scholar, whose sermons were about Evolution, history, Matthew Arnold, Emerson and such things. We were none of us christened, though we often went to Sunday school, driving way downtown in the big carriage, behind Lady.

But the fact that Torvald asked if God was a bird shows there was not much outward religion in the family. We never said our prayers, and no one ever told us how to. The neighborhood children had to say at night that frightening dismal prayer, "If I die before I wake..." Yes, it was only when I heard other people speak of church and religion and show their depressing, tinted Sunday school cards of Jesus and the disciples traipsing around barefooted in night gowns, that I became scared about graves, dead bodies, sin and Hell.

I mention all this, not because my parents' neglect of our religious training was right and the best thing. Perhaps it was not. But the interesting thing is that I, never having been forcibly fed religion or talked to about it with sanctimonious sweetness—behold, I began to have a deep sympathetic interest in it. All the words of theology (so depressing and repulsive to my friends who had strict Protestant parents) like Faith, Justification, the Holy Ghost, Resurrection, Revelation, Transfiguration, and saints and archangels—they seemed to me beautiful and as poetic as something out of Shakespeare or John Donne, and full of meaning, and I wanted to know all about them. My respect for religion seemed to grow naturally and in a cheerful way, and it expands all the time so that presently it may include all my life and consciousness. No, "respect" is not the word. I mean this: that whenever I read of great men who have been religious, such as Tolstoi, John Donne, Blake, Carlyle, Bach, Michelangelo, there spreads and expands in me a kind of light and recognition which says, "Yes, that is right. That makes me feel better. Yes, that is *it*, the way to be. That opens up life to us, instead of closing it."

And so I must speak of an ethical struggle that began in

childhood and that is not over yet by any means. I became quite a liar. Though I don't know whether it was that I was such a liar, or that I wanted to be truthful so much that I felt especially guilty about it. Anyway, this has been a life-long struggle with me, to be truthful—an inward struggle and examination.

It was always so easy for me to lie. I suppose I have a good imagination and so an unusually alert tact. I can fore-stall so quickly hurting people's feelings or displeasing them. But also my conscience just hates lying and always has. And it is cowardly, which is a thing to be ashamed of.

Well, this is one thing I have figured out about my lying. My mother was very much of a question-asker like all moth-ers. And like many mothers her questions were often per-functory and absent-minded. That is, they did not arise out of true interest. "Did you wash your hands, dear? ... What did you do, dear?" One's heart sank with boredom and ennui at answering because she was not truly interested, as a friend would be. "Tell me quick, what happened?" is your friend's attitude. It is easy enough to answer then.

So I got in the habit that all children have, when they come home— "Oh, don't ask me that. Oh, heck, what a bore. . . ." Though I never said this out loud. I was too polite.

But to save myself a narrative I would answer the ques-tions "What have you been doing, dear?" with some mono-syllabic explanation, probably not true: "I was just at Blanche's."

But one day when I said "at Blanche's," I had been at Mrs. Fahnestock's, my music teacher's, all afternoon. To say "at Blanche's" would save the effort of more words, would cut it off right there. But Mother happened to know that I was not at Blanche's. They had been looking for me, I guess, tele-phoning and so on. There it was—a lie. I had to go to my room and have dinner up there, a serious punishment in our polite friendly household. I did not mind the punishment, but felt frightful pain about the lie. The bottom of my whole character seemed to have dropped out, a feeling of miserable instability as if I were on quicksand.

And why did I lie? It was even more respectable to be at my music teacher's than at Blanche's, if that could be possible. There was not the slightest sin in being in either place. Why did I go out of my way to lie? First, perhaps, to save myself a weary narrative to one who was not excitedly interested in it, and second because of a need for privacy, for not having all my acts searched into.

And so I try not to bore my own child with questions (failing, of course, every day). And instead of trying to get her to entertain *me,* which is back of parents' lazy, perfunctory, unlistening questions, I know I should try to entertain *her*—tell something lively and exciting. And parents assume that they must know all their children's doings, and for the children to conceal anything is deceit. But all people have a right to privacy. So I say to Gaby: "Always say to me, if you feel like it: 'I am sorry but I don't want to tell you that.' Then I will really admire you."

For one curious result of my childhood feeling that to conceal anything is deceitful, is this: I now feel as though I have to tell everybody *everything.* I have been a perfect sieve. Anyone can know anything about me, if they ask me and want to know.

"What were you doing last night?" I say in a mildly interested voice to Johnny Baxter, who has certainly done nothing more sensational than go to a movie.

"I would tell KSTP but not you," he says.

"I hear you had a heachache yesterday."

He staggers in mock despair, makes horrible contortions of hopelessness.

"My Lord, I tell something to some one and it gets to you and the next morning by 8:30 everybody knows it downtown ... Now that's good service."

But I have decided, after many years and doubt, that I like this free candor in myself. Yes, I much prefer it to caginess.

My music teacher was Mrs. Alexandra Hollander Fahnestock. Anne and Elsa took music lessons first of Miss Dillingham, and Elsa sat there on the stool trying to stretch those sixths, tears of exasperation running down her cheeks. Mother let Elsa off. No music for Elsa was the verdict. Anne then went to Miss Helga Johnson and so did I. We had to make our hands like claws and hammer at Plaidy exercises, the most uphill, tiresome, impossible thing. Anne got to play quite fancily and well: Mendelssohn's "Songs without Words," Sinding's "Rustle of Spring." But I did not like Miss Johnson's teaching.

Later by some chance I was sent for music lessons to Mrs. Fahnestock. Well, she was a wonderful person. She was elderly, a Jewess, I think, with a dark dramatic head, hair elaborately coiffed, and raised black brows and a huge nose like Punch; short, fat, stubby hands, white and pulpy and covered with rings. I can see now her two opals, the size of small peas and surrounded by diamonds. She wore a blouse and skirt—a fancy silk-lace blouse, and it met her skirt neatly, secured by a hundred pins, at a belt that had a "Grecian dip" in front. This belt was strung around a hard large corset. She had that hard-shell corseted solidity of women of that time.

She lived way downtown—I had to transfer twice to get there—in a railroad apartment on Twenty-second Street and Park Avenue. In the front room were her piano and fringed portières and hassocks, and the piano was bristling with standing photographs of European singers and virtuosi. She was one of a distinguished musical family. Her brother, as I remember it, was a director of the Berlin Conservatory.

She was utterly adorable, precious, dear, good, fascinating, wonderful. Full of praise and thrilling musical excitement, of stories about Melba and Lucca, a primadonna, she told me, whose blue eyes were so heavily encircled with double-fringed eyelashes that in Germany the bakers called a certain cake "Lucca eyes." Mrs. Fahnestock told me that when she herself was young and walking down Unter den Linden, a passer-by was overheard to say: "She looks like the Ninth Symphony." And this was the greatest compliment of her life.

She made me feel that she saw something special in me. But she did in all her pupils. There was one girl, blond and sweet, named Eva. "The corners of her mouth are so beautiful," said Mrs. Fahnestock. And sure enough I studied the corners of Eva's mouth and so they were, and from that time on I saw how aesthetically interesting and important the corners of a mouth are. Yes, she was always opening my eyes to interesting, dramatic, and beautiful things.

I don't know how many years I took lessons. It seemed to go on forever. I think the family forgot about it. They just paid the bill as it came in every month, with the grocery bill. I was never catechized or pressed about practicing. And I never, as long as I took lessons, practiced enough, or at all. Through all my childhood, I never once went to a lesson with that pleased inner peace: "I have really practiced this week. You will be surprised how I have polished off things this week." Always some uneasiness and bluff. But Mrs. Fahnestock liked the way I thundered at the piano and had power in pieces that were slow. Chords. Oh, I could do those and put in expression!

And not only did she not reprove me, but she fed me. Perhaps that is what kept me going to my lessons. Perhaps she was poor and did this because it was so necessary to keep me coming. But I think not. She was married (and I caught the overtones of unhappiness) to a tall hook-nosed man who looked like a duke but was a floorwalker in a big furniture store, and she had a child, a knife-faced boy named Noel.

I think she fed me because she was an angel of German hospitality. I would arrive there after high school. We walked the length of the dark railroad apartment to the dining room, with a window on some dim backyard. She brewed tea (we were not allowed to have tea at home. A stimulant!) and she gave me wonderful fat rich doughnuts doused in white powdered sugar. And sometimes there were other special cheese cakes and strange delicious pickles and European things that my mother with her notions would not have approved of. I got fatter and fatter. Tea with sugar and cream, several cups of it. Good.

Then to the piano. She sat beside me fingering a long gold chain that hung way below the Grecian dip with large topaz-colored beads at intervals. I sat down with misgivings and played with bluff and vehemence something from Schumann's "Album of Childhood." She expounded it. It was a story, she said. "You see? He tells a wonderful story. The arpeggios. He plucks the harp."

Well, God bless Mrs. Fahnestock. All those years of lessons, I at least learned to read music and soaked in an affection for it and, now that I am thirty years older, I like to practise the piano so much that I am afraid to begin it early in the morning for fear I will keep it up all day.

III.   COLLEGE

1.

I go east to college and am shocked to find that I am a card.
The money emotions in our family. Father resists automobiles.
How my mother contended for her children. A queer adoles-
cent depression.

THEY WERE GOING TO SEND ME TO WELLS, LIKE ANNE.
Anne graduated that June. She would be at home then and
come out. Elsa was a senior at the University. As I said, a
woman's college was not for her. Too ladylike, too seminary-
like. She wanted to be where there were law and engineering schools and poor people and coeducation.

Mother thought Wells would be good for me, I think, because of my social backwardness. Mrs. Elbert Carpenter had
gone to Wells and was a trustee, and Mother admired her very
much: the beautiful Georgian house that she lived in, the
clear scholarly papers she read at the Peripatetics, speaking
in her neat, lucid, alert sentences, her fine clear spirit. (I
derided Mrs. Carpenter as I did all socially prominent and
"splendid" people, because of my own social catastrophe, I
suppose; but more because I was always trying to make people laugh.)

Miss Lindquist came that summer to make my clothes.
Name tapes were sewed on everything, on all the long black
stockings. Then Mother had her own tailor, Mr. Nilson, make
a tailored suit for me. This filled me with anticipation. I saw
myself graceful, negligent in it, like a loose-limbed Eton boy.
But it was a terrible disappointment, because instead I looked
like a club woman, with stiff buckram over my bust and

the coat tails beetling over the hips. Then we got a hat to go with the suit, a great wheel of a brown hat, held on by long hat pins. It was high-sitting and not becoming.

I began to hear talk of Wells from girls who went there. Most of it centered around the word "popular." "Oh, she is popular ... But she wasn't popular ... But I am sure *you* will be popular." I had misgivings about it. Sometimes, however, they said consolingly, a girl who was not popular at first became so after several years when it was discovered that after all she was a perfect peach.

Sitting here in 1938 and looking back at the me of that time, I see myself as a silent doltish girl. But then I remember Anne Herendeen, a Wells senior who visited us that summer, and I see that I was not unattractive, but jolly, and full of good ideas. Because Anne Herendeen took a shine to me, and I can hear her terrifically loud laugh hooting out at me, a laugh that was so peculiarly loud that I fancied it was like a hyena's, and it was full of uncontrollable amusement.

She was from Geneva, New York. Her father was rich and she didn't like him very well. They had a coachman and two horses, and her mother (I asked her for these details at once, of course) was a black-browed stylish lady who believed in woman suffrage and had really seen Susan B. Anthony and Elizabeth Cady Stanton.

In September, the Wells Special left the Milwaukee depot. My trunk was packed with all my black stockings, brassières, Peter Thompsons and cotton knit underwear. We drove downtown with Lady. The train left after dark. I was all dressed up in my new "strictly" tailored suit and my wheel of a flat hat was tweaking at my hair. I was anxious inside about popularity. Would I be popular? There would be all these other girls on the special (probably very popular). Eastern girls would begin to get on at Chicago.

Besides this, there was an uneasiness, about riding on a

train, and changing in Chicago. My ticket was so very long and complex and what if I lost some of it? And then I carried, in a suède pouch very uncomfortably around my waist between petticoat and skirt, my money. What if that should be lost? I had never carried much money like that—forty dollars—before. There was risk in taking a Parmalee bus at Chicago, from one station to another.

Well, all these trepidations were inward and no one would have guessed them from looking at me. My corset dug into my thighs when I sat down, and pushed up my bust, and when I looked in the strip of mirror beside my Pullman seat, it seemed to me I was obnoxious looking, dishearteningly matronly. Yet, in certain rough clothes and shoes, I could feel so swashbuckling. Well, it was too bad.

The Wells Special went galloping over the hills east of Rochester: Canandaigua, Ithaca. And then along the narrow track that winds along the shore of Lake Cayuga for forty miles. On a bright morning we arrived at Aurora, a sleeping Victorian-Gothic hamlet. The little wooden station is on the blue lake. The waves sparkle right beside the tracks.

That first day an extraordinary thing happened. I experienced suddenly a wonderful sense of power, a feeling I had never had before. I began to walk around free and hatless. (The awful hat was hidden in the closet.) Everybody asked me questions: "What are your brothers' names again?" they'd ask, fascinated by the strangeness. "Sigurd, Arnulf, Rolf and Torvald ... And then there was my little brother Ugla who died." "Say, Ueland is fresh." A delightful feeling came into me.

I cannot tell you how remarkable it was, to find myself that very first day a card, a wag. It was so immediate, a complete change. I can still feel how it surprised me.

You will see that later in life, two or three times the same thing happened, when I was cast out, so to speak, thrown out and all alone. That is why all submerged people should be sent away from their families, or disinherited, or divorced, or repudiated. Their powers will come suddenly to life, in the most wonderful way.

The sophomores were supposed to haze the freshmen, that is, to sneer at them and make them stand back when upper classmen passed through a doorway. I dreaded only one sophomore and that was Marion Woodward. It was probably because she veiled me with my old Minneapolis inferiority feelings, for Marion was from home and she had been at the dancing school where I was so humiliated. And she was herself a short, peremptory and bossy girl with strong sturdy legs. The whole Woodward family were dynamic, quick, bossy, jolly people.

Well, whenever Marion came near, I began to tremble with inner excitement for fear she might boss me. When anyone threatens to boss me I become violently excited inwardly. I felt this way with Father and, when I was little, with Anne. The feeling was not fear exactly, but an anxiety that they will make me so mad that I will have to knock them down. It is hard on a good-natured person.

Freshmen got homesick. Everybody watched for this malaise to come. It was a very quick, attacking illness. Sunday night in the chapel, there was a 'cello playing. Marjorie, my friend, and I sat together and the 'cello was too much for her and her homesickness struck her amidships and she arose and struggling with her paroxysms, pushed past the knees of a long row and left the chapel. "Poor kid. Homesick." After a few moments I did the same—put my handkerchief to my eyes, though I was not homesick at all but just wanted to get out.

After chapel the upper classmen came rushing up to my room with concern on their faces and there I was not crying in the least. "Well, for heaven's sakes! That crazy Ueland."

Among the others who came was even Mary Whitehouse.

She was a senior and the president of Student Government, and she had steady blue eyes and plain hair and she walked with a masculine swing from leg to leg; that is her shoulders swung stiffly with her stride. Her blue eyes, her honest clear look, were like Elsa's. I fell in love with her. This was "a crush." It did not last long, I think, only about ten days.

This incipient homosexuality in college (it is such a disagreeable, unspiritual, scientific, evil-laden word for something that can be romantic and inevitable and all right) is interesting. There were certain girls and they were together all the time and jealous and all that. We heard from time to time how they were seen kissing each other, in a sappy way. It did not shock the rest of us. We had not much curiosity about it. If it was called to our attention we thought it queer, repulsive perhaps, just as other people's love-making always is. But for the most part we did not think much about it.

Dear Father:

This is our biology teacher. Drab complexion, salt and pepper hair that is twisted and distorted into all sorts of wry angles and held in place with a couple of vicious looking sidecombs. She invariably carries a handbag, something like the one Mother gave me. (I always jeered at handbags.) In laboratory when we are dissecting crayfish, she will say: "We are all getting along so nicely today that we may be able to do some pretty little extras I have...." meaning tapeworms and liver flukes....
P. S. I haven't heard a word about Lady.

Dear Mother:

There was a special train to Auburn a few days ago to hear Sembrich. She has a smooth, golden voice that pours out slowly.... At evening we row much on the lake and watch the sunset. It is a wonderful time of year when the frogs stutter all night. I can't wait until the bridge of my nose gets sunburned. The golden lines of sunlight rippled on the sand bottom and there are dark and little green fish, parallel and then dispersing in explosion. I put water on my arms and face. Must get brown, tanned like a soldier.

Dear Father:

I can't go to the prom because Edward, Anne Herendeen's brother, will not be able to come. A great relief has cleared my brain. . . .

Louise Wyman, a St. Paul girl, is sitting right next to me in the Library now, and when I stop for thoughts (which come slowly) she talks politics. It seems to me she is remarkable. Child labor, high tariff, more battleships and the Y.W.C.A. are her platform. But of course she knows nothing about these, so it doesn't matter. . . . Of course you'd like to know about my studies. English is the best. I wish I were Lafcadio Hearn.

Dear Sigurd:

Bless you for writing and answer this right away. Tell me more about the dancing class. Oh, Gol, I am glad I am out of it. . . .

I went to prayer meeting this morning and was urged to be "cheerful" and also "not to study on Sunday." Prayer meetings aren't much, I've decided. Haven't I been cheerful all year? And isn't studying on Sunday a necessity? Now tell me about Ray Van Tilburg and the rest.

Dear Mother:

You just asked me to write to Elma and Vendla [the maids] and some mental telepathy must have been involved because I just did it. . . . Monday was the game. I had been tense all week. At night I threw basket after basket. I couldn't have been more nervous if I had been going to the dentist's. Well, we won and I made quite a few baskets, a thing which I mention to you only because you're interested.

Like fun. The conceit in this letter, which I can see better than the reader, discourages me now in 1938.

Dear Brother Rolf:

I am going to sing in an opera, "Patience," given by the Boat Club. I am merely in the chorus however, in Greek draperies n.b. cheesecloth. . . . Also, my regular Rolf, you will be interested in my baseball team, being so athletic yourself. . . . I am already practicing chinning and I can now hang very well for quite an instant, without touching the floor. But I really haven't any news at all, Rolf. All my excitement is spiritual at present.

Mother said "spring hat?" in her letter, but tell her nix. There is no necessity for a hat until I get home. Then, perhaps. (Perhaps never.)

Dear Mother:

Thanks for the fifty dollars. . . . There was an Episcopal chicken pie supper down at the prep. school. Miss Lamereaux, the head mistress, spoke of you profusely. She has heard that you are the most able woman in Minneapolis. Isn't that absurd?

I think I have a logical mind. Dr. Lowe in his history lectures, will ask me a momentous question. I answer and he nods impressively.

My letters from college are so immature compared to Anne's and often the conceit in them saddens me. (I show you only the bright, more attractive parts.) I never once comment with eagerness on something I am learning, but it is always about how *I* affect the professors.

Anne would say things like this, in her letters: "My work is so fascinating. I never was so interested in so many things. I am fairly bombarded on all sides with new ideas, a young Renaissance is going on inside me. Spencer and Stephens and Huxley and Ruskin and Carlyle and Plato and Mill and a lot of other big men that have been little but names to me till now. I hope I can keep my balance and assimilate all their conflicting thoughts. . . .

P.S.: Too bad about the little Pink-Eyed Ones. I had it myself."

No, I am bumptious and conceited and full of myself. In this kind of energy I was a little like Father.

In February we walked to Auburn, twenty miles away. We got up before dawn, in the black bitter cold. We walked five miles up the hill and there in the black trees was the village of Sherwood, its chimney pots against the rising sun.

Such a strong aesthetic feeling and memory I have of this. The sparkling stars before dawn. The morning star growing large and yellow as the east grew lighter. The smell of frost and cold. The physical struggle and thrashing and effort through the deep snow-frozen ruts. Part of the pleasure of that walking was that it was such a battle. The cold sweat poured out of our hot hair onto our blazing faces. We "stamped and raged and labored and worked." For me there was always such pleasure in physical labor and my own energy. And this too was like my father.

Sometimes I find things like this in my mother's letters: "Father feels rather downcast as his bills are heavy this month, taxes besides everything else . . ."

I must speak about the money emotions in our family. They are important in every family and run deep under the surface and affect children very much.

My father had so much ability that he had no fear about making a living, but he could not bear a debt. He had a violent temper, though it blew off quickly. When the bills were high, it exploded, perhaps just on one evening a month and perhaps for only a few minutes.

I think there was this conflict in Father: His experience had taught him that there was a reward in frugality, in saving enough pennies out of ditch-digging to study law. But he also naturally was full of generosity, and had a buccaneering swing and opulence so that he always, in the end, gave us whatever we wanted.

But once a month, when he came home and saw the bills, he blew up. "A thousand barrels of devils!" In his voice was the vicious note of awful swearing. I can feel my face turn gray at the thought of it.

It was hard on Mother, on me, on everybody in the house, even the little boys. Elsa years afterwards, when she came to understand her inner self, thinks that Father's subjecting my mother, whom she so passionately loved, to these brief trying moments, was what kept her ever from marrying. Be dependent on a man for money, for support? I guess not! Not on your life! And there is something of this same feeling in me. But remember that Father's passion was not really mean at all. It was a quick physiological explosion and he could not help it. Nevertheless these things hurt people deeply, in a family, and the effects last forever.

Mother seemed to take Father's explosions about the bills quietly. Once in a while with dignity she told him that she "just would not have it!" and this made him unusually contrite at once. But I know that it was very hard on her. No first-rate person can bear to be a burdensome expense.

"Never be meek," I have heard Mother say countless times in a pleasant but a very, very definite way. And I think it was lucky for all of us that she would not become an overworked housewife.

For example, she would never learn to sew. Perhaps she had no skill for it, but I seem to remember that she said that if she did sew, if she started doing work like that, she would be stuck in it forever. So we had two servants and dressmakers and so on. I do not think this was any unwarranted expense and hardship for my father. She knew his ability. There was no selfishness in it. Nor was there a trace of social climbing or doing "the correct thing" in it. No, she was always just working to create a fine civilized family. The children would be healthy and handsome. They would go to universities and colleges and have professional training if they wanted it. They would dress well. This for the sake of beauty, and not just to make an impression. And throughout her life she was saving money out of her, I am sure, very small allowance, or whatever it was she had. For what? To buy beautiful silver, to buy long-coveted pieces of fine furniture, a gilt mirror, or an eighteenth century English sideboard. Always economical contrivance entered into it. She used her meager savings for a more beautiful garden, a pool which she had Mr. Gunderson put in.

But she did not care at all about an automobile. We had Lady, only one horse. And when Lady died at a very old age, we bought the unused, frolicsome round-bellied Forman horse, Bessie. Bessie was eating in our pasture anyway, because the Formans next door had for years used only their limousine. Bessie and her one-seated high-wheeled carriage I think we got for a hundred dollars.

Father resisted automobiles for years. It was not until Torvald was a freshman in the University that Father bought one at last, a Packard touring car. And Father kept this car for years, until it was practically junk, with a bell like a fire engine ringing in it some place, and it would break wind horribly in traffic. Under the unshakable impression that he had a magnificent five-thousand-dollar car, when President Hoover came to town, or some tremendous dignitary, Father would gravely suggest that we offer our fine car for the reception of him.

Torvald, Toke, was the youngest and so brown-eyed, smiling and good-natured, that he was allowed to do anything he wanted to. By the time they came to Toke, every bit of parental discipline had died away, vanished. Perhaps it was this automobile that spoiled his university career, for he got very big and lumbering and, as he said, could not seem to do anything but toss pennies at a crack. He flunked. He began to work in a bank.

Mother, of course, while the rest of the family rode in the automobile, was going over to the State Capitol every day on the street car. Beautifully dressed, she would take this hour's ride. It was more than ten miles. If there were errands to do downtown, buying safety pins, toothpaste, and all the tedious shopping of a large family, she would take a street car that made a circuit way downtown in Minneapolis, transfer, and then travel on to St. Paul. But if the rest of us had to take a street car, we felt like sufferers, almost like Marie Antoinette on the tumbril. I never heard Mother complain that she never used our car, that Torvald had it, or the other children. No, she liked the street car. She liked the walking especially that she had when she took the street car.

So Mother was certainly not selfishly extravagant, but she built up a good life for us. She quietly held my father to that. She contended for her children.

Father used to say with fake mournfulness, how he wished that she were not a public character, but kept chickens like a good Norwegian woman, like Martin's wife, for example. Uncle Martin had a better education than Father; he had studied engineering and Latin in Norway, and then emigrated and took a homestead in North Dakota. But he married a meek woman who spent her life in the kitchen with the windows down, cooking bad coffee and frying pork. Their fine-looking children were under-educated and became apathetic and talked in grunting monosyllables. I think there might have been more fire and excitement in their lives. I think their mother was too meek.

But to return to my money emotions. Father's swearing at the bills or something else, has done this to me: I am always plunging away, in my mind, from the thought of money. And like Elsa, I cannot bear to be dependent on anyone for money. No, I myself must be the dispenser of it. It is suffering for me to accept money, even when it is owed to me, and I have worked very hard for it. "Oh," I will think, "you don't need to do that. Here. Please. Really. Don't do that." I like to get it too, of course.

Perhaps it is because Father did this: When I asked for money, as a child, his first impulse was doubtful. "But why do you want it?" Then resentment would well up in me. Immediately there came his second, better, tolerant thought. "All right. All right, here. Here, Poompy. Rub noses." And he would give me twice, thrice as much as I had asked for.

And there I was— What emotional indigestion! Gratitude now, charged with guilt, with sorrow to be a nuisance and an expense, with guilt about my resentment of a moment ago: "when he was so nice as to give me all this!"

Yes, around the whole question of money there is emotional turmoil, and it whirls in me at the thought of bills, investments, salaries. I wish that sometime I would become as quiet about it as St. Francis himself.

In my first year at college I had a hard experience. On my arrival I had the surprising triumph of being popular. But as the year went on, a painful self-consciousness came to me. I would make a joke and watch eagerly to see if it was effective. I would hear the words as they came out, and of course they were stilted and angular because I planned them, and people would be only embarrassed; and so I became afraid and miserable in the presence of certain girls, especially the more witty and attractive ones, the girls with the diamond bar pins and much self-confidence. In their presence I lost my power and all magnetism:

For months this was an awful inner experience for me, an unbearable unhappiness and confusion. I never spoke of it. I mentally figured, puzzled over it, sought every possible device to explain it and escape from it. I tried praying even.

But at last in June, at commencement, in the lovely weather, when there was tennis and swimming and the excitement of interesting visitors, again I began to have some small triumphs of vanity. Again I was as happy as I had been at first.

I think the explanation is this. And I speak of it because I have seen this painful rhythm in so many people, particularly in young ones, and I feel so sorry for them. That is, they find themselves popular, gay and admired, and then presently no one seems to like them at all. In me I think this is what happened: When I did not think particularly highly of myself, I was really original and free and independent, and that made me entertaining, and interesting to others. Then I began to *work* to be entertaining, contriving and planning it, and watching anxiously to see if I was. But this always automatically seals up this inner creative fountain, which is in everybody and is always changing and casting up something new. At last when we are thoroughly rebuffed, discouraged, we despair and give up all efforts, and become again independent of others and full of our old freedom. And what happens? At once the free fountain is working again, the fountain of originality and life. And there people are again —all listening! And smiling and wanting to get in the circumference of our presence as though we shed sunlight, as though we sent out ultra-violet rays.

No, children, don't work for effect, ever. Just feel free inwardly and outwardly and know that you are something remarkable (but forget it), and know for certain that the inner fountain is always there. Then everything will be all right.

2.

Wells College is remote and safe and not near enough to the trade-unions. I go to Barnard; good professors and bad colds. Richmond Hill Settlement House and a little whiff of Bohemianism.

DOROTHY GILBERT FROM PORTLAND, OREGON, WAS AN ODD-looking tiny girl with a tiny aquiline nose and slightly receding chin. She led me intellectually. When the others wanted to give a play that was "appealing" like "The Professor's Love Story" or Pinero, Dorothy and I had contempt for them. Give Shaw or Strindberg. Not such popular junk!

She led me into ideas about woman suffrage and art. We jeered at the girls with huge photographs of fiancés on their bureaus, in silver frames. They just wanted to get married.

Oh, my heavens! how homey. They had not the faintest idea of what a trade-union was, or settlement work.

Dorothy wanted to become a stage designer. So she led me into helping her make a Gothic chapel for "The Pirates of Penzance," with stained glass windows of colored tissue paper. (I am still proud of it.) And she would sing hymns, changing each word to its antonym. That is, while the others in chapel were singing "Let us gather by the river, the beautiful beautiful river," Dorothy in her tiny clear voice would sing as loud as she could: "Let us hemstitch by the lake, the ugly, ugly lake."

October 7th, 1911. Initiation for Phoenix easy. Perhaps I was too fresh.

Oct. 13th. I must keep a notebook. California has suffrage.

Oct. 18th. Read Christian Science with Inez. Too much God overalls.

Oct. 19th. Read Machiavelli. He was like father. Bal says I make fun of everybody. Not so.

Oct. 26th. Saw Henrietta Crosman in "The Real Thing." Cheap, simple. Cornell men are unenlightened pampered dogs.

Oct. 27th. Meecie said I was conceited but clever, and I was behind the door. Louise said Meecie was right about conceit.

Oct. 29th. Ione gave a spread. Felt like a vulture over that chicken. Ill all day, in spirit, that is.

Nov. 5th. Sprat is curing me of conceit. She says: "That's not funny!!"

Nov. 15th. Nellie Hoffman tells about man who kissed her. He went up her arm like a vacuum cleaner.

In the dark great forest on the hills there was Moonshine Ravine and Dorothy and I walked there. I remember one evening coming down through the November woods full of dim rain falling on the gold rust leaves. A Celtic twilight, I thought. I felt presences. I thought I saw a nymph with gray eyes, a Celtic nymph. And perhaps there were leprechauns. I have always liked this idea of invisible beings become visible, when we are clear enough.

And Dorothy talked about William Yeats and Blake. We copied, in the library, drawings of Aubrey Beardsley and of some artist who made fine drawings of ancient Britons. At a masquerade I went as a Briton. I made my long hair look like a black mane to the shoulders and Dorothy made a shield from a dishpan cover, with the ancient Celtic symbol on it, three legs running in the same direction, and I wore wrinkled white stockings with cross-crossed thongs. The others, to our disdain, dressed almost unanimously as "coons." Yes, Dorothy and I loved wild Britons and Celts—Tristram and Cuchulain—and got to know all about them.

My other best friend was Marjorie Shipherd of Duluth, who was Irish, arch, and wonderfully flirtatious, with a shriek of a laugh. Well, Junior year Shippy (somehow at college everybody became Skunkie, or Skookie, or some such thing) was taking advanced embryology. In her fancy blouse she would sit alone in the laboratory for hours, opening aged eggs, fertilized for many days, and her beautiful Napoleonic nose wrinkling with disgust, she would write down her notes nevertheless, with exactitude. She did good work in embryology, passed with a good mark.

But at the same time she would say things like this to me.

" 'Sexual and a-sexual'—what does that mean?" she would ask in her altogether arch, cute way. She really did not know. I teased her about it, but I certainly was not the one to tell her.

Shippy was Catholic. She had been to a convent where they took baths in their nightgowns so that they could not see their own bodies. In the wooden Gothic house where the Juniors lived, Shippy and I and Helen Clark roomed together. There was on our floor only one bathroom, the tub surrounded by a white curtain, and an airshaft extended from it to the third floor. And the girls up there, if they cared to be so horrible, could look down and see whoever was in the tub. Well, of course no one would do that! For all of us, when we

undressed at night, never exposed ourselves to our room-
mates. You put your nightgown on the very first thing, perhaps over your street suit and hat, and then struggling, undressed beneath it, and when that was over, hurried into a
bathrobe. But we liked to tease Shippy, who was convent-
bred and more shockable even than the rest of us.

So what we would do was this: we would stick our heads
through the chute, as though to look down at the tub below
with Shippy in it, but *with our eyes shut.* Oh, yes. We
could never have stood it ourselves to open them. That would
have been too awful, too coarse for words. Her frantic shrieks
filled the building.

To the young, eating is very important. My one-line diary
runs like this:

Feb. 24th. Gorged on Isabel's cake and candy. Gertrude Cleve-
land a-sniggering here all night.
Feb. 28th. Went to bed reading Lord Jim and eating allegrettis.
March 9th. Went to breakfast but head ached and nose ran.
Margaret Howe's family left cookies. Read about pirates
in Kipling.
March 26th. Quick walk to Levanna with Hough. Ship told me
about John Sevier, eating cake in bed.
April 3rd. Prodigious amounts of candy about house. Louise
thinks settlement people are fools because they smoke.

We had orgies. Our eating candy, I suppose, was our
equivalent for getting drunk. It is the same thing, really.

I can remember eating a large box of candy with Sue
Fritsch and someone else. Oh, how ribald, careless and jolly
we felt! A little sick, but who cares? We were in the reception room, the inner sanctum really where the Dean had tea
with visiting dignitaries, an elegant room of blue and gilt
with glass cabinets full of objets d'art and gilt-framed por-
traits and thin-legged French sofas. But here we were this
night, on our candy jag, sitting on the sofa and laughing our
heads off. I would pick up an expensive vase from the glass

cabinet, from "the gum machine" and would toss it and see how nearly I could come to dropping it, to make the others yell with fright. Or we would play catch with it, feeling like such rascals, such hobbledehoys.

Well, that summer after my third year at Wells, a curious thing happened. I was certainly happy at Wells, successful and liked. But in midsummer one day at home at lunch we were talking of colleges. (There were always many visitors at lunch, ranging from Torvald's friend, Dutch Farwell, to perhaps Mrs. Carrie Chapman Catt.) I spoke of Wells disdainfully. There were not, I said, any really great professors there. Mother, characteristically, just listened thoughtfully and said: "Why don't you go some place else then?"

"Well, maybe I will."

I sent for a catalogue of Barnard. At Barnard they had famous Columbia professors, I said. But this also was in my soul: Mother had had Anne "come out," whatever that was. I knew that she would want me to do it too, and I saw the dancing school horror hanging over me. But Elsa, the wonderful Elsa with her honest feministic gumption, was in New York. She had gone right there after the University and got a job at Richmond Hill Settlement House. If I went to Barnard I would be near Elsa and perhaps after graduating I could work in New York too. At least I could establish connections in New York, so that I could escape from home later.

Anyway, at Wells there was a feeling that life was passing bucolically by and after that there would be nothing to do but go home and get engaged, or perhaps not get engaged but just stay at home. No, this was too frightening. I went to Barnard.

I persuaded Ruth Martin, a Wells girl from Indiana, to go with me. Knitte I called her, because it was the most foolish name I could make up, a tall lovely girl who talked in a rattled, incoherent way, blinking her fine orbs, wetting her lips, tripping herself up with her own nervous questions and laughter. But she was brilliant, especially in mathematics, and I was happy with her because I could tease her and she accepted it in such a helpless way, lifting a great slow flipper to cuff me.

But uptown New York, I found, was not like New York around Washington Square and MacDougal Street, where Elsa's settlement house was. I had visited Elsa during Easter vacations, and I had thought that downtown New York was so dramatic and wonderful and exactly like literature about New York: the hansom cabs; a man with a monocle; the mellow sunniness of Washington Square and the friendly Italian slums and the horse cars trotting along their narrow curved tracks, the bells jingling; and the lovely sound of soft foghorns in the river, blowing beautiful chords. And then Elsa would take me for rides on the Fifth Avenue bus, and at night—almost every night—we went to an Italian restaurant and had red wine and Elsa smoked cigarettes and then casually looked into the evening paper and we went to a play—not just once a week, but almost every night!

But uptown New York around 120th Street and Columbia was very different. High, bald, bleak buildings—apartment houses. Drugstores. Not romantic at all. And besides there was a high nervous wind up there most of the time cutting across from Riverside Drive.

And now I had all the worry of living on my allowance. At Wells, Father had paid for all the board and room business and I had ten dollars a month to buy my fudge sundaes with. But now I had to find a room and furnish it, and pay for the rent and buy my meals. And this was an added difficulty: that I was pathologically incapable of asking for enough money. Father was insistent that I have plenty. But no, I could not ask him for it. I staunchly lied and insisted that I needed much less than I did.

Knitte and I rented a room in a high repellent modern apartment building on Morningside Drive. It was in the prosaic modern-conveniences apartment of Mrs. Staley from Iowa, and her daughter Myrtle. (What a name!) Why, Myrtle was no more dashing than one of those Christian Endeavor girls in Linden Hills—with her hair parted in the middle and the rolls on either side pinioned with large side-combs. And her engagement ring! I think she was taking domestic science at Teachers College. Something obnoxious.

Our room was small with one tiny closet. There was one window and a drop of twenty stories; and a ferocious drying steam heat. There was no draft in the room. Very little air could get in.

Then Knitte and I went out to buy furniture. I look back with great pity at myself, at this time: my incompetence, helplessness, immaturity. Perhaps, though twenty-one, I was still going through the queer mugginess of adolescence. But it seemed so hard for me to deal with anything. We bought beds for ourselves. To economize we got tiny narrow cots, with the thinnest possible mattresses. I guess they cost about three dollars apiece. (I did not know enough, was too sloppy and immature even, to see that I had a decent bed to sleep on.) These I called our "bucking cots" because they were so light and movable that at night, if we turned too quickly, they threw us on the floor. And either there was no air in the room, or if the wind came through the window, the cold froze us through our mattresses. And there was no place to hang clothes.

In a spurt of enthusiasm for beauty and cheapness, in that small creative gush, we bought a table and scrubbed it and painted it. I remember shopping in the depressing second-hand stores where Broadway sinks so bleakly down hill at 122nd Street. I bought the dirty old kitchen table for a few dollars. We scrubbed it but it still smelled. It still did not stand squarely on its pins, but woggled. I bought paint. I painted it ineptly (getting paint on the floor and my best skirt too) so that large bubbles were in the final coat, with wrinkles on them. I still feel this nightmare of laziness, incompetence, helplessness.

And all the time, I was trying to eat as little as possible (to get thin) and having to bust over on two ice cream sodas between meals. Bad food and sleep added to my feeling of dullness. I can remember trying to study in the Barnard library, looking out the window in a kind of muggy opaque despair and wondering: "Why can't I think?"

I signed up though, at once, for work with "the interesting professors," the men who taught in Columbia too: with James Harvey Robinson and James Shotwell, the historians.

Robinson was a gentle distinguished man, with a clipped gray mustache and a far-away beautiful dreamy eye. He was mild and good. An impersonal affection seemed to come out of him to all of us. I can remember two things he said. Toward the end of a class some students began rustling their papers, cloaks and so on.

"Just a minute," he said mildly. "I have a few more pearls to cast." Another time he said, just before an examination: "Now remember, when you are taking this, that you are human beings and not abject students." He meant that we should not be afraid of it, of niggling details, but just freely let out our general sense and wisdom. I loved him for that and have never forgotten it. How rare and wonderful it is when a superior shows others, dependents or younger people, true friendly respect.

Professor Shotwell had the most beautiful rich booming voice, and I admired him especially because he looked like Sigurd, the same green-blond hair and a blunt nose.

The other teacher I remember well was William Brewster. He taught English, a theme course. Poor me! Again I had hopes of being brilliant in writing. Brewster was a drawling New Englander, very big and spare with hair-colored hair and a clipped hair-colored mustache. He sat at his desk hunched over and spoke with drawling but clear-clipped consonants and stretched and contracted his wide mouth to do so, and said cruelly jeering things.

He was very hard on me. "Pretentious" he said; and "Don't try to be so clever." It hurt my feelings badly but I liked him too. I used to think with a kind of baffled impotence: "Well, if you really knew me you would see that I am something!"

Edna St. Vincent Millay was in the class but I can hardly remember her: a quietly prim nice girl with reddish hair always eclipsed by a hat. She and Gretchen Damrosch, big and beautiful as Juno, always sat in the front row. But I always sat in the back row.

We were supposed one day to write a description of someone in the class. I think it was Gretchen Damrosch who described me. I was surprised at what she saw and not unpleased. She said I was "sturdy" and had a "peasant strength," black hair, and blue eyes and big feet. In general I was very pleased with this description. I was especially glad that my eyes looked blue and that I had attracted enough attention so that she described me.

Jan. 9th, 1913 (says my diary). Feel like a warrior. Prance, giggle, snort. G.D. describes me in Themes. Blue eyes and big feet were her two mistakes.

Knitte and I took no interest in Barnard as a college. I don't think we were ever in the dormitory. We never went to class meetings. Once I went and Freda Kirchwey was talking against sororities. It didn't interest me. This was not out of coolness or timidity, but because I had cast off college spirit forever, with Wells. I had succeeded at that at Wells. Now I could give it up.

When I graduated I did not appear at the exercises, but asked to have my diploma mailed to me. I went instead up to Wells to their Commencement. There was a story going around that I had never graduated from Barnard at all (some of them were vexed that I had left Wells), but I liked this scandal and thought it was funny.

In January I got sick. "Earache," says my little diary. "Get up but go to bed after anthropology. Earache in the evening again. Sad and sick.... Dorothy Gilbert comes and I have to get up, deaf and sad as I am. Our room is hell so we rearrange it. Quite jolly then.... Nearly die in class. To bed early and frightful dreams repeated over and over."

The doctor said it was tonsillitis. So Elsa made me come down to the Settlement and Miss Beasley, the visiting nurse, took me in hand. She painted my throat at clock intervals; she starved me; she made me suck raw eggs. She was English, looked like the Mad Hatter and was as tetchy and fierce about all her tiniest orders as a prime minister would be. I will never forget what a relief it was to be under her deft power and not at the mercy of my own appetites and my diet theories (always changing) that perhaps four chocolate sodas a day was a good idea; some such notion.

I read in bed "Jean Christophe," and "Far from the Madding Crowd," and George Moore's "Hail and Farewell," and Bernard Shaw's "Man of Destiny." And that was the most wonderful reading experience I have ever had, because I had a high fever and it gave me the illusion, the dream, that the books were reality and that I moved among all the people in them, and touched them.

There was living at the Settlement a girl whom I will call Margaret Stuart. She was about my age; and she was remarkably pretty with straight-gazing handsome blue eyes and black eyelashes, and a turned-up nose, and a quiet burning seriousness. When she laughed at something, it was apparent that she had not got the point exactly, though her laugh was hearty and prolonged. But I liked Margaret tremendously and we became close friends. She made me think of a thin, watchful, lovely, young female cat. She was an orphan and had been adopted.

And so we began to talk. She liked my good-naturedly defiant ideas which held that girls could do anything that boys did. She had had boys in love with her. In fact, once, some time before, a boy had loved her very much and in the access of his feeling, had tripped her and the first thing they knew they were lovers and wondering if they would have a baby. This seemed very horrible and unfortunate to me. I wanted to believe that the young man was entirely to blame and that Margaret most certainly did not like it.

When I became well again it was decided that I should live at the Settlement. This was just what I wanted and was secretly aiming for, and in this I know I deserted Knitte in the meanest possible way. And then in January one dark day when it was snowing, she and I went up to school to see our marks, for the first semester. Outside the door of each classroom they were posted, and we went down the empty halls to look at them, one after the other. I barely got through; I had one D but enough C's so that I was on probation. But Knitte—D, D, D,—she had flunked every single thing! After while she became sick with sciatica and had to go back to Indiana. Through me she had wasted and lost a year. I went to the train to see her off, but missed it.

Well, she has grown up to have a brilliant life, ironically one of scholarship, and it was just like her to forgive me right away.

Margaret Stuart and I began prowling and exploring. We went to suffrage meetings and socialist meetings. We picketed with factory girls. We went to night court and were indignant and sorrowful over the prostitutes. "My Lord! why don't they arrest the *men* as well as the poor girls?" We went to Barrie's "Twelve Pound Look," to Brieux's "Damaged Goods."

Girls could do anything boys did, damn it all. So one night we went to Little Hungary, a café far over on the lower East Side near the Bowery. It was supposed to be an interesting, dangerously sophisticated place. We pushed our way into the dark, uproarious place, smirking and a little nervous, imagining of course that we were in danger. "The headwaiter, Oscar, was very nice to us," says my diary. "Discusses free love and woman suffrage with us."

When we walked home at one o'clock, along the Bowery and the dark empty dismal factories of Bleecker Street, a gray-haired man who had been in the restaurant followed us. We saw a prostrate man in the shadows and the gray man picked him up and gave him money. We thought this nice looking gray-haired man was following us to look out for us.

"Roemer," says my diary (Miss Elizabeth Roemer was the head of the Settlement House), "gives me hell."

Naturally we were elated.

And then in April we got a little whiff of Bohemianism, of Greenwich Village.

At the Italian restaurant on 9th Street Margaret and I, one evening, found ourselves actually drawn over to the table of the Red Ink Club, and there was Jack Reed. "That is Jack Reed." "Oh, is it? Jack Reed!" He had a snub nose and a fat but haggard face and bushy curly hair. He was an ex-Harvard man, a wayward young man, a startlingly good writer and he "lived with" Mabel Dodge. Alice Brimmer sat next to him, a dumpy Village vampire, and she ran her hand up his arms under his coatsleeves (what a funny thing to do, I thought) and they were carrying on some kind of a quarrel, for she was beseeching and lascivious and he was gruff and irritable. It disgusted me and filled me with wonder. I could not project myself into the souls of such people at all.

Eddie Ward was there, an artist, a slim red-haired young

man with long narrow feet, shod like a dancer's. And Pete
Myer, a Dutchman who did batik and had a studio on 11th
Street. He had a sallow face and the hairs in his lip and chin
were sparse like those of a Javanese. Margaret and Pete were
together at once. Pete had a wife named Mary, we were told,
an exotic looking woman with a big nose and hair parted in
the middle and falling in smooth black wings over her ears.
But she did not live with Pete and it was all right, it seems,
that Pete liked Margaret. I did not think so. I did not like
this mushy business.

And Eddie Ward began to like me, really *like* me. This
filled me with surprise and a faint elation. He even liked
my being rather fat (imagine!), my ruffled blouse, and flop-
ping hat with an orange velvet ribbon on it.

Eddie had a real studio, the old-fashioned kind. There was
a dark gallery and long dusty portières, and dark brown-
gravy paintings about, and a pair of fencing foils. He himself painted landscapes with tan barns and turquoise blue sky.
I was impressed with them and thought they were fine. But
I was more impressed by the darkness and the Rembrandtian
dustiness of that plush-hung studio. Eddie had a mother, a
raddled, red-haired mother who lived in some dark place in
the studio. I only saw her once.

Another member of the Red Ink Club was Bobbie Perkins,
a tall hollow-cheeked man with tortoise shell glasses and a
ridiculous solemn face. This was the famous Bobbie Perkins,
the artist. "They say awful things about Bobbie," says my
diary that night. And Eddie and Pete warned us too, about
Bobbie.

But Margaret and I seemed to be in his studio a little later.
It was on Washington Square South, a disorderly and paint-
encrusted room with ancient many-paned windows.

December 15th, 1913. To Bobbie Perkins': "I need you.... The
model dresses here," he says with obscene significance and yet
in a very funny way, guying me as young and countrified.

"I'll bite a hole in your waist." He makes love to us;—puts my arm around him and says: "You great big brute of a girl, lemme go."

I remember how we had a real elation-of-danger about Bobbie—that appalling sex talk to us, so funny and really dirty and frightful too.

Griffin Barry was there too, a young man with a half-smile and a charming head like a choir boy. He leaned against the mantelpiece and sighed and half-smiled, with his head on one side, and told me he was thinking about the "futility of living." It impressed me but I made jokes about it afterwards.

Margaret seemed to be sliding into love with Pete, and while I was pleased at Eddie's attention, I could not go that sentimentality.

April 22nd, 1913. I am silent and absent-minded. Eddie hints I am bored. Tries to draw me out about my brothers and life work.

May 5th. Margaret and Pete mooning at each other. Eddie thinks I am bored. Emotions put me on the bum. I ain't the girl I should be. . . . Men shouldn't let themselves get the kissing habit.

May 29th. We go to Brighton Beach. Hate to be owned. Never again.

Yes, this proprietary feeling of a beau made me restive (and continued to for twenty years more). I wanted to be free, not escorted. It meant there were no adventures, no entertaining things happened, if our beaus watched and glowered every minute to see that we were not insulted, and pinched our elbows to help us over curbs.

But anyway when I went to the Wells commencement in June, it was a pleasure to shock them a little bit with my Bohemian sophistication. For my diary says:

"At dinner I say I would just as soon be a minister's mistress but not his wife."

3.

MARGARET STUART VISITED ME THAT SUMMER. THIS WAS 1913. And presently with Margaret around I felt shackled and wished she were not there. And the whole explanation of it lies in just this: we could not make each other laugh. After she left I never saw her again. Her foster parents had given her money to go to Germany and study Dalcroze dancing, but the War came, and no one has ever heard from her since.

She got the Dalcroze notion because Francesca was in Minneapolis again, and of course she at once had dozens of people thudding around in their stockingfeet to her commands of "HUP!"

Francesca we had always known. She was the adopted child of Dr. Bendeke, a distinguished Norwegian doctor. She had been in Europe for twelve years studying the violin, a pupil of Ysaye and other masters, but now she was back in Minneapolis and Dr. Bendeke was dead and she lived in our house and taught. Rolf, about thirteen, and Torvald were taking violin lessons and Arnulf was working at the 'cello. Rolf was the best. He was as beautiful as an angel, slim and perfect. He was wonderfully co-ordinated and would run over the lawn on his toes and turn dainty handsprings. Francesca adored him and thought he was extraordinarily gifted. His hands she often spoke of, his wonderful hands. She said later that it was Father who made him lose interest in violin playing. Father, like most fathers, seeing him so talented and interested, became a little troubled about it, thought a violinist's career was no life work for a boy and began to jeer mildly at the thought. Father wanted him to play well, of course, but not to become an artist. Francesca said this attitude was a very subtle thing, but that it affected Rolf, and that it always does affect children and discourage them when parents, even very secretly within themselves, no longer back them up.

Darling Francesca. Father would shake his head over her. "Crazy, crazy girl!"

She had the warm blazing eyes of a saint and loose slippery hair that was always falling away from its hairpins, and she dressed in a cheap cotton dress that looked awkward and raw-wristed, especially because she took long pigeon-toed strides in her flat, black health shoes.

Crazy girl—I should say so! I would come down to the kitchen on a sub-zero morning and Emelia the cook would be looking out the windows toward the snow-buried pasture.

"Now Miss Bendeke...I don't know...She has gone off downtown with no coat or hat on...."

She was a Christian Scientist, and everybody but Mother teased her about it, I am sure in a stupid, nagging, wearisome way. "Francesca is giving absent treatments to the cat!" (It was true, and she healed the cat; every animal thrived and became unbelievably intelligent in her presence.) But she would just laugh until she wheezed and tears squeezed out of her eyes. Her Christian Science was fascinating to me though. The mere avoidance of bad colds and diseases did not interest her, but she said things like this: that if she ever had time for it, she was going to make her legs two inches longer. I knew that she could too, if she worked at it.

Sigurd's best friend was David Shearer, a very big tall young man with curly hair and a fine sharp nose, and he could imitate people with startling perfection. But he was not for woman suffrage and made fun of all my New York nonsense, my ideas about women being just as good as men, about smoking and social workers and artists. When Margaret Stuart arrived with her hair hacked off at mid-neck,

David said to me, making his hands bend backwards from the wrists in the most obnoxious way: "And what is *she* terribly?"

I was very fond of David just the same and my diary says: "David's best girl is back. DEM !"

And this was Henrietta Prindle. I must tell about David and Henrietta (who now live across this lake, outside my window) because I see them so often and they have become a part of my extended family. They fell in love during sophomore year at West High School. "To think," says Henrietta, who is five feet two inches tall, "that when David and I were first engaged, he was shorter than I !"

I first saw Henny at a dance and she had my ideal of a figure: long legs and wide shoulders and a round rather short neck. Slightly pugilistic. And she wore at that dance a tight white suit with black stripes in it, so tight that it is incredible she got into it. The coat had little stiff coat-tails that flared out over her tiny compact bottom. And I can still see her—the way she jumped stiff-legged from a window seat to the floor, and jumped stiff-legged up and down, and ran and slid across the floor followed by several admiring boys. She had a lovely projecting upper lip and complexly twisted stylish mouse-colored hair.

Now when I had been at Barnard, Mother had written me a letter that alarmed me. She said that she intended to keep out of too much work that winter, since I would be home. I smelled a rat. This meant she wanted me to have some social life.

But I forestalled that. In August I went down to the *Minneapolis Tribune* and asked Mr. Boughner for a job. Sure, he said. I could be in charge of the women's clubs. Twenty-five dollars a month. It was so easy, it bowled me over. Of course it was because Mother was so prominent and public-spirited. And when I told her this good luck she was disappointed.

"Oh, Brenda dear..." She thought it was too bad. She thought I needed pretty clothes, some parties, some frivolity. Of course I did. But in all this, some extra skill was needed, some understanding that went back for many years.

At the *Tribune* I was given a desk. All morning I had to telephone women in the hope of extracting some item like this:

"There was a meeting of the Lyngblomsten Society on Tuesday, September 24th at the home of Mrs. S. E. Larson, 4906 Emerson Avenue South. Those present were..." (getting all the names right). "Mrs. Hjalmar Hetland spoke on 'Conditions all over the world.' Plans were made to organize."

This was newspaper writing, journalism. That is, you learned to compress almost everything in the first sentence, and the only phrase you needed was "plans were made to organize." It took me a day to learn this, and that is all you have to learn in newspaper writing. But for twenty years, whenever I wanted a job I would say "I have done newspaper work," and a look of deep respect would come into my prospective boss's face.

After collecting several items like the above I typed and pasted them in a column and handed them in to Mr. Boughner at the city desk, who would say: "Any of the arson squad there?" He meant women suffragists. Sometimes I went to the club meetings, but the writing about them was just an elaboration of the above. Friday was a harder day because one had to cover much more space in the Sunday paper, and also one had to telephone to Mrs. Boggs, Mrs. Joggs, Mrs. Doggs, and wheedle them for photographs.

Now I must not deceive you. From my diary I seem to be so jolly and insolent, but thinking it over, I see now that I must have had an abject shyness inwardly, because my job was so hard for me.

I hated all this telephoning for items and photographs and shrank and suffered. I had to brace myself even to ask our

Tribune telephone operator for a number, she sounded so nasally tough and reluctant. "Walnut 0036" I would say, trying not to sound placatory. I thought how sick she must get of me, to have me keep asking for numbers like that. And then to hear my voice asking Mrs. Boffin and Mrs. Coffin for something in sugary anxiety. Each time I lifted a telephone it was a wrestle.

I went to work on the street car. Then because I had no exercise, which I was used to, I got sick—one of those impenetrable colds, during which I would go to bed and get up again, absolutely swollen, deaf and filled and ill with mucus. Then something happened that was to have an important effect on my life.

One evening Mother took me to the house of Dr. and Mrs. Vincent near the University. Dr. George Edgar Vincent, a strong, black-eyed man with a clipped, gatling-gun vocabulary, was the president of the University, and later he became the head of the Rockefeller Foundation. But Mrs. Vincent was even more interesting. She, I think, was a member of a rich and fashionable Eastern family, and she startled everybody because she was so waywardly athletic and dashing. Most faculty wives then were very different from Mrs. Vincent. What would she do? Why, she would start out and walk twelve miles in the morning. Most startling of all, there was a public skating arena over near the Fair Grounds, and they had music there in winter, and here University boys and girls went, and tough kids from St. Paul and north Minneapolis. And here, think of it! Mrs. Vincent went almost every afternoon, in the center where the experts were, and executed beautiful and highly skillful figure skating, swinging her long legs like a pair of compasses.

And they said that in the social life of the University faculty, she behaved in an utterly unstandard manner, was restive and paced like a lioness and frankly showed that it was impossible for her to simper and gush and shriek hostess platitudes above the din. But the criticism of Mrs. Vincent was only among insignificant people. Everybody else admired her. Me especially.

At this evening party, Mrs. Vincent was to read a play that she had written herself. It was called "The Cowboy and the Lady." The play was not very good, I guess. At least I remember thinking: how could she read all that sentimental nonsense right out loud? and as her own? But the evening was important to me because of Dr. Alfred Owre.

He was Norwegian and head of the School of Dentistry, which became the best in the whole world. He was a slender bachelor with a Vandyke beard and I knew about him—that he had one of the finest cloisonné collections in the world, and that he would walk thirty miles or more on Sundays, eating, so it was said, only a little lettuce.

Well, that evening, when there was an intermission in the play-reading, I happened to be standing with Dr. Owre. The servants brought plates of coffee, cakes, sandwiches, ice cream. I took what I was offered. Dr. Owre, however, with clipped, gentle dignity, refused. He asked for a glass of water, and proudly drank it, while I sheepishly ate my plate piled with poison, for so he considered food eaten between meals. It seems to me that after the glass of water was brought, he popped some kind of a pellet into his mouth and swallowed it. But this must be a mistake. I don't believe that Dr. Owre would ever take a pill of any kind.

Anyway, while I ate, he told me his régime, his theories. I was very much interested. This was it, in general. He walked twelve miles each day. He ate nothing between breakfast and dinner. He drank water. He ate hardly any meat, whole wheat bread, butter, cheese and lettuce. An apple for dessert. No refined sugar.

He was one of the very first diet pioneers, for he had made researches into the relation of diet to teeth. He was a brilliant and an entirely remarkable man, with a remarkable career which I have not time to tell.

Well, what about me? I listened with the deepest fascination to his account of his carefully regulated life because Dr. Owre was so wonderfully slim. Clear, tranquil, pure features, clear eyes behind aseptically sparkling gold-rimmed spectacles. In him there was no middle-aged sludge, no muddiness, no corporeal matter at all. He had a crystal, childlike texture. His teeth, he explained, tapping and baring them, had some fillings in them, but that was because his mother had, during her pregnancy, eaten "grocery store food" (refined cereals in packages, sugars, and so on). And he had had headaches as a young man. But now that he knew so much he would never have them again. Nor, he assured me, would he ever in his life again have any colds, or any new dentistry.

Well, all this gave me hope. And I began to do this: I walked to the *Tribune* every morning. I ate no lunch. And I walked home at night. That made nine miles a day.

It made me feel wonderful, much better. After getting down to the office, instead of sluggishness, I felt bright and lively all day long. I began to have a beautiful red complexion. What joyful exultation, going around Lake Calhoun in the winter wind. At night I fell asleep right after dinner. No colds.

I did this all that winter. I missed only one day when there was a blizzard. Because *not* to walk frightened me. I was so afraid of slumping back into laziness, fatness. I was still fat but stronger and more compact and I could feel my long stride pulling at my waist line. I have been told that this exercise stirred up my metabolism and was what I needed. I gradually began to get slimmer. And that is why I think many women, having inherited a ditch-digger's energy from their father, and never having carried anything heavier than a beaded bag, perhaps like me need exercise.

December 10th, 1913. See Maude Adams in "A Kiss For Cin-
    derella." I hate to see people's throats glug with emotion.
    So does Toke.

December 21st. Christmas is coming. I am going to give all the
    boys a motto for Christmas to hang up. "Less for self and
    more for Brenda."

In midwinter there was a job for fifty dollars a month on
the *St. Paul Daily News,* and they said I could have it. St.
Paul was a ten-mile street car ride. But I had to have my
walk, so I would get up at five and walk to the Mississippi
River, about six miles, and then take the street car. This
walking had become an obsession. My whole spiritual vigor
depended on it. And I was stern about it, because if you
skipped one day, it was so easy to skip many. For about ten
years or more, to start on a walk I needed always a fierce mo-
mentum of will, overcoming much reluctance. But at last it
became easy.

In St. Paul my office was a dingy room across the stair
well, far from the city room. When I had my list of women's
clubs all pasted up, I took them into the city room where four
flat-topped desks were pushed together, and Mr. Vance, the
city editor, sat with three other reporters. It was a little awe-
some. I sidled up hurriedly and withdrew with a bashful
murmur.

But my work was too easy. I began to soldier. At least I
had an almost continuous feeling of mild guilt. I came late
and there was not much to do and I went home early. I would
run up the stairs as fast as I could, telling people I did so, so
everybody would think I was busy and a live wire. I had not
the imagination to be learning anything about newspapers;
no, nothing outside my own routine. Since then I have
thought: Why didn't I learn and understand all about it?
how the presses worked, the advertising, the financing, the
boss, the cost of production, the circulation methods. But no.
I did my work and got my walk out of the way, and kept on

making up jokes and admiring them. This was one of them:

I told people that one day at last, to attract a little attention, I went in with my copy to Mr. Vance and the others, all busy pasting up copy and absorbed. "Now," I said in a low voice, "I have to go out for about fifteen or twenty minutes. But I want you all to go right on working as if I were here."

Mr. Vance was a bald man who wore glasses and he was always in his shirt sleeves. He wore arm garters too, pink ones, and around his necktie there was a ring with a large glass-emerald in it and his trousers were bright red-brown. He had the hoarsest voice I have ever heard and he smoked cigars always. Well, this Mr. Vance, so uncomely, was so shy he could never look one in the eye. He was kind too, and sometimes he came into my room to bring something, to ask a question perhaps. And when I handed him my copy at his desk, he never looked up, but I felt his shyness emanate from him. He was perhaps forty-five years old.

But presently I fell in love with Mr. Vance, for about three weeks; and with all about him—his cigar, his office grayness, his hideous clothes, his glasses and strangled hoarse voice. A newspaper man, a city editor! One Sunday morning in the spring I drank some chocolate for breakfast, and perhaps it was unusually stimulating. Anyway I started walking out into the country toward Edina Mills, oh, far beyond to Eden Prairie. It was the very first spring day and the roads were dry enough to walk on, and the wonderful fragrance was beginning to rise from the fields, and I walked in a rapture, an exultation that I will never forget. Such strength, such glory, such happiness! I can even remember the new suit I wore, a jacket of oxford black and a short tight skirt. My joyful strides split the skirt and I didn't care a hang. I strode on, thinking in the deepest emotion and inflamed imagination of what? Mr. Vance! "Darling Brenda," I heard him murmur, reaching for my hand. "I love you. I can't stand it. I had to tell you, do you understand? I love you."

It was queer because I was beginning to have a few admirers and much more likely ones than Mr. Vance, like Len Erdahl, who kept asking me to skate at the Lake of the Isles ring, whirling me around like a comet on his iron forearm, when I wanted to skate alone.

February 14th, 1914. To Pan-Hellenic dance with Len. He depresses me something fierce. I tell Henny how I scared a highwayman by cracking my joints.

March 5th. Spencer Owen asks me to party. I refuse. Next time I will write a letter: "Gents: How dare you insult my Jesus and my God by asking me to a dance!"

March 8th. Mr. Vance calls me young lady sweetly.

March 11th. Mr. Vance finds me reading scandal sheet. Says, "Why, Miss Ueland. Shame on you!" Me pleased.

Presently Mr. Vance sent me out on a story, a sob story. A girl had been found poisoned though not dead, on the lawn of the Daly family, prominent St. Paul people. One of the Daly boys had been with her the night before. Her name was Elvira Anderson and she lived in a poor little house in Midway. She was at home with a badly scalded throat.

Mr. Vance said:

"Miss Ueland, go out and talk to her mother. See if you can't get something."

And so I did, my breast full of that peculiar anxiety to acquit myself well, to get a "scoop," and inner shame at being an offensive, prying, meretricious snoop, making things harder for some suffering people. Yes. This go-getting, this salesmanship that we Americans tell ourselves is so fine— the conflict it sets up in our bosoms! Because it really injures a man's soul to be offensive. In the millennium we will think of that. For every offensive nuisance of an act, done in the name of good business, injures a man eternally, the brightness of his soul.

Well, I went out to the cheese box of a house, a bungalow.

A large Swedish mother came to the door, and I made saccharine inquiries. "Yes. I see. So Elvira was upstairs?" I pried and acted very sweet, and she told me things uneasily. "Who did you say you were?"

"Oh, I just read about it and wondered about it. My, that's awful, Mrs. Anderson ... And you say she wasn't unhappy, that you know about?" I didn't like my sugary and diplomatic voice as it came out of my mouth.

You see, I did not know that you were supposed to say: "I am from the *Daily News.*" You were supposed to make that statement at once and then *afterwards* do all the clever snooping possible. I wish I had known it, because that at least seemed honest.

Well, I went back to the office and wrote some inflated bilge (sob story), and the next morning Mr. Vance came hurrying in with the *Pioneer Press,* the rival paper. We had been scooped on the poisoning story, he said anxiously, and pointed at the headline.

"Mysterious Woman at Anderson Home."

"Who was that, Miss Ueland? Did you know anything about that?"

" 'Wore shabby hat,' says Mrs. Anderson," I read in the newspaper that he held out to me, and then it dawned on me. "Why, my gosh, that must be me!"

It was about this time that I saw the ghost. I was sleeping on the third floor in the east room. It was a luminous March night with a high fresh wind blowing from the lake. The snow had melted once, so now there was rough dark ice there, and a sweet cold freshness was carried up from it by the wind.

I had an alarm clock on the chair by my bed. I was getting up at five so that I could walk to the river. At two o'clock (I saw the clock in the luminous night) I woke up and there right before me was an old, old woman. She had thin hair screwed back tight over her scalp and the bald interstices showed between, and one crippled trembling hand was on a high cane. She seemed to me very distinct and exact, but also transparent. Or perhaps it was just the curious penetrating x-ray light in the room.

"Who is it?"

Then in terror at hearing my own voice asking such a question, I felt cold sweat in my eyebrows and the hair on my nape stood up. She was between me and the door. Besides, I did not dare fly down that dark bare hall where that invisible woman, that Boyg, had bumped into Miss Lindquist.

I turned over, turned my back and stayed so, rigid with fright until dawn. An exhausting time. Just once I tried to sleep in that room again, but I couldn't. My nerves were all sharp strings.

April 15th. There is to be a suffrage parade. Golden-haired Julie Plant is to be Jeanne d'Arc; Sigurd's best girl. I will design her costume from drawings of Boutet de Monvel. Blue tights (union suit) and over that, white mantle with petaled edges and yellow fleur-de-lys. On white charger (fire horse).

April 19th. Julie and Henny come out. We sew on costume. The firemen would not let us take their horses because there might be a fire. Me: oh, nobody would want to go to a fire.

April 26th. Francesca thrills me about Europe. Says we can work our way, if boys do. Blue and lavender clouds. Henny and David for dinner.

IV. GREENWICH VILLAGE

1.

I save three hundred dollars and go to Europe. I persuade
poor Father to let me study art. Walking to Columbia every
day or across Brooklyn Bridge. The helplessness of the tal-
ented young. I cut my hair all off. Young men are now really
attracted to me; I feel wonderfully charming.

ANNE'S YOUNG HUSBAND, KENNETH TAYLOR, WAS GOING TO
study medicine in Germany, and they were leaving in July.
Anne Herendeen in New York was going with them. Why
not me too? they all said.

All winter I planned it. I saved my money, every penny
that I possibly could. (I was living on Father, of course, and
even charging downtown lunches to him.) By summer I would
have three hundred dollars. That was enough. Sure. It certainly was. Besides, Francesca said that girls could work their
way if boys could.

A month before sailing I announced it to Father and
Mother. Mother, as always, thought it was fine, but Father—
he didn't want me to go, it made him anxious about me. He
didn't like that Anne Herendeen, with that loud laugh. I
was a child, a girl, and all that. Three hundred dollars was
not enough, he said. It was not a decent safe margin to travel
on. Poor Father, this was the first time he tried to block me
and come up against my peculiar will. And there was to be
another time when I would sit and pleasantly look at him in
our sitting room and refuse to give in, and that was even
worse.

Yes, I just sat on the piano stool obdurately, kind and

pleasant but never giving in, not one-quarter inch. This re-
sistance is not easy for me. It is the hardest thing—these
few fierce willfulnesses in my life—that I have ever done,
because I like to please people so much, to make them feel at
ease and untroubled. The unhappiness of any member of my
family (fortunately they almost always hide it) is the most
excruciating suffering I can go through.

But I won. Since my three hundred dollars was not enough,
Father made me take two hundred more from him. I took the
train alone. (Anne and Ken had gone on to New York ahead
of me.) As it crossed the bridge, high above the Mississippi,
that July evening, I had more than my usual remorse. The
sunset was behind the lovely towers of Minneapolis. I felt
just awful about Father, and when it grew dark I kept looking out the window until it was a black mirror. I felt a little
pleased with myself though. I had a fine bright complexion
from so much walking and I was slim, slim. Only 139 pounds.
I wore a striped green and blue silk blouse that I had made
myself, and I admired my shoulders, and my jaw line looked
clear and my nose straight and handsome, like a duelist's.

We sailed from Boston on an English boat. The day before we arrived an English battleship came out and stopped
us. Germany had invaded Belgium. In Liverpool a morato-
rium had been declared and so we decided to walk in Wales
for a week until we could get money.

England looked exactly like England. This was surprising and hard to believe. In every detail it was like England,
in Liverpool, in the suburbs, in the country. And all the people, whatever their costume, looked like English people. We
saw grooms and huge ladies with blue-red faces and farmers
with smocks and buttoned leggings and young navvies with
half their teeth gone and rotted, and sad and gentle clerks
with classic features, and school boys with tricorne hats.

In the lovely town of Chester people stood before a bulletin
board and waited for news. Tommies walked about. Late that

night we sat up in our room, in a turret of an ancient hotel, and looked down on the people, seriously waiting in the warm summer night. After midnight, I think, the news came. England had declared war.

But I must not write about the War because this is a book about me. At first, as I come to this point I will think: *"Now how interesting!* I must tell all about those first dramatic days of the World War. *Now* I am getting to something really *significant* in my memoirs. Why, this is regular memoir material!" And I start to tell of that visit to Europe in detail. But again and again I am blocked and find it a drag to write about it.

In the same way, just a few pages back, I thought: "Oh, I must mention the first International Exhibit of Modern Art held in the spring of 1913 in New York. Think of it! I was really there. My, what a furor it caused, especially Marcel Duchamps' Nudes Descending a Staircase! Right there I have something to tell of real historic significance, because of its far-reaching, nay, incalculable effects on the art, artists, and art world of today."

But as I try to write it, each time my angels stop me and it drags. "How can I get that in? What a bore to write about it! But I've *got* to get it in."

And now I see why. People already know about Art and the War, or they can look it up. But they don't know about me. Besides, these great events, that so many fill their memoirs with (to hide themselves) often don't affect us much. The War did not affect me because I did not suffer from it or fight it. No, the whole World War did not truly affect me and change my soul as much, say, as Dr. Owre's drinking a glass of water at an evening party.

We saw a thousand young soldiers in London march off. They all looked small and pale and chinless, these new English soldiers. People in general were thoughtful but not depressed, because the war would last only three months. The last war in Europe, the Franco-Prussian war, was over in a few months.

Anne Herendeen and I, pretending that we were refugees going in the wrong direction, got to France for a few weeks. We wore no hats, had no luggage, only a toothbrush each. The French soldiers were very short and wore their dusty too-large sagging red trousers and blue coats with long tails knocking against their dusty shoes. They were bearded and extremely sloppy, and their cannons were pulled by scrawny and unkempt horses. But the poor French. You could feel their anxiety and also their long patient cleverness. We began to hear how thousands of the very finest British troops had been wiped out, in just a day. The War began to seem no fun.

We had hoped to walk to Paris. We did walk several miles inland, but at each little town, one had to show passports, photographs, and officials were so quiet and tired. It seemed mean to burden them. We decided not to go on, to go back to London and then home.

There was such a flood of tourists leaving Europe that we could get steamship passage only in steerage with seven hundred immigrants. I was just delighted. Think of it, it only cost thirty-five dollars and that meant I would have more than two hundred dollars left.

We were in New York. It was September. There began for me one of the gayest, most jokey, intoxicating, free and jolly existences perhaps that has ever been experienced. What fun. What larks.

You see, I had more than two hundred dollars left from the trip (just the surplus that Father had insisted on giving me), and I could afford to stay in New York for a while.

Anne Herendeen had an apartment at number 9 Jane Street in the Village, a tiny unheated railroad apartment on the top floor. We slept on army cots in the sitting room. There was no heat but a Franklin stove in the front room; but when winter came, we were too careless or hurried ever to bother to light it up, to build a coal fire in it. We didn't know how anyway. So for heat we turned on the gas oven in the kitchen and, with the doors shut, this was our drawing room. I painted the kitchen black (I believe it was the first black kitchen in Greenwich Village) and put up orange striped curtains. And because I got to know a twenty-year-old artist, Gilbert Strunz, who was gently original and, I am sure, a genius, and who was always doing curious things with fabrics, I made myself blouses out of unbleached muslin ("such interesting texture") and for buttons I got those two-eyed bone buttons, the kind used in children's underwear, and cooked them in tea and salt, (Gilbert told me how) to make them a beautiful antique ivory color. Then I stenciled on the back of these blouses a design, perhaps an Austrian imperial eagle. When I took off my jacket, this would be displayed and all would laugh and admire it.

My wardrobe was this: a blue serge suit to which I was devoted (belted tightly around the waist and it made me look fairly slim), and a few silk undershirts and pants, and about three cotton blouses. No overcoat; no gloves; no hat but a small brown velvet tam o'shanter. To keep warm out of doors I generally ran, trotted, pretending to passers-by that I was trying to catch an invisible bus just ahead. I have run miles in New York this way (and still do).

The bathroom was in the cold hall. I was very clean. Every morning I took a fiercely scrubbing bath in that ice water. In midwinter the bathroom was as cold as an enclosed portion of winter. But I felt wonderfully hardy and lively. I always liked the idea of chapped, cold, rough, hard, bleeding hands, of endurance and good-natured hardihood. To be so thinly clad was uncomfortable, only when I had to tone down my pace and walk with someone in the street, and could not run; and it was really agony after the theater at night, standing on a high elevated platform, the winter wind cutting off your hands at the wrist.

At night, sleeping on our army cots, in the front room, so cold that steam blew from our nostrils, we sometimes put even the dirty scraps of floor rugs over us to keep warm. We dressed for bed instead of undressing. "Because," Anne said, "if there is going to be a fire, I don't want to miss it."

Young men began now really to like me. There was a tall Princeton boy with a milky mustache who had been with us in steerage. While Anne and I enjoyed ourselves, jumping rope with the immigrants, he kept out of it, uneasy and aloof in his perfectly creased trousers.

Sept. 26th. To Princeton with Harold Featherstonehaugh. Anemia is his trouble. Does like me though.

There was a red-cheeked manual training teacher from Minneapolis, named Peter Rostad. He really began to be in love, I think, for he got smoldering and surly.

Sept. 30th. Met Peter. He says he cannot eat on account of me.

I remember sitting in Central Park one bright fall afternoon. He talked bitter violent love. I was flattered and elated ("This is really *it!*" I thought), but it was repellent in a way, too.

Sunday, October 4th. To Russian church with Peter. "Feels me near him." Erotic! Awk.

I must tell a little about Gilbert Strunz because knowing him changed the course of things. He looked like a slim gentle Spaniard, a youth painted by El Greco. I had known his sister at college. His father was a rich German-Polish chemist in Cleveland, and I am sure a remarkable, brilliant man, and Gilbert too was eccentric, extraordinary, among other things a vegetarian, and so gentle that he could not walk past a butcher shop. He would live on ripe olives for days at a time. But he did this not from any theory, but just because of Shelleyan sensibility.

He had a fine studio on Tenth Street in a new building, with a gallery in it (there was none of the dismal mustiness of Eddie Ward's studio) and a vast pearl-blue north light. As an artist he was utterly original and unorthodox. He was himself alone, a true artist without cult or theory. He went to the Metropolitan Museum, or the Roerich Museum, or the Hispanic Museum and quietly burned with an inner fire over different things.

He introduced me to Bobbie Gray, a wonderfully kind and laughing young man, who taught design at Columbia at Teachers College. He was tender and good to Gilbert, and admired him, and his innocence and his Shelleyan sensibility and the strange gentle unpredictable things he said.

Well, I would go to Gilbert's studio while he made beautiful stenciled curtains out of unbleached muslin; or while he "antiqued" a fifteen dollar Knox hat that he had bought— that is, soaked it, battered it, sunburnt it in some way, so that it had just the softness, the vagueness, he wanted. He always looked fashionable too, though not in the neat conventional way. Perhaps Aubrey Beardsley would have looked like that. I can see his thick pearl-gray chinchilla overcoat with handsome leather buttons. When he opened it, it was lined with bright flowered silk.

We liked each other so much. One night I was there and he got me some paper and I was persuaded to draw, in pencil, a Chinese jade frog. I tried it in fright, in fear of failure. I don't believe I had ever drawn anything before from sight, though I had drawn thousands of knights on our blackboard at home.

To my surprise it was good. He thought it was *very* good. He thought I should study art. "Why, what a good idea!" it struck me, and more and more forcibly as the days went on and I saw what fun it was to be in New York, and that my two hundred dollars was dwindling.

Gilbert was painting my portrait too, and I went and sat for him patiently. It was a large canvas, and the portrait was full of life and bright and beautiful, and I posed and posed, and not satisfied, he would wipe it off and work it over and change it. Then after quite a long time, I began seeing more and more of R., a married man whom I was to marry, and one day Gilbert told me that he had slashed my portrait to pieces. He made no explanation, but I knew that it was because it was hard for him—my beginning to like that married man. I think Gilbert was perhaps in love with me. But this may have just been my hallucination (the kind many women have, and often the less attractive ones) that all, that most all the men I have known have been fascinated by me. I may be entirely wrong. Well, at least I used to say that to Julie Plant and it made her laugh.

But Gilbert and this little drawing of the frog and this talk about Art made me hit on this thought: perhaps I should stay in New York and study art. Perhaps *that* was my career. Why, I was always good at drawing. I knew it. I could feel it inside. Look at those drawings I used to make on the blackboard. (And I drew in college notebooks on the margins, but never anything but profiles; there was surprisingly little variety; I never once thought of looking at something and drawing it.)

And so I wrote planned (insincere) and eloquent letters to the family and to Father, about Art: How I really thought I would be good at it. Couldn't I perhaps stay in New York for one year and really work at it? I had met such interesting artists too, well-known artists, and teachers of art at Columbia. (This, I knew within, was to reassure Father, to make him see how serious it was, how dignified and grave.) While fine Art might not pay right away, there were tremendous amounts of money to be made by illustration, and I felt that with my ideas and my sense of humor (poor bluffing child! I feel so sorry for myself now, and so embarrassed) I could do it on fifty dollars a month. Easy . . . Father gave his consent.

And so I began to go to Columbia to a couple of classes in design, where Bobbie Gray was the instructor, and also to the Independent Art School where in a small room, in a loft on 66th Street and Broadway, there was a nude model, and you drew him "exactly as you wanted to." Homer Boss, the artist, walked among us and gave gentle criticisms. "A little more of this," he would say, with a shove of his two hands in one direction.

I still walked. I was so afraid I would slide back into sluggishness and fatness. So I walked every day from Greenwich Village way up to Columbia. It took an hour and twenty-five minutes. I had to go at least five and a half miles to feel that I had sufficient air and motion. I had three alternative walks. 1. To Columbia. 2. Up Fifth Avenue to 59th Street and back. 3. Across Brooklyn Bridge and back. This last was a fine walk especially on Sunday when it was so quiet and cavernous among the high buildings in lower New York, and the policemen along empty echoing Broadway, at intervals of several blocks, were all lonely and talkative. They saw me striding along, going and coming back. Each stopped me for a little talk.

I got to know the policemen along Seventh Avenue too, which was torn up then and gutted for the new subway, with broken sidewalks across deep holes. It was so dusty and disheveled it might have been a Wild West town.

But above Times Square, Broadway was in the morning sun and clean and fresh. Young clerks were opening the doors of the haberdashery shops. It was almost like morning in Minneapolis with dew on the lawn, though by noon the street was filled with freshly shaved actors with sideburns and male dancers with their sharp-toed shoes and chorus girls.

At 72nd Street I turned and went along Riverside Drive, walking through the winding path. At two places, I sat on a bench to smoke. This was quite a risk then, because I had to hide the fact from passers-by, or from policemen. No women smoked then out of doors. I was very proud of my smoking, of course, and that I craved it so much that I had to step into doorways for a quick drag. I wanted to be a little tough in a fresh jolly way, and also I thought it would make me thinner. Also there was feminism in it. Of *course* women can smoke if they feel like it! My God, why not?

The trouble was, though, that by the time I got to art school it was ten-thirty or so, and I would be quite tired. The night before, of course, Anne Herendeen and I had been up late, talking, giggling, or at a Liberal Club dance or the Masses Ball. There were two classes that I had at Teachers College: one in design under Bobbie Gray, and one in fashion design. Now, they might have been all right if I had worked along patiently all day for a year or two, but in the circumstances it was so vague and useless. I remember making a silly little design and thinking: "Why?" I was not learning anything and they were not interesting or good. The fashion designs were even more pointless. And at the Independent Art School (it was started in defiance of the old-fashioned Art League, by some modern artists) I liked to try to draw the model as I saw her, the infinite inflection of every wonderful line seemed so subtle and beautiful and was worth struggling over. But Mr. Boss never liked mine. It disheartened me. But I felt better about it, and entirely indifferent to his opinion when he liked the horrible, writhing, confused intestinal torsos that the others made, particularly one simple little girl who kept needing bigger and bigger canvases and never put on them head or legs—just torsos, intestines.

But that I learned nothing, of course, was not the fault of the art classes, but of myself, for after all that walking, smoking and lack of sleep, there were really only the meagerest hours left in the daytime for work; perhaps an hour and a half; at most two. No work arrives anywhere unless it is at least a steady, impassioned, illuminated eight-hour day.

When I got to Columbia I would be so tired that, after forty minutes or so, I would have to rest. I found empty rooms on the top floor with a piano in each. I went up there to smoke and played Norwegian folk songs, which I liked very much, although as I played them I thought most of the effect I would make playing them for people in Greenwich Village. "That interesting Brenda Ueland, and she knows some pretty Norwegian folk songs."

Then back to the class room to trace and paint in India ink. Bobbie Gray came around and gossiped and said: "That's nice." I think there were no credits to be got, so it did not matter at all if I passed. All the time I felt guilty underneath at the peeweeness of this effort, and guilty at how I had got Father to support me at this nonsense; though I would only let him send me fifty dollars a month, which, of course, was not enough.

There was a still life class too. We drew crockery jugs next to an apple, and such things. I was astonished at how good my first one was, especially because I had never tried it before and it was such a pleasant shock. I could have become a fine draftsman. I knew it then and I know it now. But there was not even the beginning of any perseverance in me. I never learned how to work patient hours at anything—not until now, until after forty. And I have not learned it yet perhaps.

All the time I had an uncomfortable apprehension of what I should be doing to be an artist—the vague mountains of experience and knowledge I should take in about canvases, about the mixing of paints, the manual dexterity. My imagination had a glimmer of that great patient labor. I wanted to do it. But in the pressure of my other wants—cravings to talk, to dance, to think about whether this man or that liked me, were my jokes of last night successful? and so on; the smoking which made me weak; my absorption in the struggle to starve myself so as to get thinner—patient work was impossible. This makes me sad now. Such vaunting plans and so little perseverance. Oh, that art year. How pretentious and not a nickel's worth of real work.

But underneath there was real talent and a strong serious spirit longing to unfold and show itself. This is in millions of young people, I know now, but all their various cravings smother it, and nobody can think of any way to help them but to scold them. "Where's your grit? Where's your stick-to-it-iveness?"

Just now I go to the telephone and I hear my daughter's friend Polly, aged sixteen, talking on the extension downstairs in the kitchen. "Honestly, when he acted that way. Well, I'm sore. Well, wouldn't you be? He said and I said and he said and I said that he then said. When he was dancing with Maura he gave me a kind of funny look and I didn't think anything about it but then I began to kind of think I *thought* it was funny. But wouldn't you be sore? I mean really? Because last week . . ."

The understanding which is in all, needs so much help and discipline, though I do not mean by "discipline" what most people do, i.e., just a kind of nagging and pushing. The only discipline is to be associated with wonderful generous people who are working too. These may be parents or teachers or favorite uncles. But the association must be close and daily and full of affection.

But in me, at twenty-two, as in all girls particularly, it was floods and deluges of the above telephone conversation that drowned my ability, and for more than twenty years. A few years of it would have been all right; but there were twenty years of it. And sometimes I think in 1938 it is much that way still.

And it occurs to me that there is a tendency to patronize

and make lofty fun of oneself when much younger. We are at a safe distance. You see right now I am treating myself at twenty-two with a kind of patronizing Booth Tarkington drollery, while in the present, now, I take myself so seriously and consider myself a serious, struggling, suffering human being. Of course I was that *then,* too. As much as now. I was serious inside and as full of agony and effort as I shall ever be; a battle between one's soul and gifts with childish egocentric cravings, for fun, to make a sensation ... But I am almost sure of this: that I understood less about it then than I do now.

But the fun of New York! I can remember running home from Fourteenth Street to Jane Street one bitter December afternoon, at top speed through the dirty frozen city, the wind blowing bits of cut-glass dirt in my face, and feeling how wonderful life is. At home there would be cigarettes and apples (I took to eating Jonathan apples between meals; that bright hard oval apple, three for a dime. I had read that President Taft ate apples between meals to reduce), and I would talk to Anne and tell her all that had happened, every detail. Anne was a fascinating, original creature; she had the blackest eyebrows I have ever seen, a wide mouth full of pointed teeth, out of which came that extraordinary laugh, and a gold-colored face like a Tartar princess. In the evening when we went out to dinner at Polly's restaurant on 4th Street we knew we would talk to somebody "interesting," some denizen of the Village. Perhaps we would come upon Max Eastman or John Reed or Big Bill Haywood or Emma Goldman, and impress them with our well-bred Wells College wit and radicalism.

The next thing that happened I had my hair cut off, not like Irene Castle's in a long Joan of Arc bob, but very short. Once as a child I saw a little girl who had had typhoid fever and she looked just charming, her neck going up into those short standing curls, and the glimpse of tight little ears.

But long hair was really sacred then. Even my mother seemed to think this. At night you braided two long heavy tails over each shoulder down to a thin wisp at the end, and then you scraped old hair out of a brush and quickly wound it around. There were hair-receivers and rats. When you come to think of it, this seems shocking now.

One day I had been to the dentist's. My hair was disheveled, homely. I went to the Brevoort and sat in the barber's chair. Henri was the barber's name, a rather coquettish man with a long soft virgin beard.

"I want it all cut short. Like a boy. But not exactly like that, but as though a wind were blowing from behind. Like Lord Byron."

He didn't know Lord Byron. "Like a bad little boy," he said finally.

He started to cut. I directed him with a hand mirror. He was frightened. I felt as though I were being beheaded.

I was utterly delighted with the result. And so was Anne. And so was everybody (so I thought). Everybody looked at me and that was nice. My pug was gone, my maternal pug. Gone were my weakness, motherliness, please-look-out-for-dear-little-me meekness. Honest and free now. It is curious, but I never had a proposal until my hair was cut, and this is probably because magnetism emanates from one's own inner state of confidence.

I think there is much that is masculine in me, just as there is in all women we like, and just as there is nothing so unmoving and tiresome as an undiluted he-man. But it occurs to me now that I may have given you the impression that I was always one of those gruff women with a gravelly voice and a neck shave. I don't think so. I like them and they are fine, but I was not like that. For I have, I am sure, a slow and quite a pretty voice and I have always felt tenderly kind to everybody. I could not be short and bark blunt facts at people (much as I would have liked to) to save my life.

"Oh, the Village in 1915 was really interesting! Not as it is now," people say to me. Now there are big apartment buildings, where there were then old residences and gabled roofs and low picturesque hovels. But I suppose the people there now, as they were then, are serious and good people, as well as lost and mistaken people.

I have had a middle westerner say to me, a polo-playing stock-broker, an extremely flirtatious and worldly man, with more love affairs (so called) in a decade than three Greenwich Villagers could have in a lifetime: "I hear you belonged to a love cult in Greenwich Village," and the idea was quite a shock to him.

It turned out that he meant what was probably the Liberal Club, i.e., two pleasant demure rooms in an old house on MacDougal Street, where unusually serious, mild and intellectual people talked about Henry George or trade-unions or the unfair divorce laws. You see, externals are usually shocking and vulgar (all gossip makes them so) while internals never are. Say that someone tells you how a certain business man is "keeping a woman." It sounds so vulgar, so coarse. But who knows what is inside those people?—the guilt, the regret, the love, the sadness, the confusion, the loneliness. No, no matter how bad things look externally, inside there is dignity, the sad battle of the soul, as Dostoevski was always trying to show us.

In general, Greenwich Villagers were just more serious than other people. Take Harry Derk, "the Vagabond Poet," he was called. He walked all over New York with his burly shoulders thrown stiffly back so that his stomach stuck out a little (Harry told somebody that I walked so wonderfully: "Just like me") and hatless and his thinning brown-gold hair blowing.

He had once eloped with Nelson Dingley's wife, I was told. Nelson Dingley, they said, was a very tensely idealistic man, like so many radicals, without wisdom or fluidity. He was rigidly idealistic on every tiny thing. His wife drank coffee, which he could not approve of, for he was a crank about vegetarianism and all that. And they said that when Mrs. Dingley and Harry Derk announced to him that they were leaving, and together, and they went out the door and through the iron gate, Nelson Dingley came running after them with Mrs. Dingley's percolator in his hand.

"Here!" he cried with dramatic bitterness, a magnificent gesture of despair and scorn: "Here. Take your percolator!" (But this story, of course, may be too good to be true.)

Well, Harry could elope with another man's wife, but it was really because he was so serious and had so much responsibility about love, and what it was. He just would not lie about it or conceal it, in a comfortable way, as many respectable people do. You see, there are two kinds of unmoral people: those who are more serious and pure than the rest of us, and those who are vulgar and callous, or irresponsible. I admire the first kind very much.

Greenwich Villagers were really those who had more conscience and sensibilities than conventional people. They loved art, music, social justice, progress. Only once in New York did I encounter some truly horrible people and that was uptown in a restaurant on West 40th Street. There they talked sexual talk without wit or ribaldry in it. It was as shocking as if a lot of idiots were cackling and guffawing and finding something funny in cancer.

But I don't think I was ever shockable in the usual sense—that spinsterish flight where a compartment of the mind is shut with a click, never to be looked at or considered—though I thought a lot of peoples' acts were kind of obnoxious.

"Because as for sex," I would say to Anne (it was one of my jokes), "I am unequivocally against it."

In the evening her beau came over. They sat in the sitting room by the Franklin stove, and I went to bed and trying to sleep, I knew they were kissing each other—the low voices, the occasional laugh. It disgusted me very much (such saps!) and in the morning I could not look Anne in the eye and she knew why and felt guilty. (Imagine her not saying to me: "Why, of course I kiss my beau! What do you think?")

In midwinter Anne went home to Rochester and stayed for two months. I moved all our flimsy bubble-painted furniture to an apartment on West Fourth Street, where there was steam heat. And so I was living alone and, out of tact, did not tell the family. This new apartment was on the ground floor back. There was no lock on the front door to the building, and one could walk straight back and push into our flat, because there was no lock on our door either. I didn't mind in the least.

There was a sitting room that faced a sunny court, a pitch dark kitchen, a dark bathroom with an extremely short tub. I put up striped denim curtains everywhere and arranged our cheap furniture. It seemed quite all right to me. I missed Anne because she had a feminine way of shedding comfort and charm. That is, she actually made toast for breakfast and set the table, on a big wicker tray, in the sun. I missed this, but did not mind being alone. I took a hot bath now, in the morning, cooked some black coffee and gnawed at a loaf of pumpernickel. I used to joke that my pumpernickel, after I had it several weeks (I gnawed off a little bit each day with my teeth) was hard enough to kill a person.

Swithin Johns, a small pink-faced Socialist who looked like a cupid, an eternal boy, took a shine to me. I was amused, though, because I felt that he was physically afraid of me. Once in a coltish, hobbledehoy skirmish I went to get the tea kettle in the kitchen. I was going to pour it on him. Anyway he was alarmed. It made Anne and me giggle afterwards to think of it.

Well, one night when I was alone in the flat on Fourth Street and the light was out and I had gone to bed, my unlocked door opened and Swithin came in.

"There are a lot of people in my apartment," he said, "so I decided to stay here."

I was at once the battleground for excitement, for shock and confusion.

"Well, all right. Sleep over there if you want to."

I could not be mean. As a feminist I could not turn into a prissy conventional woman and cry out: "Oh!! How can you!" As an equal and a brother (feminism) I could only say: "Why, sure. There is the bed. Fine. Do it."

But I knew that he was sophisticated about sex and thought that everybody should be, and that in coming he hoped for some kind of palaver or drama; that he had some stupid idea of making love or talking about it.

It was a long room and the two army cots were at opposite ends of it. He went to bed in the darkness. I lay on my cot in a turmoil of feelings.

He talked a little.

"I suppose I should make love to you."

An ominous silence from me.

"You better not," I said in a low boiling voice.

"I should not have done this. I won't do it again, Brenda," he said.

There was no more talk. I could not sleep because of anger, so I practiced on the mouth organ all night. Just before dawn, at five o'clock, I got up, dressed and walked across Brooklyn Bridge and back, to ease my feelings. He was gone. Later he said contritely he would never do that again.

Apparently what gave me this violent convulsion of feeling was the suggestion that I might take part in anything the least bit erotic. But I did not bother to lock my door after that (it involved a trip to the hardware store), and I slept there alone and did not have the slightest fear of thieves or thugs. I just didn't want anyone to come in there as though I were a sexy Greenwich Villager. Ish.

But presently there was really a romantic adventure.

Mary Heaton Vorse lived in a pretty white house on Grove Street. She was cultivated, a Bostonian, I think, and had two thinly handsome children who talked with clipped inflections and scholarly idioms, and she was married to Joe O'Brien, a newspaper man whom everybody loved.

Mary herself looked like a blond Madonna of the Annunciation by Giotto or Cimabue; that is, she stood that way and had that same gesture, the lifted meekly protesting hand. And her speech was slow, mysterious, and elegant, and she looked askance always and, by her manner, held one way off. She was a passionate radical, though. Wherever there were terrible strikes with shooting, or protest meetings of huge growling miners, or I.W.W.'s like Big Bill Haywood, Mary was there.

I was invited to Mary Vorse's one evening. It was a serious, almost conventional evening party really, and it was to discuss something important (though I never seemed to be much interested in what they were discussing). Mr. and Mrs. Amos Pinchot were there, and Mr. and Mrs. John O'Hara Cosgrove and other ladies and gentlemen. And me, with my short hair, bashful and noncomittal but pleased with myself.

One of the guests was the most fashionable looking man I had ever seen. His name was Raoul Hendrickson. He was blond with white eyelashes and a profile like that on a Greek coin. He wore a bright brown tweed suit with plaits in the trousers, and in the breast pocket of his coat there was a large much-exposed flame silk handkerchief. I thought of Oscar Wilde, of English lords; for he did have an almost-English accent and also a very opaque expressionless face, an eye like a ram's; that is, there was no play of friendliness and communication in it. But he wanted to talk to me, to my astonishment, in one corner of the room. He was Norse, he said. I looked very Norse. I had a head like a Greek youth. "Very Norse! May I call?"

"Why, sure, I should say so, Mr. Hendrickson. That will be fine."

I had heard of him. I think I had heard that he was a philosophical anarchist who had taught something at Columbia, that he was a poet. He told me that his father was Hjalmar Hendrickson, a Norwegian novelist. His mother had been rich and American. He had a brother named Algy in the British Royal Flying Corps and he himself had a farm in Massachusetts where he lived most of the time and bred horses.

"Yes," he said. "Norse! You are very Norse. I will call."

One afternoon in number 9 Jane Street, there was a stentorian rumble of voices coming up the stairs. It was Hutchins Hapgood, short, deep-chested, spectacled, kind, and always talking. And here he was coming up our stairs and with him, carrying a cane, was Raoul Hendrickson.

Hutchins Hapgood left right away. Raoul stayed. I sat in our sitting room, on the edge of an army cot (a couch in the daytime) trying to talk to him in a surprised young-lady way, not quite knowing what to say because he had one of those faces so unresponsive, such a blank of unlistening egocentricity perhaps, that everything you said sounded very flat, discouragingly flat.

"Well, it is nice to have you come. Are you staying in New York for a while? Did you have a good time last night at Mary Vorse's?"

He came over and sat beside me on the army cot. I wore my only costume, my blue serge suit and a white cotton blouse which opened at the neck. My neck below the clavicle was tanned and sunburned from being always open to the weather. He kissed it and continued to do so for a few seconds, to my embarrassment, sheepishness. Impossible to know how to behave gracefully in such a situation. So I did what I always try to do—say just what I was thinking.

"Why," I said, "this is fine for you. But look at me. I have no particular feeling at all."

He got up abruptly, let out a groan and paced back and forth, smacking his hands behind his back, the back of one in the palm of the other. "Oh!" he exclaimed.

It was very mystifying. I didn't know what to say next. Soon I made a few more young-lady remarks. But soon he left, taking up his hat and stick. I could not penetrate at all the opaqueness of his elaborate and punctilious manner, to see what he was thinking. It seemed queer to have such a Bond Street figure going down our tenement stairs.

Well, when I told about this experience with Raoul Hendricson (making it very entertaining) one day I heard this: that he had told Mary Heaton Vorse that he had been very much hurt, cut, by what I had said to him.

This astonished me. And pleased me. I then wrote him a letter. (I have always known how to write good letters, I think.) He wrote back. It was a solemnly grave poetic letter. He was a kind of D'Annunzio (whom he mentioned), and he talked of "a beautiful gesture." I cannot quote it at all, but he said in fine language, something about my being so Norse, the strong feelings I had created in him ... Anyway, when next he came to New York he would come to see me.

And so he did, in the spring, a month later (there were quite a few letters exchanged), and by that time I had (as I so often do) become imaginatively in love with him. I had worked him up and inflated him and bedizened him so wonderfully in my imagination. Why, look what he was: handsome, rich, a landowner, an anarchist, a philosopher, a Norwegian, blond with a profile like a Greek coin, dressing more wonderfully than Oscar Wilde or an English viscount. Why, he combined everything. He was a fine one to fasten love on. And I thought a good deal of my own dashing originality, to have arrested the attention of such a person.

Well, he came. He took me to dinner at the Brevoort, and

it was an uptown kind of dinner, the kind you might have in Rome or Paris. Venison, huge mushrooms under a glass bell, several courses, and the right wine with each, white and red. (I never could take an interest in these arrangements, and did not care much for wine anyway.) I wore my serge suit and my tight brown velvet tam o'shanter. But I always took it off in the Brevoort and showed my short ruffled black hair, many locks pointing sharply awry.

It was hard going to talk to him. His face did not respond by any movement or light, to what I said. He talked himself and said often the same thing, i.e., that "a beautiful gesture was everything." He was a poet, or that was what he wanted to be. He admired and knew Isadora Duncan and Gordon Craig. I was admiring and full of awe and my natural freshness felt restraint. But I talked the best I could. He was not a person that would ever laugh.

We went home to the apartment. We sat on one army cot. He took off his coat and he put his arm around me and I had my head on his fancy and expensive waistcoat. And he was very chivalrous and kissed my hand beautifully, and I thought it was wonderfully romantic. And his embrace, his beautiful chivalrous quiet, unfrantic, and occasional kiss, that was pleasant, I liked it very much.

"I want to stay here with you all night."

"Oh, no. I couldn't do that ... It wouldn't be honorable to my father, for instance."

"How do you mean?"

"Well, he is supporting me. If I were making my own living, it would be different."

"Well, then, I must go."

"No. Don't go."

And he stayed on for a time and at last he said that he must go or stay with me all night. "Couldn't I stay?"

I disliked having him go and did not want this romantically interesting episode to come to an end. But amongst all the other reasons why I could not consider such a thing was that I could not bring myself to say to him candidly, (from embarrassing ignorance):

"Well, what about this having-children business anyway? My gosh!"

(I don't think there is anything admirable in this. It is just interesting that I set up to be and was generally considered a Greenwich Village heller and was really so sub-adolescent.)

We wrote letters. I thought about him every day, and was in love with him in a way, but, more than that, I was elated, pleased at the situation and its color and triumph. I wrote him love letters. The vague plan was that he was to come down in June and we would be married.

He said: "I do not believe in marriage. But I would marry you, if you wish it that way." (He would rather, as I told people jokingly, that I shout from the housetops, "I love you illicitly." I was still immune enough from being in love to joke about it.) He was an anarchist and did not believe in marriage, the mere external forms. Oh, yes, I appreciated that, I said; and I thought it was fine and sensible.

But I said that I could not have a love affair as long as I was dependent on Father. That did not seem fair; he was helping me and he would not like it. Perhaps in June . . . when I had got a job . . . maybe. . . .

But one day a letter came from him. He was going to Athens with Isadora Duncan. A grave, studied, aesthetic letter about the beauty of Greece and how Norse I was and the beauty of my Byronic head. But no, he must go. With Isadora. "A beautiful gesture is the only reality," and so on.

I cannot remember feeling badly at all. A mild disappointment that there would be no more of this particular romantic fun. But there were no pangs of despised love.

Once or twice I saw him again—in his stylish clothes but horribly bunged up, with a blacked eye and swollen lip and vaguely drunk in a half-smiling, stiff-lipped trance. He got to drinking very badly. He married a thin, sighing, ill, pathetic adoring kind of girl and treated her badly. But it was her fault too, I suppose, because she, like me, had insisted on loving and then marrying his aura, his glamor and not himself. She lived with him up on the lonely estate, and always he was going to write poetry.

At last he got down to it. (She told me this long afterwards and of course it may be the perfected story of a divorced wife.) There were orders to give him utter peace, to leave him alone, not to come near his study. He wrote, wrote, wrote for three days. Sheets of paper flew on the floor like autumn leaves. And at last in an ecstasy, he rushed out into the forest, rapt and intoxicated by his inspiration. His wife tiptoed adoringly into his room to see what he had written. There was only, in all that pile of papers, one sentence written:

"Who dares to look at a tree!"

2.

Father comes to New York and shows his ignorance about Art. Hopelessly in love with a married man. Merian Cooper, a Southern gentleman.

IN FEBRUARY, I FIND, MY SISTER ANNE IN PARIS WROTE THIS to my mother:

I've thought a good deal about Brenda. It is what I feared when she stayed in New York. I don't know what can be done except to see as much of her as you can—and wait for her to grow out of this stage. Of course it would be very bad to have the slightest breach. I don't think you can absolutely count on her reassuring letters. Anne Herendeen sent me one of her letters, and it presented a contrast to the excerpts *you* sent me in the same mail. I mean the attitude was so entirely flippant. It bored me very much. I think you simply have to wait until she grows up a little more.

Well, this depresses me now. Bamboozling my parents! So trivial and stuck on myself! My silly and misspent efforts! I had some talents too. I could draw a little bit and could hear music and take in ideas intelligently. Well, in writing this book, I have rubbed my nose into myself of 1915. It has been a painful experience. And what makes me feel worse is, that in comparing the letters of Anne and Elsa and Sigurd with mine of that time, I can see they were already thoughtful fine people who knew what was true and important.

"Father is coming to New York," it said in a letter from home. This was very upsetting. It was in February. I had not told them at home that my hair was cut—all gone. I had put off reporting that.

"Well," I thought, "he is a very absent-minded man and I will just wear my velvet tam o'shanter, which is tight and covers it all pretty well. And I will sit some distance from him, and perhaps he will not notice."

What also alarmed me was that he would find that I was living alone, with Anne Herendeen in Rochester. And even more, there was guilt about my Art. Where were all my drawings and paintings? There were just a few little piddling ink designs and a charcoal thing or two. Oh, dear. It was not fear of him that was as painful as true remorse. Guilt! guilt! that I had not worked harder and had something to show.

He came one cold morning, walking out of the train at the Grand Central in his bold quick way, his crumpled hat thrown on his head so jauntily. (Father's hats were always disreputably battered and old, but no one ever wore a hat with more style.)

We sat in the apartment, I in a rather far corner with my velvet cap on, and glad that it was a darkish day so that he would not notice my haircut. But at last he said gently, sadly, after a long talk during which he looked at me under anxious brows: "And you have cut your hair off too."

I took him up to Teachers College. Bobbie Gray helped. He praised my ability and put up a fair story for me. (I don't believe I was so heinous as to ask him to do this.) What if he had told the truth? that I was an incorrigible loafer and had accomplished only the most measly and feeble things? I showed Father (with shame at my bluffing) the muddy painting I had made of a waiter, as an advertisement for a Greenwich Village ball.

Dear, darling Father! He stayed at the Seville Hotel, and I remember that in the quiet lobby he looked about at the old-fashioned pictures on the walls, realistic pictures of the school of Bouguereau and de Tadema, under glass.

"Now what do you tink of dis? Dat is pretty good now." (He always had a Norwegian accent.)

I felt superb pity for his lack of sophistication and began to explain, to talk about Whistler and the Japanese (one or two things that Gilbert Strunz had told me), as I did so, my conscience growing lighter, and my anxiety about his visit. He didn't know anything about it, anyway, I realized with relief. At home we had a few paintings by Norwegian artists, and once Father and Mother had helped to send a young artist to Paris. This and the information that Michelangelo and Leonardo were good, was all he knew about Art.

"Now do you think this is good?" he would ask, going up to one picture and then another, with his hurrying walk, to scrutinize it.

"Oh, my heavens!" I thought. "Poor Father. He doesn't know anything." And I explained tactfully but firmly why they were no good at all.

He was distressed at the state of my clothes and made me go to Wanamaker's and bought me an overcoat and some gloves. The coat was pale tweed, hip length and flared at the bottom. I thought it had a good swing.

I sent him home thoroughly fooled about me and my work.

Or so I think. I was glad that he was gone and safely out of the way. But do not think that it did not hurt me to fool him. I was painfully, excruciatingly ashamed of myself and sorry! sorry! And I resolved to work hard, much harder. But I couldn't. There was too much doing.

When Anne returned from Rochester, Samuel Merwin came to see her occasionally. We thought he was very wonderful because he actually had stories in *McClure's Magazine*. He was a round man: a circular bald head, a circular face, large circular glasses, a circular stomach. He was lymphatic and unromantic in appearance but it awed us to have him actually there, at tea.

One afternoon as he was going into the flat with Anne, I came walking home, diagonally across Fourth Street, eating an apple, and I was introduced and stood talking, with one foot in the gutter and one on the curb and eating the apple. This made an impression. Bang, the idea came to him! Just that attitude was what he wanted.

He was writing a serial about the younger generation. It was about the time of the "salamanders." Owen Johnson, I think, had written about them in a novel, about those young ladies who go through the fire of immorality without being burned, i.e., they get money out of men without having love affairs with them and losing their "virtue" as it is mistakenly called. (Imagine identifying virtue with virginity!)

Yes, Samuel Merwin said, he would put me in his serial. I was just the note he wanted. I would be Sue, the heroine. And so the story appeared, to my immense elation and pride; and there the illustrator had drawn my tweed coat, my short hair, the tam o'shanter, the apple, the foot on the curb, and being introduced to a tall, lean, handsome man with round glasses.

My conceit grew and developed happily. My enormous self-approval. Or rather, I should say, my sense of being very wonderful without doing anything to prove it.

I now come to the story of my marriage. An autobiography is no good unless everything is exactly true. But now there is much I cannot tell about myself because then I would have to tell about my husband. And this is unfair, like hunting—like shooting something at a great safe distance. Besides, I know what is in my soul, and so I can tell it. But I may be wrong about what was in his.

My marriage was a mistake, as far as I can see. Though we never really know. For it may have been necessary for me to make a mistake, to have been forced into a restless, striving life. But it was a mistake in that it ended in a divorce.

My theory is that my marriage was bad for these reasons: because of my dancing school humiliation, whence came my self-protective scorn of boys, and then because I went to a woman's college, where I saw no men at all. The result was that I was a sub-adolescent at twenty-three and had not one bit of immunity in romantic things.

Most children get this immunity in high school, especially in coeducation, where they learn about romance, love, jealousy, jiltings in a hundred homeopathic doses, and finally, with unconscious wisdom, select the one who is right. But knowing nothing of men until I was twenty-two, I could not make comparisons: "This young man when he is in love is ardent but a liar. That one is kinder and more fun."

In New York, where I felt that I was becoming so wonderfully experienced, come to think of it I knew well only about five men: Swithin Johns, a couple of young publishers, a drunken newspaper man, an art student or two, Barney Gallant, and a married man.

One evening Anne and I were at dinner on Waverly Place, a sedate and pleasant place with pretty blue china and candlesticks.

"That's Minerva Newman's husband," Anne said as we went up to pay our check. (That is not her real name.) "That is Mr. R."

And that was not *his* name either, or even his initial. But I find that I have to call him R. because it seems easier to write about him that way. When I call him by his name I keep feeling embarrassed and hesitant. I still like him as a human being, and we try to help each other, but when I write about my marriage as still existing, it makes me uncomfortable.

He was dressed like a stockbroker, not like an artist or radical, in well-shined tan shoes and a striped necktie. He wore gold glasses and had that tough hair which is the color and texture of a doormat, and a short nose, and his eyes, slightly magnified by his glasses, were very bright and round and brown.

He wanted to meet me. From what I know of him later, he may have arranged to come and pay his check at the same time we did. He was always strategical. And that was a thing I never agreed with him about, for I hate strategy.

I went home that evening with another pleasant little feeling of triumph. Why, Minerva Newman's husband, he liked me too! He too thought I was independent and original.

Anne and I admired Minerva Newman tremendously and knew all about her. She made speeches all over the country for woman suffrage and was big and free and fine looking, with eloquent dark eyes, flashing this way and that.

The next day, right away, there came a special delivery letter from R. asking me to see him at his office. He wanted me to make a little drawing. I made the drawing (with great uneasiness, for I certainly did not know how to draw). He accepted it, praised it extravagantly, paid me ten dollars for it.

I saw him often among all the others, in that winter. (He and Minerva were not happy together and they might separate forever, he told me. She was away.) He was very persistent in seeing me, a sender of telegrams and messengers.

Sometimes I liked him and sometimes I did not. He was twelve years older than I. I liked his University of Wisconsin appearance and practical nasal talk, cutting right through anything sentimental or idealistic. His middle western looks, knowledge of football games and automobiles seemed so reassuring. But he would do this: if I broke an engagement with him, he made me feel that then I had to give him *two* engagements, to be forgiven. And I have three serious weaknesses. 1. I cannot disappoint people. 2. I cannot be a poor sport. 3. I cannot take a dare. (The first is due to an abnormal sympathy; the others to lack of insight.) And so you can see how it is that I saw him oftener and oftener and got to know him more and more intimately.

But I think this marriage was a mistake because it was not a case of true love at all. It was his persistence and my good nature that brought it about. I think it was not love because it took me so many months to like him deeply. There were these differences between us: When we took a walk together, he set out singing so loudly and talking, while I liked a walk to be quiet and easy, with eyes on the horizon. He talked so very much and usually about things that did not interest me or make me laugh. I remember thinking: "Now if he were a girl, would I like him? Would we have any fun together?" The answer was "No." And this is a good test of real love, I think. I still use it, but sadly do not always go by it.

"Just the same, he is a likable and very bright man," I thought, "and he knows a great deal about mathematics, engineering, and world trade, and built up a successful insurance business in Milwaukee before he sold it." And he believed in suffrage, though in a practical, rationalistic way. He could not stand sentimentality about love or religion. He had not a touch of the poet in him, or the believer, or the nobly imaginative man. He could not stand it when women in love put on that earnest spiritual love. I agreed with him; or thought I did.

And at last he asked if I would marry him if he got a divorce. Well, Minerva, approaching a permanent separation from him, had pangs for a little while, and asked as a last favor that he and I would not see each other for two months. But first, before parting, we might have one last walk together, she said.

Again we went up the Hudson and walked over the mountains into New Jersey. I was full now of seriousness. We were parting forever. An unwonted romantic devotion filled me. And even R., so materialistic and physical in all his conceptions, was full of feeling too. I really fell in love with him at last.

Naturally we did not keep our promise to Minerva. We decided (with no struggle) that we had to see each other. Minerva was told. Gradually it was understood that there would be a divorce. Minerva was wonderful in her magnanimity and goodness. "Marriage," she said, in her interviews in the newspapers, "is a link, not a handcuff . . . No, I will not have alimony. Women must be economically independent." She lived up to all these things.

But as for me, this going from freedom and a kind of jolly innocence to being in love was frightfully hard. You cannot imagine what an inner cataclysm. There were emotions like jealousy and fear (I had been so remarkably free from jealousy and fear before) that I had not the faintest idea how to explain or escape from, because I had so little practice in it.

I lost my power to charm people, and this was because I was split down the middle, full of self-doubt (how could I like or trust myself, getting jealous like that?). And though it was romantic, you understand—why, Isolde never had any more serious and radiant feelings than I!—there was so much pain and confusion in it, trying to explain to myself why I really *did* love him, and how all the things I did not like about him were just my own vile egotism, the evil, ungenerous meanness in *me*.

I think the trouble was—and I suppose it happens to millions of poor human beings—that I was tied emotionally to someone I did not really admire. Dead in love, yes, but what also were the facts about it? At the same time I was bored to be with him (our conversation) and yet afraid to be away from him (my jealousy).

Well, when summer came there was no more art school and I had to go home. But I loved summer and Lake Calhoun and knew that I would get back to New York some way, so everything was all right.

"Brenda," I find that Sigurd wrote in a letter to Elsa, "is appearing on the front pages of the *Sunday Journal* minus her hair. When she comes home, she is going to have an awful job to get any of the family to be seen in public with her. Rolf and Toke are already on record to this effect."

And such talk always made me feel pleased, and like laughing, and gave me more self-confidence than ever, if that could be possible.

At home I began to campaign to get even slimmer. (New York had shrunk me to about a hundred and thirty pounds.) I ran each morning far out in the country and then around Lake Calhoun. It was seven miles. I ran about half the way and I just loved this exercise. It was not hard work at all, but something buoyant and wonderful to look forward to. When I got home from the running I swam a quarter of a mile out to the buoy and back again. Then I dressed very sprucely and took a street car downtown and had lunch at Donaldson's tearoom, with some girl, Henrietta Prindle or Julie Plant. I got down that summer to 124 pounds, which is what I weigh now. There was one drawback. Lack of vitamins. Expending so much energy and living on strong tea, cigarettes, sugar and bread, was hard on my teeth.

"My teeth are like rubber: they bend when I bite," says my diary. "$75.00 dentist bill. Good night!"

But my short hair was a success at home too, because such a remarkable young man began coming to see me. This was a reporter on the *Daily News* named Merian Cooper. I can see him sitting on our porch, very pale with a damp gray complexion and pallid reddish hair. And at first he seemed insignificant, softly drawling his vague Southern accent. But he had such startling ideas about honor, his word, fighting —a rigid, chivalrous code. He was a Southern gentleman. I had never seen one before and I admired him, though his ideas seemed so unsensible that I was wonderfully entertained by them.

Here were some of them: He had been expelled from Annapolis for some drinking escapade. He swore a vow never to see his father again, to cross the Florida state line, until he amounted to something. Also he had vowed not to take a drink again for some incredible period like two or three years. And the implacability of his vow was like that of Genghis Khan. He had many stern, strange phrases like "the law of fifty-fifty" (though I didn't know what it meant), and he had a scheme to break the bank at Monte Carlo. He was very, very anxious that there be war for the United States so that he could go to it. He loved war, fighting. That was the thing for him! and a little later it was a great relief to him when Americans were sent to the Mexican border and he could tear down there to get into it. As for when the United States entered the World War, that was too good to be true. So fiercely adventurous and soldierly, yet he was himself so gentle and good. He was always the one to spring up to do the helpful thing, to insist on paying the entire bill for every party. He had written an article "On the Right To Lynch"; so our friendship was interesting in view of the fact that my favorite pronouncement was that "the Negroes are the coming race."

But sitting on our porch on a midsummer evening, the steel twilight shining from the lake, he liked me, and what I said, and my black fur cap of hair, my freedom and jokey candor. We went to a dance at Christmas Lake. He said he liked my way of walking, straight ahead and untrammelled. In the black soft night we went down by the lake. It was smooth, and musical far-away oarlocks clinked under the stars. Suddenly he burst out laughing.

"What are you laughing at?"

"I am laughing at what the Florida matrons will say when I take you down there."

"How do you mean, 'Take me down there?'"

"When I marry you."

I said that perhaps it would never happen. But I am sure I did not tell him that I liked someone else. This is a species of character-strength that I have never had.

And then he spoke very beautifully about how two certain lovers swam far, far out together in just such a lake as that. I forget whether it was to drown together or just why they did it, but I liked it and felt that he had beautiful and poetic ideas.

Yes, he was a darling. His gentle, unselfish politeness to the other youths who were with us.

"Ah'll get it, Ed" (the car or whatever it was). "Here, Ah'll pay 'at check. Wait, Ed, don't do that. Ah'm payin' 'is."

He would come out to our house in a taxicab from way downtown, a great cumbersome lumbering taxi that cost about five dollars for the trip. In it we went down to the Radisson Hotel in style. They had dancing on the roof garden. But after paying for the cab he had very little money left.

"We can have a bottle of gingeh ale and there'll be enough lef' fo' the waiter. Twenty-fav cents."

Of course we had to go home on the street car. But as we crossed Hennepin Avenue he murmured something politely and went over to a policeman.

"I borrowed a dime from him fo' carfare," he explained to me. "I ran out."

"Why, how crazy!" I cried. "Why don't you let me pay for it? Why, that's ridiculous." I jingled my pocket full of money and said it was just absurd of him not to let me pay for part of our evening, or all of it.

"A gentleman never takes money f'om a good girl," he said with haughty finality.

I called him "Shooting Cooper" because there was hardly any situation he could imagine getting out of honorably without shooting. For example, I would be rattling along telling him about New York doings, how Barney Gallant gave me a birthday party at the Black Cat in New York and we had some fine sparkling burgundy that put me in a blur and how when I came to, I was dancing with the waiter. (I meant the nice handsome Luigi, who owned the restaurant and was a fine dancer.)

"What did you say yo' escort's name was?" said Cooper quietly, taking out a notebook and pencil. "What's his address?"

"64 West 11th Street. Why?"

"Because I've got to shoot him."

"Oh, you crazy Cooper. I never heard of anything so ridiculous. Oh! Southern gentleman! But you are so nice."

I had the greatest admiration for him. I loved that honor business really. And he probably liked me for trying so hard to make him share my money, and not being such an exquisite little bundle of Southern womanhood. For I would cry out: "What a fool idea! Why shouldn't women have the pleasure of supporting men? Just to even things up a little! You bet your life. If I were married I would insist that my husband take bridge lessons and be careful to get his nap. Just to even things up a little for the poor men."

One night we drove down to the Radisson in the lumbering taxicab. We ordered a bottle of ginger ale. But when the bill came he looked serious. There had been a miscalculation. There was not enough left to tip the waiter.

"Oh, say!" I said. "Now of course. Here." I dragged a handful of money out of my pocket. A little pale, Cooper had to borrow a quarter. But he really brooded over it, was very silent. Presently we were out in the mezzanine corridor sitting on a red plush davenport. He was still silent, really troubled, thinking hard.

"What's the matter?"

"You know," he said at last, "there is only one way I can make 'at right—borrowing 'at quarter f'om you."

"What?"

"If you will be engaged to me until I pay it back. Would you be willin' to do that?"

"Why, sure."

"Ve'y well . . . Will you marry me?"

"Sure."

The next day he gravely paid his debt.

"I release you from yo' engagement," he said.

That winter in New York I had dinner with him and his best friend, Tracy, a tiny, thin young man with a flashy suit and clear, quiet eyes. Tracy too was the kind of a person who wanted a war. At dinner with me, they were both gentle, talkative, polite, shyly enthusiastic, and it was the last time I saw them.

But they came one afternoon to my room, and left a note. My landlady gave me a picture of two swashbucklers, saying how Cooper had crumpled the paper. "Throw it on the deck!" he said like a pirate and slammed it on the floor until it bounced.

He became an aviator, was shot down in Germany and imprisoned. After the war he joined the Poles against the Bolsheviki. He was for years a prisoner in Russia. Later he made the moving picture "Grass" and that made him famous. And then "Little Women."

I saw him again in New York in 1929. And at that point *I* had become idealistic, and he the cynical man of the world. But probably there have been many changes since.

3.

Working for Bruce Barton on Every Week. *An anxious life. Getting married and the War. What the various Uelands felt about the War.*

IN SEPTEMBER THE PROBLEM WAS, HOW TO GET BACK TO New York? I had barely a hundred dollars. I now come to one of the worst things I ever did. I lied. I claimed to have been offered a job in New York which would pay me sixty dollars a month. I would have been more honorable just to have gone. Yes, I wish I had done that. But I was demented because of this being in love.

And so there was the second combat of wills with Father. Again I sat on the piano stool. It was in our sitting room, a large room with a bay of windows toward the east and a great oblong window toward the south. Mother's large portrait is on the wall. There is an upright piano, out of which comes thin, but tender, singing music. Above it there is a large painting of a fjord at sunset by a fine Norwegian painter. Mother's Duncan Phyfe secretary is in the room, with a worn, ancient set of Plutarch's Lives in it, and there is a beautiful gilt mirror that belonged to her grandfather. The room is bare and filled with sunshine that fades the rug.

Father sat there looking at me, inwardly despairing. Why did I want to go? Why not stay at home with them? Why wasn't I happy? What could they do about it?

No, I had to go. I sat there like a Sioux Indian stoically taking poison. Tears sprang into his eyes and for a fleeting moment he cried. Yes, that was one of the hardest things that ever happened to me.

In New York I made a skimpy anxious living. Anne Herendeen was on *Every Week,* a thin magazine that cost three cents. They began to give me assignments for "double-page spreads." That procedure went like this: First I had an idea. Say that it was "Famous Bachelors." Then I collected twelve good pictures of twelve world-famous bachelors, including Eleanora Sears of Boston. Then to the public library and the *New York World* morgue (this was a library of clippings from old newspapers) for information about each of them. Then to write a hundred-word caption for each, crammed with much labored wit. For this—after innumerable pictures and captions were rejected and not found satisfactory—I got fifty dollars.

Bruce Barton, a big, red-faced young man with stiff curly hair and sharp nose, was the editor, and he passed through the office and joked in his hearty way. Anne Herendeen he called "Staff" and Johnny Mosher, a thin Williams boy with a spasmodic laugh, "Gus," because it was the least apropos name he could think of. We liked him, Bruce Barton, though we disdained him for his businessman ideals. Oh, Lordy, go-getting! Success—what an ideal! But sometimes in a sentence he would reveal the most deep inner depression: "I never can see why the whole human race doesn't jump in the East River!" Yes, he always seemed to me deeply split, as though a man who really wanted to be a scholar and a saint had an overwhelming power and gift for business promoting and money-making.

But our real boss on *Every Week* was Edith Lewis. She was the best boss I ever had, the most intelligent, the most just, the kindest and the bluntest. Her warm hazel eyes looked at you and she would say right out: "These captions

are no good; they are all over the place!" and at the same
time, because of bashfulness, she would be almost lisping and
blushing deeply. From anybody else, it would be an unbearable wound (unfeeling, mean editors weazen all one's
ability, just as mean employers do) but not from her. And
I respected her so much. Yes, it was true, I saw at once: the
captions were frightful. I went and did them again. I was
grateful to her for all her guidance.

Dear Mother:
Miss Lewis was pleased with the two things I have been work-
ing on. I still have my twenty dollars. It's like the magic purse.
I have always that much.

Brenda.

But that winter was not fun like the one before. I had to
work very anxiously for every little scrap of money. Just to
give you one glimpse of what my "free-lancing" was like.
(It is such a joyful, buoyant expression: "free-lancing.")

A young Icelandic dramatist came to town, who, George
Brandes said, had a great future. I read this in the newspaper.
"That might be a good story," I think. I search him out, find
him in a small room with lace curtains and a brass bedstead
on Seventh Avenue. I talk to him, pump him uneasily (your
questions in interviewing always seem so tiresome and prying). I write the piece with immense labor, rewriting it and
polishing it fifty times. (Writing was a fearful travail for
me until twenty years later when I learned just to say what I
meant and nothing fancier, that the only way to impress people is not to try to impress them.) I mail it to the *New York
Times*. It comes back. I am paralyzed with discouragement
and self-doubt. What an anti-climax after all that difficulty,
embarrassment, and anxious, pretentious labor! And they
send it back! Life becomes too hard.

After several days I have the courage to mail it to the
Sun. After ten days I hear that they accept it. They give me

eight dollars—for that Herculean struggle! But I could
write to Mother:

The *Sun* has taken a piece of mine on a remarkable young
Icelandic dramatist whom George Brandes has written about.

It sounded very fine.

Miss Lewis and I [I continue] have a secret liking for each
other. She is pretty shy and we both have the same trouble of
jerky talking. I have been working in the same room with her
for the past month, and, strange to say (for me), I love her.
I went to her house with Anne Herendeen last Friday. She lives
with a short story writer named Willa Cather.

Miss Cather and Miss Lewis lived on the top floor of an
apartment on Bank Street and Miss Cather was beginning
to be repected as a true artist. She was a young woman with a
sturdy comeliness, clothed in dark velveteen. Her thick light-
brown hair was in smooth braids about her head and she had
even white teeth and a strong, round, rosy face.

At these Friday teas there were always music critics, like
Louis Sherwin and Pitts Sanborn. And John Mosher and I,
young and nobodies, listened to them in silence and made a
little fun of them afterwards. There was so much highbrow
talk about what this music critic had said of that music critic's
criticism of the opera. Miss Cather loved opera and wrote
stories in beautiful culled prose about prima donnas. She
worked in the morning and walked in Central Park in the
afternoon. That is why she had such nice red cheeks. There
was something affirmative and masculinely intellectual about
her, and her talk was pleasant and fluent but very, very definite; while *our* darling, Miss Lewis, was always shy and
quiet, gently blushing if you said something that made her
laugh, and she just quietly saw to it that we had a nice time
and that there was hot water for tea. She was from
Nebraska too, like Miss Cather. Anne Herendeen said she
had once written beautiful poetry but gave it up. "I bet she

would be a hundred times better than Miss Cather!" we would say afterwards, defensively.

But that winter I was not very happy. This was because I was in love. You see, plunged into this strange state, my whole energy was turned toward one person and there was no true interest in anybody else, I had no attractiveness in me. Yet I wanted people to like me. But they don't when you are like that. They sense that you have nothing to give them, no affection nor warmth, no bright rays. They sense you are a yawning, sucking vacuum wanting only admiration, and they fly from you.

I was twenty-four that October and it was the only time in my life when I really dreaded getting old, and had that objectionable female terror over it. It was because of jealousy of R., and his talk about how men's physical passion, biologically, lasts so much longer than women's; that is why, as he would say, it is better for them to marry much younger women. The fact that he was twelve years older than I, he said, meant it would perhaps be possible for him to stay true to me. Just think, next year I would be twenty-five! How old! how passée! Would he still be attracted to me?

Minerva had said she would get a divorce, but she kept procrastinating because it was an unpleasant and trying thing to do. These procrastinations were always a staggering blow to me. And I can feel now that curious desperation I had to get married. It was as though something I wanted very badly was just out of reach and suspended on a thin thread which might break and it would fall into the abyss. There was no patience nor quiet nor philosophy in me. I have awe now, for my mountain-moving will, my devotion.

For example R. had lost his job and had not a cent in the world and you can see how rickety, teeny, and thread-hung *my* money-making was. I remember walking along 13th Street with him and trying to make us both feel better about everything.

But at last in the spring he persuaded a company to send him to Spain on an economic investigation. Now I was left in New York, and this was all I had to do: try to make a living "free-lancing"; to keep asking Minerva to hurry with her divorce; and to hold off my family, who were deeply troubled and sad about it. From the letters I dig up now I discover that a vast circle of people thought that it was too bad—my attachment to a man so encumbered—and they were doing all they could to draw me away.

March 1916. Lunch with Geoffrey Parsons. He said I lacked continuity. But, my Lord, he doesn't know what I am aiming at.

R. came back from Spain in April. I was on Front Street waiting for him that bright morning. That was happiness, and immeasurable relief to see him. I had a little stuffy room smelling of rotting carpets, on University Place, near the Lafayette, in a rooming house with only beaver board between us and the next narrow cheap room. Through this partition there came lovely music, and it was Rachmaninoff playing, for this was his miserable rooming house too. After hours of that music R. burst out crying. He cried and cried. He was afraid of the future, of the divorce, and most of all, of the reporters, and losing his job, if it got in the papers. I summoned all my powers of sympathy and encouragement. They are very great too.

On April 29th, 1916, lovely generous Minerva wrote:

Off you go, Brenda. Got the decree today. Good luck. I hope it means happiness to you. It certainly is a relief to both of us.

And so we went to Goshen, New York, and were married, and went to a movie afterwards. Walking along the quiet sidewalks in the soft dark night, it was an odd anti-climactic feeling to be married, and I felt something like regret inside about it, an indescribable feeling of nothingness.

Now I must tell something about the War because by this time it was really beginning to affect us; it grew all the time more frightening and depressing. I know that almost every day for years I would think: "What would it be like if there were no war? What would that feeling be?," because such a heavy cloud was always over us. But when you made yourself imagine there being no war, at once, a flood of purity and sunlight filled the world! Why, if there were no war, you knew that never again would anything be of the slightest importance—loss of money, sickness, earthquakes, pestilences—such an unfathomable cheerfulness would be in us all. Because there is no malevolence in these things.

On Election Day in November, Hughes seemed to be elected and we were sunk. That meant that the horror in Europe was sucking us in. It meant that pro-militaristic sentiment was swinging the country. But the next day Wilson won after all. "He kept us out of war" had been the slogan. And that meant the country still had an honest abhorrence for the whole thing. Wilson would save us from it.

Kenneth Taylor, the young doctor who was my sister's husband, was surprising us all by his work in London and then in Paris. He was a quietly energetic young man, so modest and incoherent that his talk was a kind of mumble. He was utterly unassertive and shyly smiling, with eyes full of searching kindness and green fire. He had gone abroad for post-graduate work in Germany, but the War bent his course to England, where he worked under Sir William Osler, and then to Paris, with the famous American surgeon, Dr. Joseph Blake.

Ken [Anne wrote] goes shooting the other day at Blake's chateau—I don't know how many acres of park and forest near Fontainebleau—and they had a shooting party for a game pie for the blessés New Year. Several Englishmen from the hospital went and Blake and one or two others. Ken came home very pleased because he had shot all but one pheasant, and more than half the rabbits. The others were so annoyed because with one shot he got a rabbit and a pheasant, the poor bird having accidentally got in the way.

This was symbolic of Ken. From Minnesota, mousily quiet and unobtrusive, in whatever it was—hunting, card playing, golf, carpentering, gardening or medicine, it always turned out that he had done better than all the others, to their mystification. And when they spoke of it, he would shyly mumble and look embarrassed. I had a theory that because he could not *talk* he acted ten times more than the rest of us. For example, one summer day at home, sitting on the lawn under the elm trees, we all talked about Art and discussed it volubly from every angle—about Elie Faure's book, and Matisse and Cézanne, and how fascinating it would be *really* to have the time to draw or paint. Ken, who had been sitting there, apparently had disappeared, for here we saw him again, driving up the driveway in somebody's car. He had been downtown, bought canvases and paints. Before noon he had stretched several canvases, painted a landscape and a still life. He is still painting and much of his work is very beautiful. Sometimes I think he accomplishes so much because there is no egotism to stand in his way (as in my case). Michelangelo said, when they asked him why he worked with a light on his cap, like a miner: "Because then I never stand in my own shadow." That is what I do. But Ken does not: He just worked, searched, worked, tried and acted, and thought and tried some more. He never bothered to think whether it would be good or bad or better than somebody else's.

August 30th, 1916. From Anne:

Ken had another paper in the *British Medical Journal* which he expects to turn out something of a hornet's nest. In it he goes after some of the theories of Sir Almroth Wright, who is the great god of British medicine. Also the author of a ridiculous book against suffrage, and women in general. Ken is quite sure he has him in several mistakes. Of course his presumption is like

David with a sling shot, but he feels sure of himself and it will be amusing. . . .

December, 1916.

Ken heard a rather interesting thing about Metchnikoff's death the other day, from a man who had worked with Metchnikoff at the Pasteur for years, and who was present at the autopsy: it was given out that he died of "heart failure," but that is a vague term of course. The verdict of the autopsy was that he died of cirrhosis of the liver caused by his having eaten lactic acid for the last five years. He took it to prolong his life, you remember. Quite ironic, isn't it?

In the first months of the War, gas gangrene poisoning was killing off wounded soldiers in twenty-four hours, and Ken made some researches that saved them. He became quite famous for it, much more than he wanted to be, for the newspapers got hold of it and made a to-do over it. I tell these things just to show that Anne and Ken had a close view of things in Europe. What they said affected my feelings about the War, very much.

Well, in March, 1917, in spite of President Wilson, it began to look as though there would be war for us. What had changed Wilson's mind in two months, from the man who "didn't wish either side to win"? Probably only the Recording Angel knows. External reasons were: 1. the submarine campaign; 2. American investments in the Allies (and so tremendous pro-Ally propaganda); and 3. Wilson's growing belief that if we went into the War he could arbitrate the new peace.

But I think back to all the people I knew then—Greenwich Village radicals, middle western families, school teachers, business men, Anne and Ken in Europe—and every single one of them thought that the United States going to war would be just a contributing to the nightmare, that it was better that the War be a draw and not a victory, that England and France were as culpable as Germany. It was not only me, whose political ideas were based on thrice-removed hearsay. It was every person I knew.

March 27th, Elsa writes to my mother:

I am interested that in spite of Anne's French experience, she seems to feel no more the necessity of our country entering the War than I do. I can't see what we could gain by fighting and I am praying that the middle western congressmen will insist upon being shown before we are plunged into it. I thank God for every day's delay. The Russian revolution isn't the only thing that can happen with unexpected swiftness.... I am not so worried about Arnulf with his middle western surroundings, but I feel nervous about Sigurd's conscience in these days, when even Bryn Mawr is "mobilized to a man." The only silver lining I see is that wireless telegraphy and automobile repairing have been introduced into Bryn Mawr in place of some Latin and Greek.

But it came about. War was declared. In Congress Senator La Follette made a passionate argument against it, but he and twelve others were branded "the willful obstructionists" by Wilson, and, almost over night (for doing what all good Americans are supposed to do, and especially Senators, i.e., to speak up and argue for what they believe), they became "traitors" and suffered all sorts of contumely. But we thought La Follette's arguments were wise and reasonable.

The young men I knew were depressed and cynical. John Mosher made jokes and burst into his spasmodic agonized laugh. "I have a friend," he said, "whose mother is very anxious for him to go to the Front, to see the stuff that is in him."

Women began to behave in the most loathsome way. Some organized ladies were offering their automobiles to rush the virgins inland in case of invasion. John liked to plan who would be in those automobiles, naming very plain but patriotic women. Members of the D.A.R. and debutantes were asking men on the streets why they were not in khaki, and if they were slackers. It made my blood boil and still does. Think of doing that! *Go* to war. There is dignity in that. But to ask someone else to!

Jack Rochester, who was as athletic and adventurous as anyone, could not see one hint of sense to the War. He went about with ironic humor, balancing from day to day, whether to enlist or wait for conscription. The trouble was his rich cold-hearted father was frowning at him. He called himself: "Piece of meat no. 296."

Gilbert Strunz, who could not look in a butcher shop window, was finally pressed in. He joined the marines because he liked the red stripe on their trousers. He was at the front and died of wounds.

Elsa wrote:

"Social work is in a great turmoil . . . trying to avoid duplication and at the same time defend itself from the fire-eating preparedness ladies who want to run the universe."

Now Mother and Father in the Middle West, with agonizing conscientiousness had studied and sifted all the facts about the War. I think they came to the conclusion, with the greatest sorrow, that it had to be; it was the only course; the President could not do otherwise.

But Anne, our firebrand, did not let them rest in it:

Aug. 4th, 1917.

Dearest Mother,

I told you that all the boxes have arrived. The sugar you send comes through perfectly, and increases my little store. Our sugar cards give us about two lumps apiece a day.

I do not see how you can be so optimistic about the war and the boys. You seem to have just the attitude of the Britling family. I am very melancholy and bitter about it, much more so than before. I am not at all sure about the war "being right." To begin with, it shows no signs whatever of finishing for a long time. Five months ago you said that surely our boys would never have to come over, it must be finished before very long. The end looks further off than ever. Now the Germans have all of Galicia, today we hear they have taken Czernowitch. The great British offensive seems to be stuck in the mud in Flanders. The worst of it is that the political part of the war seems to be in the hands of doddering old men who have secret conferences and decide that millions of boys shall go on fighting jusqu' au bout, and none of these people who are fighting have the least idea what they are fighting for, how long they must go on throwing their lives away.

It is a shock to learn from Germany, from Michaelis, what passed at the last secret session of the French chamber, the first and second of June: to learn that in January the French sent a diplomat to Russia to get the consent of the Czar to France's taking certain German territory west of the Rhine, from Germany; and that as late as the first of June this year, this remained in the plan of the French Government. Of course Ribot denies the truth of this, but his denial is very feeble, unsupported by any proof. He only says that the idea was to make a "buffer state" of this German territory, but that is very much like annexation. At any rate it is not calculated to encourage the liberal and democratic element in Germany to continue its efforts for peace.

At the first sign of the desire for peace in Germany, the Allies get drunk with the idea that Germany is weakening; they stiffen up their demands, talk about complete victory, etc. This naturally scares the liberals in Germany, makes them willing to go on fighting because they think it is for their very existence. It is a vicious circle.

Just recently the Allies had a conference in Paris—Lloyd-George, Sonnino, etc., to talk over Balkan affairs. Although the Allies are "against secret diplomacy" not a word comes out about their arrangements. It is well known that Italy wants Valona, in Albania, and Dalmatia, wants to control the Adriatic. Now what have our boys to do with that? What have they to do even with Alsace-Lorraine? Why should they give up their lives to right historic wrongs, settle historic quarrels? They might as reasonably go to China to take part in some dynastic struggle. When I say "our boys" I mean, for that matter, any boys.

I do not think for a moment, that if the French Armies were told that they were to go on fighting just for Alsace-Lorraine, they would do so. The younger generation does not care about that. It's the old men, wicked, stupid, old men who remember old feuds, who go on throwing away young lives! Of course France has to fight to free her territory and that of Belgium. And I accept that we should help her to do that. But if that were all, really, that we were fighting for, the war would be over in a month! If the Germans knew that that were all, they would accept it thankfully. But all these lies, these speeches about humanity, Liberty, the Right—and underneath, the secret plots to grab territory.

Take Balfour answering the accusation of Michaelis, saying that Great Britain is thoroughly disinterested in the war, that she has never made, and would never make, any claim to territory in Europe. It is a little conspicuous that he does not speak of Africa or Asia. Do you think the British are planning to give up all their conquests in Africa, or to give up their footing in Mesopotamia? They don't say so.

Perhaps we had to come into the war. I admit we were shockingly affronted by Germany. But once in, what has become of the idea of Peace Without Victory, of the Society of Nations? What are our ends in the war? Wilson was demanding that the belligerents declare their ends of war before we came in. Well, what are his? What are we fighting for? How long will we go on? Until France gets the left bank of the Rhine?

Sometimes I think the "mad" Russians are the sanest people on the planet.

Of course now that the boys think that "the war is right," they can only go on to the limit. The war is now popular over there. It is "the thing." It makes me sick. The American papers with their blatant patriotism, their pictures of society ladies in Red Cross uniforms, make me want to vomit.

Do you know that the average length of life of a British lieutenant after he gets to the front is eleven days?

A friend of ours in London had a boy of sixteen. She was so happy to think he was too young to get into the war. Now he is killed. How can you be so blind? So optimistic? So placid. [Of course Mother was not inwardly these things, though she tried to seem so.] Six months have gone by since we came in. The war is no farther along. Another six months and another. And it won't make any difference. There will never be a military victory. Finally the people will see the folly of it, get up and kick out the stupid vieillards who keep the thing going. It is the only end I·see.

Being in a milieu of screaming spread-eaglism, I have not been at all happy. I get into black rages. Perhaps I am all wrong. But my melancholy is very deep. Ken is naturally more hopeful, more cheerful than I am, but I am glad to say he is no more for the war to the bitter end than I am.

I am getting so that I can't think of you or Elsa or anybody, or a lovely summer day, without tears. You see how morbid and melancholy I am. You used to say about any trouble that loomed very big: "It will pass; everything passes." But that, instead of being a comfort, is the very saddest thing. The French say all the time, bravely, "Tout passe." But that's just the worst of it. I think so often of that big clock in Spain over which is written: "Each hour wounds; the last one kills."

Well, this is not a very gay letter. Much love, anyway, to all of you. I wish I were home. I wish I were twenty, and making wet tracks on the hall floor after a swim!

Anne.

But Arnulf, who was twenty-one, was more cheerful. I just loved Arnulf. He was young and limber, with thick brown hair and fine sliding brown eyes.

I hope [he wrote from an officers' training camp in Iowa] they call our regiment the Black Guard or Mrs. Wilson's Own, or the Wrist Watch or something, don't you? The 337th is too prosaic. I think I shall study a little now. Well, good-by.

Sigurd was up at Harvard studying law. When I now read Sigurd's letters I am sad that I was not just like Sigurd. He used both his intelligence and his conscience and then quietly did what they said. But how was I? I tried to, but then always something violent or frivolous inside threw me off.

Of course, in reading this autobiography, you must take into account my disrespect for myself of the past. It may make me out worse than I was. Yes, my disrespect *now,* for myself of *then.* In reading old letters, when I come to those of my own, I quickly and irritably draw lines through them and discard them. "Oh, *that* fool!" I think. "Brenda. *She* didn't know anything. What twaddle. A smattering, a bluff!"

But perhaps I was as competent and as likable as I think I am now. I probably was.

But let me show a few thoughts of Sigurd about the War.

April, 1917.

Dear Father:

I don't feel the slightest obligation to volunteer. I am a pacifist to the extent that I am out of sympathy with the Administration's war aims and peace views. I think there is great danger of making a hell out of this country, because of our sentimental enthusiasm due to being at war. General Wood is reported as saying that the war may last ten years and that anyone who says that it may end next spring is "a public enemy." Well, if this is fairly representative of the men who are conducting this war, I am convinced that one who stays home and tries to learn how to think straight is doing far more of a service to his country than one who gets himself bayoneted over the boundary of Alsace. In other words, I do not think that those who sacrifice the most are necessarily performing the greatest service to the country.

On the other hand the idea of being an officer has certain attractions.

If I should go to this camp and lose a year at the law school, I doubt whether I would come back. At least not until I could pay my own way. After one gets to be a certain age it ceases to be pleasant to be financially dependent. Furthermore, if my plans for acquiring a legal education cannot harmonize with my plan of getting married in two or three years, the former shall have to wait. I realize that there is a maxim which says that one should sacrifice present for future happiness, but it can be overdone. This is especially so if the war is going to last ten years, in which case I say to hell with the future. Pardon the profanity but that is the way I feel.

November, 1917.

Dear Father:

. . . But I lost my optimism that the war would end sometime this winter. After the unfavorable reception given Lord Lansdowne's letter, which seems to me the only intelligent piece of writing we have had from one of our prominent statesmen on the subject of the war, for some time, I began to feel that it will be a long time before men begin to be rational once more. Indeed now I am not sure that we could get peace without victory. We passed up our good chance this summer when the Pope made his overtures. Now Germany's military star is so much in the ascendant that I doubt whether we could have peace without being licked. In fact, I rather expect that we will be licked, that is, that the Allies will be licked more than Germany will be licked. Everybody will be licked except Japan. . . . Then by clever publicity and distortion of the facts, we will deceive ourselves into thinking that it was a great victory and sensible people, like myself, who argued for a similar peace two or three years earlier, will go down in history as traitors.

. . . But I promise you that no man of military age has examined into the rectitude of his conduct and listened more carefully to the promptings of his conscience than I have. If I am at fault, it is a mental not a moral weakness. One thing I have learned from you, Father, is to have the highest contempt for the opinion of the multitude and of the orthodox when that opinion is contrary to my own.

I want to say how much I appreciate the attitude that you and Mother have taken toward me in regard to this war. We have not been in perfect agreement about the best method of ending the war, nor the best method of carrying it on, but you have both wanted me to act for myself. . . . How different the case of the Jamison family who for all practical purposes coerced Joe into the service. . . . Yet Joe is a real cynic about our part in the war, alongside of whom I am a raving patriot. Well, in the eyes of the world, the Jamison parents have done a very noble thing, but my feeling is that they have shown a pseudo-sentimentality where they should have used reason. Well, I hope to have an opportunity to demonstrate to Mr. and Mrs. Ueland, how tremendously I appreciate them, but I probably won't have, and they will have to take it on faith.

Sigurd.

V. MARRIAGE

1.

To Philadelphia and I am supported like a regular everyday wife. Some things that were wrong with our marriage. Alone in New York again. I become a little fast. John Reed; Biff.

THAT SUMMER R.'S COMPANY SENT HIM DOWN TO THE NEW York Shipbuilding Company in Camden, New Jersey, a subsidiary company. I did not feel well. And I was discouraged about my looks. I was so pale and really aged-looking, with sharp lines from my nose to the mouth-corners. I had worked in New York for a year and a half without vacation (at last I had got on the staff of *Every Week*) and I smoked once every fifteen minutes, and also forced myself into a five-mile walk every day. A doctor said that I was anemic and that I did not use my lungs enough when I walked.

And so I gave up my job on *Every Week* to go to Philadelphia with R. I was going to let myself be supported, like a regular everyday wife.

"We decided," I wrote home from our boarding house on Spruce Street, "that I should not look for work until the first of the year. In the meantime I want to do some writing at home, on my own book."

Oh, yes! this optimism of one who gives up salaried work to do "something I have always wanted to do" (as they always say) . . . "some writing."

But it never happens. How many times have I discovered that? Instead, you procrastinate and dawdle and time passes and is filled and consumed by small errands, and you do not, after three or four years, see why nothing has been accomplished.

But at least my health improved. I stopped smoking and even drinking coffee, and breathed when I walked and ate more. Julie Plant, who had graduated from the University, had a job in Philadelphia. She was one of the most golden, frivolous, stylish, wonderful creatures that ever lived. Red cheeks, Julie and I agreed, in our interminable talking, were about the first requisite of being good-looking. In five weeks I was pleased, because looking in the mirror (and I kept doing it again and again with amazed satisfaction), I saw that the pinched, sallow, sharp-nosed Greenwich Villager, constantly sucking cigarettes, had become handsome and florid again.

I don't need to say much about my life, just along here. R.'s work became magnified. The Government built a large village for shipyard workers, and he was put in charge. His salary in a few months had climbed from three thousand dollars a year to ten thousand.

"But I am not satisfied about not working," I wrote to Mother. (There always has been this work-compulsion in me.) "Miss Lewis wants book reviews and interviews and will pay two cents a word. That is about ten dollars apiece. If I do four a week that will be forty dollars. The main thing is that all my ambition has come back, and before I go to sleep I think up plots for short stories."

Is that so? I think now jeeringly in 1938. How many hundred times have I planned and pinned my determination, only to have it bleed away? And spent days making schedules and whole days remaking them? But how hard I am now, on my aspirations then. I seem to sneer at them always. I must not do that. I was struggling as sincerely then to discipline myself and work, as I am now. It is just that now at last perhaps I have begun to learn how.

As I said, there was something underlyingly wrong with our marriage. It was not that we were not good to each other. Shippy used to make me uncomfortable by imitating my Griselda-sweetness to R., my voice of sweetest music crying out, "Here, let me do it! I'll get it! I'll do it!" as I ran lightly upstairs and down. That is, it shocked and surprised her and others too, that I was not more bluff and insubordinate.

And he was very good to me, talkative and volubly admiring and indulgent and pressing all his money on me. He was what is called "a good mixer." His obstreperous conversational powers could over-ride a roomful of people. But when *I* talked he would police the crowd. "Now, listen. Listen to Brenda. Now, darling, say that again."

But the trouble was that in me there was always a lack of trust, and then that non-communication and boredom because we did not really interest each other. That is, when he talked I was not really listening but waiting to have *my* say, and so it was with him. We did not admire the same things. I loved abstractions: truth, greatness, heroism. He liked plain facts and cleverness. I liked transparence and open candor about things and he liked subtlety and using his wits.

I thought then that I was as practical, factual, and materialistic as he was. But it was not so. I was really religious, or going to be, and had all sorts of spiritual longings. I remember being distressed when he would say there was no life after death.

"What's the use then?" I cried. "Why not shoot ourselves right now! What are we then, but a stomach with legs on it! What's the use?"

Of course I had not then thought out things as I have now. But this now is my explanation of our marriage. Or part of it. There is much that cannot be explained or told.

I think his materialism made me feel insecure. He liked comfort, good times, his own success. I felt (though I did not understand it as well then as now) that you have to love something *outside* and greater than yourself, or you are a goner. I don't care what it is—the sky, or a great man, or an abstraction like courage, honor, goodness, or what some people call God. But it must be above your own pleasure and success. If love between men and women is only something that is pleasant, well then, where is the stability in it? Then the common-sensible thing to do is to get pleasure wherever you can and in the most pleasant undisturbed way, i.e., by lying. That is, R. was one of those thousands of nice, well-meaning men who hold that you may flirt with other people to have a nice time, but you must not tell your wife because it would "hurt" her. And he said that if I flirted all right, but please not to "hurt" him, to tell him.

Well, this seemed terrible to me. I felt it was not love unless there was something clear and truthful about it; that you should walk about freely in each other's souls and see everything and try to understand it and then to help each other if possible, even if it is to become free of each other. I still think this. There are married people who keep their most important thoughts sealed off from each other. They may be sleeping together and having meals together and discussing the month's bills, but there is no sympathy, intimacy, communication, that lovely, friendly alternating current. This condition in marriage always seemed to me monstrous, an immorality, for if you hold back the most important thing, you hold back everything else. "You might as well be two sexually cohabiting street car conductors!" I used to say in agitation and excitement.

I have known so many unhappily married men who have said they just could not tell Edna, about not loving her in the least, but somebody else, because it would "hurt" her. Why, I think they would prefer even to quietly murder her and dispose of her body, and then always be glad that they never did really "hurt" Edna. But what a blessing the truth

would have been for Edna! She might have got a job, changed
in some way, been shaken out of her muggy dream, married
someone else who really liked her before it was too late. The
truth always puts some chemistry on things, so that they can
move and go forward.

Or they say: "I don't tell her because of the children."
But the children know it anyway, and all about it. They always do. At the very least, they know their parents really
don't like each other or tell each other anything important.
And the children's lives are made anxious and miserable by
it, and they develop their own secretiveness and evasion.

No, I am sure the truth is right, the truth plus some genuine love, I mean the real thing. That is, if you really love
someone as a human being and wish him well, it is always
easy to tell him, or anyone else, what is true. When we cannot tell it, it means that we really hate and are afraid of
them.

Not that I can behave always in this magnificent way. Not
by a long shot. But I think I always grow a little better.

To go back to my marriage—there was no rest in it. If
this is so, I said to myself, then it is no good at all. Because,
look: the whole point of marriage is that it be a rest, a re-crea-
tion, so that we can work and fight better. It shelters us from
the loneliness and adventures of a single life, which is a fine
kind of life too, as I had found. But if marriage both cuts
off all fine danger and also gives us no rest, but only doubt,
anxiety and jealousy, why, then it is no good at all.

But the above seems to be taking a very noble view of myself which is not the truth at all. I was confused about the
whole subject of sex—restive and independent, restive at
being caught because it was so much fun to be free and get
all that attention.

After the Armistice R. was to go to France for some Boston engineers to study the rebuilding of the devastated areas.

He was to be gone more than two months and I felt very
badly. I could not go with him. Women with male relatives
in Europe were not given passports.

So before Christmas I came to New York and found a room
at 14 St. Luke's Place, in a pleasant old Georgian house looking out on the concrete playground of Hudson Square. I had
one large square room with a fireplace and two big windows. I
loved that room, and the morning sun came shining in sweetly.
I began to see all the people I had known before: Anne Herendeen, Hugh Ferriss, Jack Reed, Nina Putnam. My self-confidence came back, for R. was far away now. And when I am
really alone some power seems to grow in me. Because then
I am *one,* not two, not conjugal. Conjugality made me think
of a three-legged race, where two people cannot go fast and
keep tripping each other because their two legs are tied
together.

And now I have to tell of a blow that I had just at this
point, because it was the tiny cause of all those unfoldings
that were to make me extricate myself from marriage at last.
It was not that R. did anything bad. It was just that it disil-
lusioned me and broke the spell.

One day a very pretty woman told me how R. had flirted
with her one day in New York, when I was waiting for him
in Philadelphia, struggling not to have what he called "the
iron face."

She was such a simpleton of a person (though very nice)
and I felt so serpent-clever as I drew her out.

"Why, Arabella," my attitude was, "you and I, modern
women who know all about feminism and psychoanalysis, *we*
don't care if our husbands flirt with other people, or drink
or say foolish things. Sophisticated people like us! No, we
don't care in the least. It is just interesting, scientific, a manifestation of the sex impulse. For heaven's sake, why *not* flirt,
anyway?"

"Well.... But I really suppose I should not tell on him. Heavens, he told me never, never to tell."

"Oh, why not?" I said with a jolly, good-natured grin. "What of it?"

Well, she said, they had had cocktails at the Vanderbilt and he had told her how fascinating she was, how he had always been attracted to her, and so on and so on.

It was not very bad, you see, but it was a terrible shock to me because it was a symbol of how he was, a true symbol of him, as are all the unimportant things we do. That is, if he had been steadier, deeper in his feelings, perhaps I would not have minded. At least not for long.

That was the most sharply painful experience I ever had. All night I was brilliantly awake, a two-edged sword through my breastbone.

That experience was one of the three sharp turning points in my life. For again I felt the peculiar strength that comes from being cast off. The blissful power rises in one. Where there is still something to cling to, this is not so. But as soon as there is no hope, there you are—disdainful and fearless. I suppose men before a firing squad feel this way.

For instance, the next day, what an extraordinary one! I must now, I said to myself, be independent of R. At once I looked for work—job-hunting, usually a thing to procrastinate about. I never covered the ground like that. Something in me made barriers fall away too. I got into places, saw important men, asked for jobs that I would not have dared to before. One man, a managing editor of a newspaper, followed me out into the hall and, to my indifference, gave me a friendly, half-fascinated kiss.

And this period became one of the most interesting, alive times in my life. One Sunday afternoon I had been skating in the country with Amos Pinchot and Ruth Pickering, who had recently married. She was my age, a serious well-brought-up Vassar girl with a beautiful figure and shabby clothes, who had been poor before and believed that women should work and always do what they damn pleased. That is, in many ways our lives were alike. But now I felt so sorry for her, happily married and to a rich man and cozily going home with him, to be fed by a butler; because my lonely and free and slightly frightened state was so much more interesting.

"Don't you wish you were me?" I said as I left them. "Look. You are happily married and just have to go home. And you know what will happen tonight and tomorrow and the next day. But look at me. I don't. The future five minutes hence is mysterious. Just as in a play. Something remarkable will happen."

And it always did too.

That particular night I went to the Greenwich Village Inn and found Jack Reed, whom I just barely knew, and talked to him that evening and several times thereafter.

He had been present with Lenin in the ten days that brought about the Russian Revolution. And he had had typhus and only one kidney was left. He looked pudgy and liverish, his face almost the color of his disorderly ginger-colored curly hair; a broad vigorous face and a small snub nose, almost an insignificant nose. A light tenor voice. I told him about my passport troubles, and he giggled and said that he was going back and forth to Russia all the time, whenever he felt like it.

"Perhaps you can go on my next trip."

"Oh, say! I'd like to."

He had recently had such violent adventures. He was always speaking against the War, on the street, anywhere, and for the world revolution, and they arrested him again and again. Just a week before he had been beaten up by the police, in jail. They threw him in a roomful of masked detectives and then shoved him about, a kind of gantlet, hitting him, slugging him, from one to the other. But he knew that if he fought back he would he broken to pieces.

I admired him so much, probably because he was a pathologically adventurous man. He seemed to have compulsion to hurl himself against danger, like a June bug whanging against an arc light. I used to feel this about him, though, as well as so many other radicals and revolutionaries. They could love the general—Humanity, the Proletariat—but not the particular, i.e., this or that human being, or kitten, or spider, for that matter. But after my fairly long life, I have decided I would rather be able to do the second. "For he that loveth not his brother, whom he hath seen, cannot love God whom he hath not seen." Because if you can really love a kitten, you will be much farther along on the way to knowing what love is, and will do a lot of good. If you love only Humanity (or Art, or God, so-called) and cannot love the kitten, the person, you do not know what love is at all, and consequently in the name of your Self and your own theories (whether they are from Karl Marx or the Republican party) go about doing a great deal of splendid harm.

Now in these two exciting months, I find there are many things I cannot tell about. In a curious way, for two days just now, I found it was so hard to write this part. Why is this so dull? Why am I struggling so, trying to make this or that little incident interesting and clothe it in fancy English? Why am I saying "I am a girl of many moods" and bilge like that?

After two days it has suddenly struck me why: It is because I am hiding something. For I have also learned, after many, many years, that whenever you hold something back, in writing or in life, immediately everything you say becomes vitiated with a kind of hypocrisy and prissiness, and you seem to be making yourself out to be so dear.

So I must tell you now what I am hiding, and then I can go on. I fell in love with somebody, though for a very short time. But it was just long enough to see that there were other men who were more serious and kind than R. I won't speak of this man at all in this, or say his name. But I was never to forget it. And that too was always to make me want to be free and unmarried.

But although I had sought for a job so magnificently I did not take one after all, because things became too entertaining. I began to have so much fun. And having fun and feeling free and happy, I automatically became magnanimous and forgave R. Presently he arranged it in Paris to get me into Anne Morgan's Committee for Devastated France. They were young women who wore horizon blue uniforms and Sam Browne belts and drove ambulances and so on.

The cables went back and forth. This device, R. thought, would make it possible for me to get a passport. So I got an expensive blue uniform and applied for a passport. But I could not get it. Besides, they were changing the rules every day. R. was very good at that sort of thing, pulling wires and all, and would cable somebody to wire somebody to see the secretary of the Secretary of State, and so on.

And just then I got to know the most entertaining young man named Biff. He was a tiny blond naval officer, as perfect as a watch charm in his blue uniform and brass buttons and swinging cape. He had an evenly pink face, a snub nose and ice-blue eyes, and the most original measured way of talking. "Suggest shove off," he'd say, "and man a bus, to the Matron Conklin's." That would be some fashionable lady in the East Fifties who was giving a cocktail party for officers. Biff's friends were always "shipmates." The floor was "the deck." Every sentence began with the verb and he never used the word "I." In telephoning, instead of saying: "Hold the line," he would sing out: "Stand by!" "Waiter!" he would shout in a restaurant, in his free, clear, swinging voice, like a pirate. "There's a sou'wester in the bread plate!"

He was what he called a "hootch hound," that is, he drank very much. But the more he drank the more measured and remarkable his sentences, the more erect his bearing, and grave, and the more elaborately entertaining. The only way you could guess he was drunk was by the fixity of his blue eyes and a stiff half-smile, and the clapping monotone of his stentorian laugh. He had been appointed super-cargo on a freighter. He thought he could get me to Marseilles without a passport. That seemed a fine adventure, and how astounded (and admiring) Anne and Ken and R. would be.

But he disappeared for weeks. A spree and then the hospital. At last this is what he wrote to me:

The Mariner's Scrawl
(An Episode of Our Village)

Hard by our village there dwelt a certain sea-faring man. Unknown and unsung lived this man of the Sea between cruises. "Hombre" he was sometimes called. He had sailed the Spanish Main. He had sailed the Seven Seas.

Unlike the proverbial sailorman of fiction, he was the exception who did *not* have a sweetheart in every port. He had always called them "gals" until he met this maiden fair. She was different. She was strong, not stout; she was strangely fair without the need of camouflage. Her head was almost always bare and over her ears disordered hung a tangled mass of midnight hair; her eyes, crystal dew on diamonds bright; her cheeks, the glow of the evening sun upon the water; her teeth, deep sea pearls.

"You, the Queen of the Sea, I'll make," vowed he, "on our trip to sunny France," but the hand of the law had sternly said, "Not without a passporte, my good and earnest man."

Then, like a Gladiator bold strode he to Washington. "Death before dishonor," he wrote upon his shield.

Meekly waited the maiden, nose upon the window pane of her cozy little chamber. Footsteps, always on the other side, until at last but true, the sluggish thud, and thud and thud of Postman old, who a letter for the maiden brought. In characters bold and strong, these lines they said:

> "Manned Wash.
> Radiance you gave me stood by
> So glowing.
> Passporte, Yes.
> Bring back all dope,
> Until ship comes in.
> Unalterably
> Biff."

Abiding hopes she had, until one day a breakfast would be manned. Sailorman ne'er did come. Day and day and day, no word. Great the maiden's wonder grew.

Until one black foul Stygian night, wakened from a fretful sleep, these lines by radio came:

> "Science's Gull bears this:
> For me uncharted channels new;
> Old familiar beacons left for you."

. . . and the next morning little drops of blood could be found all over the streets of Greenwich Village.

That was too bad that I never got abroad with Biff, without a passport. I saw us stealing ashore, rowing in a boat across the oily black harbor of Marseilles, sliding past the muffled voices of sentries and gendarmes. Like Garibaldi.

2.

To Cambridge. I am afraid of domesticity, until I sell a story. On East 58th Street. Minneapolis conversation. Regretfully having a baby. I become maternal now and from this time forward will always be kind.

WHEN R. CAME BACK, I WAS GLAD TO SEE HIM. BUT THE RO-mantic illusion had been broken. Now I, too, had a kind of sensible cynicism about marriage. And I had learned that to be alone was better than conjugality. And from this time on I was to secretly want to get out of my marriage, although it was to take four more years.

R.'s work took him to Boston; so we lived in Cambridge, and I liked this because Sigurd and David Shearer had both gone back to Harvard Law School again, and they were now married to Julie and Henrietta, from Minneapolis. David used to refer to all four of of them as "Ueland versus Ueland" and "Shearer versus Shearer."

These two girls were my favorites in all the world. They both worked in Boston. During the War, young men's financial independence was sadly put off, so when they married, the girls insisted on working. Of course. When David, a private in a miserable army camp at Allentown, Pennsylvania, married Henrietta, and the minister said: "With all my worldly goods I thee endow," he whispered to her: "You can have my extra pair of pants."

Then one day to my dismay R. was appointed by his company to manage a big carpet mill in Saxonville, a sleepy little Massachusetts town. We would live in a new little house with a Dutch-humped roof, white clapboards and green shutters.

Well, this prospect upset me at first. I threw myself back on resisting heels in alarm. You see, I thought of myself as a young woman with a fine career ahead, who must live in New York, or perhaps temporarily in centers of culture like Cambridge, where at least there were opportunities for my intellectual progress. I saw myself taking playwriting under Baker of Harvard, advancing my literary career in useful steps. The one thing I dreaded was being a housewife, a cooing little homebody running a house for my hubby. A most repulsive idea—putting on the ruffled aprons and fixing dainty Sunday night suppers. Horrors and Ish! Julie and Henny agreed with me and laughed obligingly hard at how I described it.

Julie was the most spirited, comforting girl I have ever known. You could hardly wait to get to Julie to tell her things and she would respond in her free, high, rollicking voice and she would slap her thigh and let out a peal of laughter that squeezed her green eyes together, so that the blond, stiff, curling lashes intertwined and tears streamed out. She made everything exciting, hopeful and interesting. When I was in pain over my asininity, my procrastinating, my failures, I just told Julie about it in such a way that she let out her wild gale of laughter. That seemed to exorcize it. And she had such enthusiasm for what was lovely and delightful: ideas, people, architecture, hats, old furniture, art, literature, new hair arrangements, paste ear-rings. And she was so excitedly interested in every faint inflection of thought that you told her, in every comment, in every tiny adventure, in every introspective discovery. Whenever I was on my way to seeing Julie and came within a half mile of her, my heart quickened with excitement and fun.

"Yes, that is the trouble with love and marriage," I said to her. "You have to follow your husband around. You are no sooner located in Macon, Georgia, and have at last made the grade and been taken into the Ladies' Aid Society, when you are jerked out to Tacoma, Washington, with a letter of introduction to Elmer Johnson of the Sewage Disposal Plant, whose wife is the first woman in Washington who had the courage to use a vacuum cleaner."

But while we were moving, something very promising happened. I had been writing a story. It was about love, of course, and I was the heroine (and very adorable). I sent it first to *The Saturday Evening Post* of course. When it came back, I experienced that usual realization (corroborated by reading it) that I was a repulsive, fatuous sap. But presently this paralysis of discouragement gives way to a tiny hope, because you see a sentence or two that are not so bad, and a little spurt of energy is born in you, to try to make the story better.

What rewriting, struggle, pains and rewriting! That rubbing out and polishing down each paragraph, to work out of it that dreadful sound of fiction ("Great work, doctor!" cried young Ramsey enthusiastically, "you certainly are a wonder with the knife!") until it was something truer and more convincing.

Then *The Metropolitan Magazine* bought it. A hundred and fifty dollars. What caper-cutting joy! Now it was all right, moving to Saxonville and living in the homey little house. Fine. Wonderful. I would write stories.

There was that year thick, slowly falling snow day after day. We had an upstairs sitting room with a pretty brick fireplace in it. I sat here mornings with a typewriter on my knees. I wrote another story, "The Hootch Hound." This was about Biff, that tiny blond naval officer. And *The Saturday Evening Post* very nearly bought it, they wrote to me with true admiration, but they had decided against it because of the drinking in it. I always had then an impulse to shock people and to affront stuffy, low-spirited and dull people.

Then I sent it to the *Metropolitan* and Carl Hovey, the editor, bought it and said that he liked it especially much, more than most stories. But this success burked my career for a long time. It is always apt to do so. Because the story about Biff was so good, I was afraid of doing less well. And then I began to want to write "more serious things." These were no good at all, for reasons that I have discovered years afterwards. They were manufactured, unconscious preaching, and a thorough bore. But the word "bore" is too mild. You would not read far enough into them to be bored.

One Sunday in Saxonville was the most beautiful day I have ever seen. There was deep, pure, magnesium-white snow. The sky was pure unflecked blue. In the midst of yesterday's blizzard it had suddenly rained, so that now there was a glass enamel of perfect ice on every twig, bud, leaf, pine needle. The bright white snow was flung with tiny blue diamonds and the spruce trees were jeweled and behung with huge sparkles,

red, white, lavender, pink, yellow. I do not exaggerate. Our
house was on a high wooded hill and this sloped far down into
a lovely vale, with a black stream wandering through it.

Julie and I were skiing with Mort Winterbottom, an earnest Back Bay young man with a black bristling mustache,
thick glasses and energy.

Mort Winterbottom [I find I have written about him in my
diary; we didn't know any Boston people and liked to think they
were all ridiculous] looks like a gorilla and Teddy Roosevelt. I
tell him he could be an agent for the carpet mills, etc., and we
talk about executive jobs: "positions of power," he calls them.
"Power brings sadness," he says, thrusting out his under jaw,
tightening his lips, looking at the ring on his finger, and then at
me, shyly. Other mots: about "Jean Christophe." "It's a book
that makes you think. Because, gracious, I think the book that
makes you think is the only book that's worth while." . . . "When
I marry, I've decided that I want to marry a girl who's a worker
and who will share the expense" (he is very tight) "and I think
that then I would have reached the heights of camaraderie, because then you could feel absolutely free and she'd be a comrade."
Says he would like to go to Paris and study art for a year, has the
money and absolutely no one dependent on him. "Yes, that would
be fine," I say, absent-mindedly, "but I think . . ." He: "It would
be selfish?" furnishing the word farthest from my thoughts.
"Gunness!" he then exclaims, "what do I do? I never have a
chance any more to help someone, because I want to help, and
make people feel that I want to help them. Paps . . ." (wisely,
shrewdly, significantly) "I do help people and may never know
it!" !!!

Well, this day he would put on the one pair of skis and
start straight down that swift hill among the great trees,
going like a bullet straight for the creek. And when he came
to the bottom he would make what I called "a rocking horse";
that is, he would fall on his face grinding his chin in the
ground with such violence that his heels swung up and nearly
hit the back of his head. And he would spring up and shout
to us on the far hilltop, in a stentorian voice:

"Bully!"

So I would go down and then Julie. And so we skied and fell and by the end of the morning, Julie's skirt was split to her waist and her bare thigh was exposed and bleeding, torn on snow crust, and we were wet from top to bottom. She went home that night and had inflammatory rheumatism.

And this gives me sadness and I wish I had kept her from skiing that day, because this rheumatism injured her heart, and presently, after several years, it was going to kill her.

All the time I was inwardly wanting not to be married any more; to be free, alone. Presently R. left the carpet mill and was sent by his company to New York, and that pleased us both.

Anne and Ken had come back from Paris. Ken was going to practice medicine in New York with Dr. Blake. To Anne, who had liked the flowers and river and bridges and open sunlight of Paris, New York seemed frightful.

"A wen!" she said angrily, "a skyscraping wen!" So hard, noisy, iron-encrusted.

But at last Anne found a place where she would be willing to live. That was on 58th Street right by the East River. It was a slum, and to get to it you walked through miles of slums of the most depressing sort, under the horrid iron forests of elevateds and through dark streets full of cold, smelling wind and lined with dirty brownstone houses. Funeral crêpes seemed to be on most of the doors and people with cold sores looked dolefully out the windows.

But a company had bought a block of houses and tenements right on the East River bank, and this property would be sold to people who would remodel the houses. Then the rotting backyard walls and washline masts would all be gutted out and cleared away and a common garden would be made for all. Yes, it would become a bosky garden and a shady grove and lawns of checkered sunlight right on the river. Queensborough Bridge swung overhead a few blocks to the north and far away was Brooklyn Bridge in the pearl-colored mist and you could almost imagine that the prison on Blackwell's Island was the Houses of Parliament. Well, Anne and Ken bought one of these houses in Sutton Square. So R. and I bought a brownstone house a block inland, on 58th Street.

Now Anne and Ken remodeled their house, and the lovely ships slipped by right under their windows. But suddenly there was a post-War depression and R.'s salary was reduced. We could not afford to remodel ours. So I began washing it myself and painting it and scraping the floors.

I missed the country sadly, where I could walk with my head bare, in the fresh wind from the far blue mountains. My walk now had to be up First Avenue, a long strain of wincing against the freezing wind and biting dust blown in the face. No grass. The wretched people. Our backyard was rotting concrete enclosed in high boards and there was one sickly tree and the sun shone only in a few square feet of it, on a very bright morning.

The house had been inhabitated by a Japanese food importer and was full of big rats and millions of brittle cockroaches and in the sitting room there had been piled to the ceiling, strange bad-smelling kegs of Oriental food. "Pickled horses' eyes," I used to say it must be. I started bravely to paint all the floors and walls of the house. The high ceilings were beautifully molded in geometrical plaster and in every room there was a lovely pure white marble mantelpiece.

But the kitchen was depressingly dark and dirty. Cinders rained in the area way every day, no matter how much you swept it, for there was a heating plant nearby with two huge towers belching this dry rain. And the Orthopedic Hospital was a few doors away, so that sometimes in the night you would hear a child crying, calling, in a way that was unforgettable. As soon as I was in that house, I knew that I had in me something Scandinavian that wanted things fresh, clear, bright, simple, austere, and open.

I got a bad cold. My cold became so thick, so corrupt. My ears were filled with it. After staying in bed for a week I would get up and there the cold was again, a morass of discouraging clogging sickening mucus. In February R. said that I should go home to Minneapolis for a month's vacation. And so I did.

It was just delightful to be at home. Julie had written, and this describes it:

But Brenda, you simply must come out here [she said]. A trip is what you need. Two maids—one whose passion is cleanliness; the house gleams; your bed is made to taste; silver all polished once a week; even glass in the downstairs halls washed on her own initiative. The other an exquisite cook with charming singing voice and a wonderful repertoire of Norwegian folk songs. These two adore each other and constant laughter and merriment intoxicates the whole house. One day a week when the ironing-woman is here, the happiness in the house irradiates all of Linden Hills.

You could have a large airy room with desk and typewriter. Breakfast in bed. Then locked in your room, could create. Then whenever fancy willed, could step out and find me, with your skates in one hand and skis in the other.

Julie and Sigurd lived in a tiny house west of our pasture, owned by Mr. Simmons, a plumber who looked like a mouse with a mustache and whose light truck had painted on it: "'Doc' Simmons, specialist for 'sick plumbing.'"

Well, it was lovely to be walking in the snow around Lake Harriet again, and talking endlessly to Julie about figures, complexions, D. H. Lawrence, bangs-versus-hair-off-the-brow, and the meaning of life.

That Minneapolis talk. It went like this. We would all be having tea or grain alcohol cocktails (there was Prohibition), the girls doing all the talking. After a prolonged hair-argument as to whether hair should be long or short, a chignon, or just cut and have a loose wops of it behind, David would say dreamily:

"Here yesterday the Cabinet goes into session and decides that it should let all wops grow behind the ears, and today that Cabinet is out and the hair is going to be cut and wops are going to be bought for wearing behind the ears."

Rolf would then object, in his thoughtful measured speech, to our idea of a good figure, that is, a small waist, broad shoulders, long legs, and no hips.

"The current female idea of legs, as far as I can make out, is a couple of thin gutta percha tubes full of chains and pulleys." He thought it was no good. "Why not a few curves?"

"I have lost weight," I would say in an undertone, turning to Dorothy Lewis, radiantly beautiful and too fat.

"Oh!" she would cry, discouraged, "I wish I could get some virulent disease. That is the only way I would ever lose. ... But aren't you afraid your stomach will collapse, or something? They say the stomach collapses to the size of a walnut. ... But then I wish my stomach would collapse."

Then Henny, Dorothy Lewis, and Julie and I would talk about buying clothes.

Sigurd absently says at last:

"Julie maintains that she doesn't spend as much money on clothes as Henny and then proves it by adding up the cost of the dresses that Henny has looked at but hasn't bought."

Dorothy maintains (to Henny's annoyance, whose tendency is to look for dresses and not buy) that you should *look*, but you should buy the first cute thing you see. Henny, defending her stand, tells of shopping for the Franklin knit dress she has on (at my request, she tells this). Well, she kept looking at it about once a week, and waited for it to be knocked down in price. ...

"Knocked down or up?" asks Sigurd.

I suggest it would be good merchandising to knock dresses up.

"If that evening dress at Bjorkman's, when you look at it again, has gone up to $105, and then the next week to $115.90, you'll grab it quick, on the stock market principle."

David finally begins to mutter:

"Oh, I don't know—I go downtown and I see a cute pair of pants in the window, cute cut and cute made, and I think I better grab them, because you don't know—when you get a pair of pants that looks cute on and then you send them home on approval and try them on and they may not be cute at all, and you'll just *hate* them."

Now after two or three weeks, as luck would have it, I felt not quite so lively and external. A tiny bit nauseated. Why, that was funny for me to be sickish day after day like that, to have a faint feeling always as though there were a bread pudding on the chest.

Gradually I began to be scared. I must be pregnant. Now, in so much of the literature I have read, and in plays, women who find they are pregnant begin to behave in the most peculiar way, weeping or scurrying out of the room when their husband asks them a pleasant question, such as, "How are you today?" only to be found weeks later sewing on something. But in life I have never seen that. You find that you are going to have a baby and say so—and either you like or do not like it.

I did not like it. I did not like it at all. It was not because I don't like children, but because my marriage seemed shaky and uncertain, and because R. did not want children. I always felt, a little bit, that he wanted to be the child in the family himself. If he had been maternal, like many men, it would have been all right.

But instead, I was quite beside myself. I ran around Lake Harriet one night in my fur coat and with overshoes on, in the deep snow, and ran every step, about four miles. But it did no good. I even went to a malpractitioner, a very fatherly, rather dirty old gentleman who lived in a pleasant little house. He said that it would cost a hundred and twenty-five dollars, but he must have the verbal consent of my husband. I worked on his feelings by my earnestness and he consented. But I caught a glimpse of his dirty operating room and vaguely and indecisively left.

Of course it scared Julie and she was against it. There was the relief of making her laugh about this awful situation. Moreover, she began to say how adorable, how delightful, the baby would be: black-haired! "Why, you will have a glorious brunette girl with narrow hips, while I will have a lank towhead with high broad hips and a hook-nose." (She liked to exaggerate frightfully, what she considered her defects, such as her slightly curved nose). She said how I would have spruce dresses made for the baby, yellow and blue with stiff piqué collars. And I would cut a thick wops of bangs on the baby (it wouldn't be bald very long) and never, never let it be drooling or unattractive. Why, even new-born babies were charming, delightful, if one did not get dejectedly matronly about them.

For maternal sensuality disgusted us: those milky women who nursed an infant for years, with such nostril-quivering pride; the kind who would be horrified at a jolly ribald joke about anything sexual, and yet could say across a roomful of people, in an unctuous deep moo-cow voice: "Is your baby still at the breast?" One kind of sensuality is just as bad as another, we said.

But by the time I got back to New York, I had to be resigned to it. And then R. lost his job. That was hard on us both. Because I found that when pregnant you have a curiously helpless feeling. You seem to need a strong, active partner badly. Energy is whirling inward, but you cannot function freely and forcefully on anything outside. Even your attention is dreamy and unfocusable.

I had physical energy, though. I worked furiously painting a nursery on the fourth floor. I wanted it perfect, clean, ivory white. The day before the baby was born Anne came over and was amused at me on a high stepladder painting the ceiling, with a huge stomach.

The evening of November 4th I began to have the faint recurrent stomach ache, which meant it was time to go to Miss Lippincott's maternity hospital. And when I was there and in bed in my room, not in the least dreading tomorrow's effort, but rather looking forward to it, I heard the new babies in the nursery upstairs. They made a strange pleasant sound like a lot of chickens. A musical crying. I felt impersonally about it, as if it were not unpleasant music in a remote room.

"Dress and walk around," said Miss Nivin in the morning, a Scotch nurse with a thin ruddy face and a little lovely nose sticking out, and tender adorable spinisterish hands swollen and red, from eternal fresh soap and scrubbing.

And now the rhythmical pains got worse. Sometimes a nurse came and sat beside me and timed them. Oh, they were fierce and seemed really unbearable. I tried not to groan, for I don't like groaners, but it was a help to murmur, to say to yourself, "Incredible. Just incredible." The pain was like bombs bursting inside me.

In the operating room the doctor and the nurses were casually leaning against my knees and talking.

"They say they give anaesthetics," I thought. "Why, what a curious thing for them to say that. Because they don't at all."

At last a cone was over my face and I breathed it and sank away into the sweet roar of railroad trains and came to and heard murmuring: "If she would help a little at the top of the pain."

I tried it and went mercifully out.

When I came to, the baby had been born, though I didn't see it. R. bent over me and burst out crying. He felt so sorry because my face was so distorted from the effort.

I had no private nurse, but just the regular night nurse and Miss Nivin, and I fell in love with Miss Nivin, a passionate adoring love, which was full of light and gratitude. It was very queer and I cannot explain it.

But the night nurse was a strong, hard, monosyllabic, good-looking young woman. I didn't like her and my dislike made me uncomfortable. She brought the baby to be nursed. And now I saw the baby: very tiny and red with pitch-black hair, and the hair grew nearly down to its brows, its frowning red brows. The Neanderthal man. "I will name her Julie," I said.

The baby would not nurse sensibly the first minute, so that night nurse clapped her on the back and said: "Now, Julie, nurse!" and the baby shrank, I thought, even gasped with fright. I hated that nurse. What rage. I could have torn her to pieces. "Don't do that, damn you anyway!" I did not say this out loud but over and over to myself in rage for many hours.

Fortunately she disappeared from the hospital for a while. A vacation, I guess. I will never forget that frightened gasp of the baby. It disturbs me to think of it even now.

And here is a curious thing: the crying of the babies upstairs in the nursery, which at first was no more to me than chickens gently cawing, became distressing and more and more so. When it began, my heart would quicken in a lively anxious way and I would prick up my ears and strain them. "Is that mine, crying? What is the matter? Why don't they take care of her?" This emotion and agitation at the crying increased and got worse every day.

"Julie" was her name on the birth certificate, but presently

it seemed not right for a dark child. For a golden one, like
Sigurd's Julie, yes; but a black-haired Julie seemed French,
petite—something that she would not be because she was
Scotch and Norwegian. After a while we thought of the name
"Gabriel," from Ole Gabriel Ueland.

I took the baby home to the brownstone house, where the
cinders rained and the million brittle cockroaches were and
the gas jets whistled and hissed, but whose walls at least were
pure pink and yellow, because I had painted them.

I remember the first night at home. I was playing the piano.
The baby was in bed at last in her veiled crib on the top
floor, and I listened on tenterhooks, for fear she would cry.
That crying set going in me some primitive fright and
anxiety that was just awful. R. and I were waiting for a
little neighborhood girl to come, so that we could walk to the
end of the street and visit the Taylors for an hour or so.
Think of it! I thought, reading Mozart half-heartedly—not
being able to leave the house, because of a baby. No more
stepping out-of-doors again with a light foot. Never. I had
that sad, queer, captured feeling which has never left me
since. Never, never would I be free again. "Just think, never
to take a train again without a little paw in mine!" I think
that this having a child woke up in me my compassion. I
think I have been deeply, painfully, unnecessarily kind ever
since then, to all people and children. A burden of kindness.

And in all my life, there has been no compassion-wounded
anxiety like that of taking care of a baby. For example, each
month I took her to see nice Dr. Bartlett and he weighed her
and felt her skull. I would be told to take a little sugar out
of her milk formula, and presently observed with relief that
she looked more pink, less bluish and pale. It was not fear of
her becoming sick or dying that upset me so, but I felt so
sorry, sorry for little Gaby always. Was that a pin pricking
her? a stomach ache? I would put her in the perambulator

out in the area way in front, where the brief sun was, or in the backyard, and in half an hour there were cinders on her face. Oh, dear!

Well, R., who was out of work, went into that hopeful unconnected dream of the man who has lost a ten-thousand-dollar-a-year job. He did not take work at fifty dollars a week, but waited, waited, for some huge, worthy executive chance. (Though I don't blame him; I am always doing that sort of thing myself.) And so he diddled at home on all sorts of money-making devices, really an excuse to avoid the misery of asking for work. He invented what he called "a kiddy cabinet," to be sold by mail order. Though he was revolted by everything that pertained to a baby, such as milk, diapers, baby-talk—this cabinet was to contain bottles, nipples, sterilizing apparatus. But presently we sold the house and made five thousand dollars on it because Mrs. Vanderbilt had bought part of Sutton Square, where Anne was, and real estate went up precipitately.

And then at last R., after many psychological flights, such as taking a course in baking at an industrial school for several months, invested in a chain of bakeries in Connecticut. I went up to Stamford and found a small house on a high-sitting cobblestone foundation and moved in.

That was February, 1922, a winter with many blizzards of wet snow and sleet. Leaving Gaby, who was thirteen months old, in Minneapolis while I moved, I then hastened out west to get her. And there she was standing and looking out the sitting room window.

"Hello, darling."

She turned and looked at me seriously and came thoughtfully and carefully walking toward me. She could walk! They had wanted to surprise me. She quietly sat on my lap, unsmiling, unspeaking. Just sat there. Oh, dear, I felt such sorrow, such pity. Just her sitting there and saying nothing made me see how hard it had been for her. How did she know if I would ever come back? And she looked pale. I felt this, but we all talked along in a jolly way.

You might say it was foolish of me to have my heart wrung by nothing. How could it sadden a baby to be alone one month in a bright house full of nice people? And dogs and cats and nursemaids and other babies, for Julie had had twins. But I knew it did. Julie told me how, one day, there had been company, and they all wanted to see Gaby walk. Her nurse brought her in and set her down. So, standing on the floor for a second, she then gave a lurch and walked toward them. All burst out laughing because her stomach stuck out in such a charming, cute way. She stopped, looked at them, and wept.

I knew why. It was because I had not been there to back her up. She was forlorn, alone, motherless, friendless. And when they laughed, I knew it was too hard for her, a humiliation. This cut me to the heart.

I was right too. Because after that, for years, Gaby could not bear to have anyone laugh at her. Though a jokey little girl, it always hurt her feelings sharply, and so badly that it was impossible to keep the tears from springing into her eyes. I told her why I thought it was, about that day when she was a year old, and I was not there to back her up.

"Because, look, darling. Why should you mind? Take me, for instance. I always like it. Because I will say to myself: Why, they think I am especially nice! Funny and waggish."

This explanation helped very much and now I don't think she minds at all.

Yes, children need backing, and we must always remember that—someone behind them to be always stanchly thinking they are dear, important, perfect. They should have it until they are twenty or more, until they are ready to discard us. That is why I must live until she is at least twenty-two. Then

I can die, which won't be bad; or go to Moscow or Shanghai, which I shall enjoy. Because if we have backing until twenty-two or so, then we can stand alone and back up our own children and friends. Though perhaps throughout life it is hard to stand truly alone.

VI. WORK

1.

Marital misery. To my surprise people are glad when I want a divorce. I become extraordinary, for a short time. Mr. John N. Wheeler. Reading Tolstoy on the train.

AND SO I TOOK LITTLE GABY BACK TO NEW YORK, AND OUT TO Stamford in Connecticut. We were now, at least, to have some family life and a little house in the country and there would be no cinders on her face when I took her outdoors. And R. would have this new business and get along just wonderfully with his ingenious good ideas and energy.

He met us at the Pennsylvania station. We got in a taxi, and I was thinking how healthy and important he looked, like a youngish Wall Street financier, with his good clothes and plump fresh cheeks and bristling golden mustache. The taxi turned into Seventh Avenue. He began to cry.

It seems he had made a horrible mistake to go into the bakery business. He had overlooked something very important, I forget what it was now. I think it was that he had not considered enough the leases and rents of the bakeries; in some instances they ate up all the profits. But I won't spend time on these business details. And anyway I don't remember them.

I patted him and summoned all my powers of optimism, of consolation. "I am sure something will work out, darling." But I felt misery and sadness and a long inner sigh. With every change, when we thought all was established, it was just the same: everything had gone wrong and awful difficulties were ahead.

We lived in the little house. I made a hundred curtains out of white unbleached muslin, with three ruffles across them, so that they looked like old-fashioned ladies' panties. Very inexpensive. Fresh, white, and charming, I thought they looked. I got Viola to work for us, a huge colored girl, so wonderful, dear, good, interesting and fun. She was very tall and stout and had a nobly handsome head with a straight blunt nose like a statue's and a wide horizontal smile curling back from beautiful level teeth. And she talked so softly and with such fine figures of speech and had such sense and wisdom, and was such a sport and would take a taxi from Stamford to New York if need be, and sent telegrams and knew Harry Wills the famous prize fighter. She never said a boring thing in her life. She was all intelligence and fun. She would laugh in a curious way. Her knees would give and she would let out a liquid scream and drop her forehead to the edge of the sink as though her neck had suddenly become broken.

R. came home in the evening and we drank cocktails of grain alcohol and orange juice. One drizzling, raining, gloomy March day we drove in the slush across the hills behind Stamford. I can feel again my thoughts: "Think of it. Here I am, so reduced to a poor, dejected married woman, that my only freedom is to take a drive in an old Buick with the baby. Will it be so for years and years?"

But spring came and I felt better. Little Gaby was so perfect, so utterly charming with her straight cherubic nose and black hair. Her hair I cut like mine so that she had a thick black bang in her eyes like a Shetland pony. And she was so well made, and toed-in so charmingly in her tiny buckskin shoes, and so delightful in the brisk short dresses with tiny collars. Julie and I designed them. She had a tricycle and went up and down the bright warm sidewalk with the lovely microscopic Hogan children next door, who were undernourished and always eating sugar buns so that their tiny teeth were eaten with black decay.

I raked the backyard. The smell of smoke rose. I took walks in the beautiful country back of us. I played golf alone on the golf links with two clubs in my hand. I got very good and could sometimes drive three hundred yards. I was so sunburned that the caddies told people that I was an Indian.

But I was more and more disheartened about R. and me— and out of love.

He was home very much in the daytime and this was painfully boring to me. I would hear him coming and in a flight from his voice, his talk, I would go out the back door and walk far over the hills. He restively always wanted my attention. If people that were interesting to me were there, like Julie, and we talked together, R. would wag his foot impatiently and want to divert the talk to *his* subjects, which always bored me.

"My gosh! what do you know about this?" he would cry. "This train gets in at 8:30 and you can make connections and save seven minutes if you take it at New Rochelle, etc. What do you know about that? Say now, isn't that interesting?"

It gored my brain with boredom. I had a mental hemorrhage of pain at such thoughts, coming at me again and again. Or the talk of golf scores.

Not that my talk was necessarily more interesting than his. He could have talked about engineering and mathematics, which I certainly could not. It was just that we were different and could not hear each other. I still think how sad and terrible it is that people do not escape from this misery in marriage, this inability to communicate. But perhaps when people are really fond of each other it does not matter.

You see, I was this kind of a person: so ductile and amiable and wanting to do what the other person wanted. "Shall we go to a movie or stay home? Which do you want to do?" Nothing, not wild horses, could make me say, "Go to a movie." No. The other person must say what *he* wanted to do, and then we would do that. But that is why, after a long time, I always must escape from dominating people—escape! smash up my marriage! get away and never be seen again!

The turning point came one afternoon in May. In those few minutes I knew: "Now it is over; now it is finished. We will be divorced." We were playing golf and he was very irritable and angry at a little starveling Italian caddy. The boy was carrying two of those huge loathsome golf bags, full of countless, fussy, expensive brassies, niblicks, spoons, that men like R. shop for and talk about and fuss over and examine and try, and then don't play with them so very well. "Damn it, hurry up! Run!" The boy on his rachitic legs ran staggeringly, struggling obliquely up the hill.

"Well now, I am through with him forever," I thought, and so it was. From that time on I was never angry again, but polite, anxiously polite as you are to a guest you do not like. Anger means there may be affection left.

It was not that it is so terrible to be mad at a caddy, or that tempers are so bad. They are just physiological explosions. But it brought the turning-point in me.

Soon afterwards Gaby and I were going to Minneapolis for a summer visit. We took the train from Stamford to New York. R. went with us. I sat by the window. She was restless and stood up and sometimes stood on his thighs. He kept brushing off his trousers and coat. It was a handsome new suit. I looked on quietly. Yes, it was all over.

But what finally screwed up my determination was this: My vehement, beautiful sister Anne was in Minneapolis too. That first morning I went out on the lawn where she and Julie were smoking and drinking and having their usual exciting, laughing, exclamatory talk. And presently I spoke of it: "You know, something has happened. I am sick of being married. I want a divorce."

Now I thought they would pull long, thoughtful faces and

look regretful and say: "Oh, Brenda, really.... Oh, too bad. Poor R. Of course he has his limitations. But, poor man."

But to my complete astonishment they were utterly delighted and their faces broke into wreathèd smiles and they burst out into hearty congratulatory exclamations, interrupting each other in their relief about the whole thing. "Oh, thank heaven! It's about time. Oh, Brenda, really, now everything will be better. You *must* do it, now. Now don't, *don't* be kind, Brenda. Weak. See it through now. Don't flinch."

This was a startling revelation to me. You see, here I had been longing to be free for four years, and yet everybody, my closest friends, had protected me from their thoughts and what they could see about my life. I wish they hadn't. And ever since then I have felt with distress how there is a conspiracy to protect married people from the truth about each other. Why should that be? If a friend is misusing you, pulling your leg in some way, people tell you about it. Yes, I wished they had told me all this from the beginning. For when the truth is put on muddy and blocked situations, they begin to dissolve and move and become clear.

And that is why I have always been, as my friends sometimes protest, angry and anarchistic about marriage (until now when I have learned more gentleness), particularly at people who lie to each other, and those men who say they don't want to "hurt" Edna. How do they know that Edna may not be longing with all her heart to get away from them?

For myself, at least, pain and danger proved to be much better than muggy adjustment, than trying to "make a go of it," as low-spirited people so pathetically say. No, never again will I live in the house for a day, with anyone, even with a washwoman in the basement, unless I love her, unless there is happiness between us.

That was a hard and frightening summer. I could not seem to sleep and eat much. I felt that I must return to Stamford and tell R. Out of a kind of decent courage (which surprises and pleases me now) I could not do the easy thing, i.e., write and tell him my decision, and then just stay in Minneapolis, comfortably at home with my parents. I thought: 1. I have to tell him in person, and 2. I have to make a living for Gaby and myself. That is, I could not leave him, taking the child for myself, and then make him support us. I would never do anything so unchivalrous as that. And I could not let Father support us. And it was frightening because marriage makes you so slack and you lose all tenseness and briskness about working.

I forget telling my mother about it, so perhaps she was away. But I told my father and was not comforted at all. He said: "You should never have made the mistake to marry him." He seemed hard-hearted but I think he was deeply distressed and felt terribly sorry for me; and I now think that the explanation of it was that perhaps he thought from my off-hand manner that I was taking it lightly: What was a marriage or divorce or two? What old-fashioned ante-Shavian hocum, to take it seriously!

Well, when Father was so uncomforting, I was thrown back on my own strength. Not for anything would I ask him for help. I can truly say that I did not feel self-pity or resentment. I did not blame him. I felt forlorn, though, and it was going to be a hard row to hoe. Of course the thing that made it hard was having a child. The vulnerableness of that! No, you cannot be a spear-thrower very well with a child.

And so this was my third desperate departure from home. Marie Rainey, Irish, a flirt, a friend and a giggler, happened to be on the train. She was a comfort, though she didn't know it. I told her about the dragon I was going to kill in such a way that her gigglings went bubbling through the Pullman, among the dark swinging curtains and waking up the traveling men. Just the same it was hard, in quick intervals, to keep the tears from spurting out of my eyes. Yes, it was not very much fun.

And now I come to the time when I became actually a live wire myself. (I guess it is about the only time.) The moment I arrived in New York, what action, what pulling telephones to my chest, sending telegrams, demanding interviews!

I heard that the *Chicago Tribune* was about to publish a new magazine, and John N. Wheeler, an ex-newspaper man ("Very hard-boiled," they said) was the editor. As soon as little Gaby was at Anne's house, I telephoned him and his curt hoarse voice growled in the receiver.

"Mr. Wheeler, I want to see you."

"What do you want?"

"A job."

"Haven't got a job."

"Well, I want to see you. You better talk to me. I am the best person you could get. It is an important chance for you. I know everybody, Bruce Barton, Max Eastman, Nina Putnam, Willa Cather. I am intelligent, lively, the best writer you could get."

"Well . . . come at three."

And think of it—me so polite and undemanding!—I at once telephoned all those people to write letters for me. Yes, that is the kind of gall you get, when your back is to the wall. And it even seems natural and easy.

Wheeler was in a barracklike building some place downtown, near the old *World* building. I liked his kind of looks. Again, they were a little like Sigurd's. He had one of those blond, clownlike faces with a slightly receding chin; fresh color, curly hair so brushed and wetted that the highlights slid about on it, and steel spectacles. And he had a loud, growling, impersonal voice and spoke with an utterly unemotional face, from the left teeth.

Later when I worked on *Liberty* I got to know him. He was one of the most formidably blunt men I ever hope to see. I never saw such an unsensitive dead pan of a face as Mr. Wheeler's. He frightened other people. (I refused to be frightened). You said something pleasant and simpered a little. A dead cold pan. No dislike in it or meanness or egotism. Just no emotion.

"Do you think perhaps it might not be a rather good idea. . . ."

"No. Don't like it," the rusty, strong curt voice snarled out without one touch of ill nature in it. But once in a while he would joke, or something that I said he would consider a joke. Then a sudden mirthless Cheshire cat of a grin appeared, with all his level strong teeth showing. I liked Mr. Wheeler always. I was always a little in love with him even. I liked his heavy slouching walk through the office, in a big blue chinchilla overcoat, so golden and pink, his face and hair, his steel glasses shining, his blue eyes as shallow and cold as a sheep's but just and hearty and intelligent and energetic.

But to go back to that first day when I bearded him: at once I told him he should hire me.

"Why?"

"Because I write well. Everybody will read it. I am intelligent, energetic, witty. . . ."

"Do you know Willa Cather?"

"Yes."

"How do you know her?"

I told him.

"Well, we aren't going to hire a woman staff writer now. Perhaps later. But I'll give you couple assignments."

We went into another bare office to see Harvey Duell, a fat young man from Chicago.

"Here, give her couple assignments."

He did. One was to be: "Are Women Getting Uglier?" based on a statement made to the newspapers by a lecturer on heredity, Albert Edward Wiggam. The other was: "Short Cuts to Divorce."

I worked on these at once (me, the procrastinator)! I went straight to the Public Library, and the same afternoon I tracked down Albert Edward Wiggam in a rooming house in Chelsea. Oh, to be scared is such a release from all the logy weight of procrastination, of dallying and pokiness! You burn into work. It is as though gravity were removed and you walked lightly to the moon like an angel.

But I must say here that I did not know how to write the articles. Within a week I had given them to Harvey Duell, and they were very lumberingly written and sententious, and Harvey Duell told me so, very kindly, and I knew what he meant at once. But it was Mr. Wheeler who told me the most important thing of all about writing.

It happened that day that he was going uptown just as I was, and we were on the subway together. We hung on straps. He was hard to talk to and I was proudly silent. I could never burble any polite nonsense to a man like that. But I said:

"How do you want me to write these articles?"

"What do you mean?"

"I mean should I write them seriously or flippantly or what?"

"I want them *interesting*," his loud rusty voice ripped out.

Yes, of course. That explained all writing to me. It must be interesting. That was the most helpful thing ever said to me about writing.

And so I rewrote my articles many times. I tried to make them lucid, direct, clear. I cut out all the verbiage. I read them to myself, and wherever my voice dragged over the words I cut that out. I tried to make them so that a simple person or a very erudite one would sink into them and perhaps be interested, be drawn along. This meant you had to say something too. There must be something true, interesting, in every sentence. I don't mean startling, but interesting.

I mailed them. I remember (so often this happens) experiencing a kind of slump of will, such as: "Oh, they won't buy them, and I never did really put anything through with dispatch and briskness." But they did buy them and paid for them immediately, a hundred and fifty dollars apiece. To support Gaby and myself and Viola. I needed three hundred dollars a month. So that was just fine.

But to go back to that first day in New York, that day of fire and sword-thrusts, when I cut through everything and accomplished so much and made Mr. Wheeler give me the assignments, and I worked on them all afternoon and evening in a deep trance of unbelievable (for me) concentration. I still had not done the hardest thing: broken the news to R. that I must have a divorce, told him that he must get out of the house and let me and Gaby live alone.

When I took the train to Stamford, it was after eleven o'clock, and again seeing my reflection in the black train window, I was not suffering now, but wonderfully alive and even happy, though I stumbled off the train at Greenwich by mistake and had to take a ten-mile taxi ride to get home.

The lighted house with all the white ruffled curtains seemed very natural and familiar and so did R. For there are these two layers in our feelings, in situations like these: on one hand you feel that here is something familiar, friendly and dear; but also something terrible that must be faced and ejected.

When I told him about it, he took it sensibly, cheerfully, and like a friend. Why, that was all right, he said. He would do just what I wanted. He would stay living in the house until he got a job; for the bakery business had entirely collapsed now, but the owner of it, who had duped him, was compelled to pay him a small income for six months. "And you can have all that," I said, "and I am sure I can earn enough for myself." I felt immense relief, a sunburst of happiness almost. I was very fond of him again, for taking it so helpfully.

After that I went to New York early every morning and came home late at night. The interesting thing is that, during this crisis, I was all the time so clear and alive. There was no nervousness at all. I seemed to need so little food and sleep. Going into New York on the train in the early morning, I would fall asleep for fifteen minutes, and wake up as lively as ever. I could recover from a long night's work, in brief naps, like a puppy. Although a little later, when I had been given a steady job and had the safety of a salary, I became an ordinary person again, normally tired, normally hungry, and normally reluctant to start work again. In fact, I am apt to wonder much more than most people: "Why am I not bright today? I know: only eight hours sleep..... Should I give up smoking?... I had a chocolate cream two days ago. Is that what makes me dull? Candy is the devil."

My regular job was working on the staff of a magazine in Newark, with a salary of seventy-five dollars a week. It took me five hours a day to commute there, from Stamford. Yet I got used to this very soon, and read some wonderful literature in those nine months: Tolstoy, Dostoevski, Emerson. I got so that I could almost keep reading when I was changing from the train in the Grand Central to the subway, and then walking through the caverns of Wall Street to the Hudson tube.

But one thing that was very hard for me was leaving Gaby every day. I shall never forget that once she cried just when she saw a photograph of me, in hat and coat and carrying a suitcase. She apparently had a feeling I was deserting her. Sometimes I would wonder if this feeling was pre-natal; did it go back to the time I was so anxious to avoid having a child and ran around Lake Harriet in overshoes and a fur

coat? For many years, whenever I was walking downstairs
with Gaby and happened to get a step ahead, she would sit
down and burst into a bitter wail of despair, of desertion.
"If only I had a wife!" I used to think, "who would stay
home and keep the children happy, why I could support six
of them. A cinch."

And another distressing thing was R. He did not leave
at all. At first I would be happy and amiable because he had
promised to go. But weeks passed and he did not. Gradually
I was cold and angry, "the iron face"—until I burst out into
bitter talk again, and he would promise to go ... very soon.
And again relieved, I would become bright and friendly.

But at last he was offered a fine job in New York. He went
to live at the Brevoort.

2.

A staff writer on Liberty *and why I can never ask for good
salary. Tomola. The last assignment. Free-lancing and a
slump of the Will. The divorce.*

IN THE FALL I WROTE TO MR. WHEELER. "ARE YOU GOING TO
get a woman staff writer? I think you should hire me." (I
was still bold and pressing, you see. This effrontery was not
characteristic of me).

He asked me to come and see him.

"How much will you work for?"

"Well," I said, scrupulously truthful, "I work for *Charm*
(the Newark magazine) for seventy-five dollars a week, and
I would work for you for that."

This was literally true, of course. I had weighed it: that
is, if both magazines had paid exactly seventy-five dollars a
week, I would choose *Liberty*. Though any practical (or perhaps sane) person would have said: "I want a hundred dollars a week."

This was characteristic psychology. I always felt that it was so extraordinary, so altogether fine and excellent that I was making a living for myself and a child—that seventy-five dollars was just wonderful. And everybody seemed to think so too, my father and others. "Remarkable, clever, wonderful Brenda." I suppose it was because it was still exceptional for a woman to make a half-way decent living. As Dr. Johnson said of a woman making a speech: like a dog standing on his hind legs, it was not so wonderful what she *did,* but that she did it at all.

Walter Davenport was another staff writer on *Liberty,* and he had a wife and only one child and his salary, I heard, was about three times as much as mine. It did not occur to me to feel that this was unjust. But there is something quixotic in me about money, something meek and guilty. I want it and like it. But I cannot imagine insisting on it, pressing it out of people. I always vaguely feel: why should I have money when other people have it not? It is like taking the biggest piece of cake. And I can never feel that I have earned it. That is, even if I am more energetic and clever than other people who are dull and incompetent, all the more reason for my getting *less* money. Because it is so much more fun to be strong and clever.

Now I come to the story of Tomola, for knowing her affected my life for about five years.

One evening I went to a party in the country. It was at one of those clapboard Connecticut houses in a lovely field edged with falling stone where, in thickets of dogwood, the whip-poor-wills began musically swallowing and gurgling at twilight. Many people were there, among them several actresses. And we sat on the lawn in wicker chairs and had cocktails. I saw Tomola coming over the lawn. I had seen her before on the train and had stared down and felt almost indignation that any one could look so eccentric. She was older than I (sometimes she looked a thousand years old and sometimes like a child of ten). She was as slim as a jockey (she weighed only 86 pounds) and had that look, that snub-nosed-boy look, and she wore a tiny tailored suit, uncompromisingly masculine. But the second or third time you saw her, you began to see she looked charming, so smartly dressed, a gardenia in her button hole, saddle soap on her perfect shoes, a steel-blue suit, her face very tanned and her blond hair looking almost white. She was a fashion artist and made drawings for *Harper's Bazaar*.

Every morning after that I would encounter her on the train and talk to her; and gradually it got so that if I did not find her I felt quite lost and disappointed. I loved Tomola. More than any man or woman I have ever known, she had the soul of a true gentleman and hero, so austere, stoical, uncompromising, and tenderhearted. And the soul was in a tiny body which she scorned and despised and never indulged or made comfortable. I think she was something like T. E. Lawrence in this. As a child she had cut off her hair until it was short, close to the scalp, and she would tear off the ruffles and trinkets that her mother put on her, in a rage.

She had gone to work at seventeen to help support her family, and now she made twenty-five or thirty thousand dollars a year. She threw it away and supported all the people she possibly could with it, and never indulged herself in anything but taxicabs and enormous tips for all.

One Saturday afternoon I went down to her office. She would not call it a studio, because she disliked the Art artists with their grubby smocks and paint-encrusted palettes. It was a penthouse on Park Avenue, a large square room painted sulphur yellow, with French doors to the roof. And there were beautiful books on drawing and art and a maid who was always squeezing orange juice. Tomola sat at her drawing board, always erect, quiet, patient, her legs crossed, one polished tan shoe pointing to the floor.

I talked while she drew and I walked up and down and told about my life and what had happened. There was a fine mirror built in the wall, in squares, with a brass star at each intersection. I walked back and forth and talked. I can see myself in that mirror: a green coat with a Kate Greenaway cape trimmed with brown fur, and my hair criss-crossed and on end.

Suddenly I heard an explosion and jumped and stared. Tomola had thrown an ink bottle at the ceiling and it was dripping down. It was rage at what a hard time I had had. I began to love her. How comforting it is when someone feels that we have been wronged. A knight.

We took a cab to the Grand Central Station and though it was only four blocks away, she always took a cab and tipped the driver a great deal, with the gruff haste of a financier. She always carried money loose, even if it were in ten or fifty dollar bills, in the pockets of her tiny jacket, and in a certain book on the paintings of Ingres, in her office, she always kept a ten or twenty dollar bill so that servants, friends, could take it when they needed it.

But though so tenderhearted, she was wonderfully blunt.

"Tomola," I would telephone her in the evening, "a friend is here. Anne, Countess Jones from Iowa. She is the one who wants you to make a drawing of her. Please come over."

"No."

"Oh, Tomola. Really. Please do. Why not?"

"I don't want to."

There was not a touch of annoyance in it. It was just true. It made me laugh. And oh, my, I admired it, I whose weakness is to be so soothing, easy-going and full of blandishments.

She did not like people, only one or two, and kept quietly aloof from them. But she loved animals—horses and dogs. She loved and knew beauty more than anyone I ever knew— the water of the Sound before her house, the lights on the ship masts, the gulls walking on the hard sand when the tide was out, under a cold November sky. When she stayed at my house in the evening, we smoked cigarettes and looked out at the poplar tree in the moonlight.

"See how the leaves turn over in the breath of night air, and suddenly how each one, in all its clear shape, is bright silver."

"Tomola," I once said to Gaby, "is the nicest person that we will ever know, in all the world."

"Yes," she said. "Tomola and Santa Claus."

At *Liberty* I had a room off the open arena of stenographers. I wrote out on yellow paper my ideas for articles and sent them in to Mr. Wheeler, and he wrote out his, and sent them to me. This made a list. I did one after the other. The third member of the staff was Hugh Fullerton, an old newspaperman, thin, very talkative; stiff, fine hair cut close but always mussed; dry fingers always rubbing at his eyes; smoking and spilling tobacco and ashes from both ends of his cigarettes.

Mr. Wheeler I did not see very often, just his slow hunching walk through the office, a brief case under his overcoat arm. Sometimes he sent for me. We had short gatling-gun talk. I was always a little scared. No, not scared. But I had the nervousness where one is too alert; you want to acquit yourself well and are controlling an impulse not to be too pleasant or affected in any way.

His talk would be a rough, hearty, gravelly shout and scarcely any consonants would be sounded.

"Ha yah?" (How are you?) "Here's story, good idea, story women fascinating to men. Hod ay do it?" (How do they do it?) "How bout it? Write at."

And so I quickly went to my room and began. An article took me about a week. I rewrote them many many times, worked very hard. I could not stand anything superfluous.

Walter Davenport and Hugh Fullerton dashed theirs off, but they left verbiage in theirs, I thought, which was just dullness and fog. No, I had to make it brighter, clearer, more laconic than that.

But much of my anxious rewriting then was just because I was not yet bold enough to put down at once what I thought. That is, at first I would spin out many very elaborate things and splendid complicated adjectives that meant nothing, as one does in school for the English teachers. And the polishing was really just cleaning all this away, to something honest that I should have said in the first place.

Ring Lardner often came through the office, a fine large man with a dead brown eye. He seemed bashful and good and afraid to look at people much. He walked slowly and shyly and kept his eyes straight ahead. I never saw him smile.

After a year or two Mr. Wheeler left, and this is what I wrote home about it:

Judging by the assignments I have been getting they are going to turn *Liberty* into something very cheap and sensational. It seems the circulation stopped going up for a month or so. The circulation manager wanted to put in more contests, and such things. Wheeler objected. Then he left. So now a new policy is under way.

Then Joe Patterson had come into the *Liberty* office to take Mr. Wheeler's place. He was the owner, from Chicago, and now he would run it. He had a charming boy-face and boy-hair, though he was over forty, and a loud shouting voice. I wondered how happy Joe Patterson was in his married life. Because he always liked (and thought the public did) marital violence and meanness. For years he had an artist paint covers for *Liberty,* and the subject most of the time was a man quarreling with his wife. They would be yelling at each other, their mouths in horrible parabolas of meanness and recrimination, or expressing some kind of vulgarity and ill will. I think he felt that everybody would be amused and relieved to see this, a kind of vent for the hidden facts of all married life.

Well, Joe Patterson's first assignment to me was this: Rudolph Valentino's wife was getting a divorce; my assignment was to interview her and write an article: "Has a Wife the Right to Deny Her Husband Children?"

It made me low-spirited, and I did not like it. Natacha Rambova was a nice, intelligent movie actress. I don't know why they wanted a divorce. I suppose for sensible reasons, as most people do. I don't know if she had ever "denied" him children, or if he thought she had. I guess that in the divorce, in which cruelty was the grounds, he said that his wife kept Pekinese dogs and did not want children. Perhaps he did not say it though. More likely some reporter or editor, all of whom seem to be lightheartedly vulgar when it comes to their work, twisted this into the story.

I went and talked to Mrs. Valentino, confided in her my predicament, what I had been told to do. She was very kind and helpful and told me sensible and nice things about Rudolph Valentino and herself and why they found it not good for either of them to stay married to each other. I wrote it down truthfully, laconically.

My story was changed and doctored up with photographs. A young man in the office was photographed and they put Rudolph Valentino's head on his body. A girl in the office became Mrs. Valentino. Across the page, they pointed at each other: "Has a Wife the Right..." etc.

Well, this sort of thing nauseates me, not only because it is so mean, but because it is so tiresome. For in writing you cannot possibly be interesting if what you say is not true, if it is what I call "a true lie," i.e., a truth which gives the wrong impression. For no matter how subtly you lie in writing, people know it and don't believe you, and the whole secret of being interesting is to be believed. As William

Blake says: "The Truth can never be told so as to be understood and not be believed."

And so I decided to leave *Liberty*. Then I could work at
home—in the house with Gaby. She would like that much
better.

So in a week or two, I wrote to my mother, November 17th,
1925, I will probably be a free lance. It doesn't scare me at all—
or very little. Think I will make much more money. In fact, two
years ago when I first came to New York and was a free lance,
I made as much money as I do now, and I had not worked for
seven years. So don't worry.... I have a lot of money in the
bank.

But again that free-lancing was surprising. The most surprising sloth drowned me. I could only sleep and go walking. To have the external pressure of a job removed is very
astonishing. Your own will now is your only motor and it
has no horse-power. Sometimes I think that perhaps the most
competent business men, and lawyers and doctors, who must
be at the office at nine o'clock every morning, do not realize
this and take more credit for initiative and industry than they
deserve. And it is why all the bright women of the world,
who if more were expected of them, might do important
work, but who instead have a chronic feeling of ineffective-
ness and sloth.

I am still in 1938, now, struggling with my will, which
bleeds away into shopping, telephone calls and talk, every
third day almost. And I have found this: that if I am told to
do something for someone *else*, to write a paper on Plato for
a University professor, say, I will sit before my typewriter
all night and get it done, in a happy trance of concentration.
But to make myself do *my own* work, that is often so very,
very hard. Why, I do not see. Are we used to working only at
others' orders? Does this come from childhood? Is it because
as children we are never urged into what we want to do, but
jerked away into something that we are *told* to do? Is it a

feeling that to work at one's own orders is conceited and selfish? Well, there is no logic in it, because women, especially, will unnecessarily wash dishes and woodwork, run foolish errands for anybody, and put off their own secret work they really long to do. This is too bad.

For myself, I have at last worked out this logic. It is one of the secret arguments I try to bolster up myself with. If there is an ache in my chest that will not be dislodged, which makes me long to write a novel, say, then that ache is significant and I must do it, for there is a possibility that the future lies all about us (as the metaphysicians now say it does), and the ache means that I am coming near to a path in my destiny that I am supposed to take. That is, it may mean that the order to work comes from an archangel and I should obey it, just as willingly as I would that of a cross employer or a fretful husband.

But to go back to my free-lancing. For nearly three weeks I was alarmed by my lassitude. I wrote in bed, tried that. Perhaps I was really tired; but I think not. It was just that the stiffening of a job was melted out of me. I wrote a love story, but it took five or six weeks and I sold it only after several rewritings.

And why was I so much more limp than before? I think it was because I had psychological cushions now. Tomola was my friend and sympathetically backing me, and my father was full of respect for me, and this probably made me relax, not press so anxiously.

The divorce came along in July, 1926. There had been no hurry about it because neither of us wanted to marry anybody else. I asked Mr. Homer Cummings to get it for me, for his law office was in Stamford—a large blondish droll man with glasses. But Mr. Cummings did not take the case himself, but turned it over to Mr. Hacker in his office, a prim man with round, literal brown eyes enlarged by pince-nez. The witnesses were my sister Anne, Viola, who had worked for me, and my friends Margaret Norris and Meecie Foote in New Canaan.

It was tried in chambers in the court house and the judge was a darling man, a mustached, slender, elderly man. He looked like a Holbein drawing. He sat at the head of the table and wrote down what we said. I told my story first and had that trembling fear-eagerness to do it well, like a horse about to go over the jumps. I talked. I felt my face flaming with bright blood and the words came out so well, so clearly, fast, accurately.

Dear Mother . . . Yesterday my divorce, before a referee. . . . It went off all right and I will get the decree in October, for then it will be handed down, or whatever the lawyer-talk for it is. So that is all over. A great relief. . . .

In the afternoon I and all the witnesses went to New York, Viola and all. Anne made us come in at her house and have a cocktail, and we relaxed for the first time. By that time we began to see how ridiculous it had been. For instance Mr. Hacker was very pleased with Meecie's looks because she looks like a gentle, blonde girl-angel from Heaven. So whenever he addressed Meecie, his voice became soft and he beamed gently.

He was trying to prove that R. used bad language to me. "Did he not, Mrs. Foote?" (Of course all this was one of those true lies, because I often used bad language too, in a not unamiable way. That is to say, bad language was not necessarily an ordeal to me.)

"But it is not, Mrs. Foote," Mr. Hacker said, "the sort of language *your* husband would use to *you*, is it, Mrs. Foote?"

Meecie swallowed and finally said, "No"; thereby losing a chance to say: "Well, I am sorry, Mr. Hacker, but it happens to be just the identical language. But I divorced my husband for it seven years ago."

Well, it was over. A great relief. A blessing for R. as well as myself. That door was shut. And immediately all miserable suspicions and ill will between us vanished. We hardly ever saw each other, but we tried to be as decent and kind and helpful as we could.

I did not ask for alimony or any support for the child. I could do that myself. "Because I want to be," I said, "the sole owner of the child (although he can see her whenever he wants to), I ought to pay for her."

This of course sounds very noble, but there is an element in it of my invertebrate weakness about money. I cannot bear to get money out of people, even when it may make them feel better to give it. And the divorce was a true blessing for R. too, although he had not thought it would be, and suffered very much, because he became in a short time an extremely successful man, more so than he had ever been in his life, the vice-president of a New York bank. You see, he needed the divorce as much as I did.

For a long time, really until just recently, I mistakenly thought (as we are so apt to do) that all the causes of the divorce were in *him,* in his inadequacies. But of course they were in me too. For I find to my surprise, in studying my past for this book, that I wrote this in my diary in September, 1936.

I have been dreaming much. Saturday night I dreamed that I remarried R. and we lived together (no child with us) and we kept house, an apartment it seemed to be, and there was a strong resemblance to things in Stamford—those cocktails we made out of orange juice and grain alcohol. He was much nicer and I felt that I had not been right in my appraisal of myself and him, when married to him.

Well, there he was, brown-eyed, his bright, round brown eyes, short nose, tan strong hair, alert, drawling good-naturedly, and a little nasally. But inside me there was the sense of oppression that had almost the sense of a nightmare, that I was not free; that I must be with him, could not strike out, go where I pleased, but he would be there always, and I would have to listen to him and could never act as one, alone and debonair. Such a strong painful feeling that I would burst nearly, and could not endure it. It was the same as in New York last spring when my beau seemed like a husband and took me places and walked slower than I could bear to go. A quiet weight and ego-force insisting, implacably, on his power and authority, in buying things, and making me go to this and that art gallery. Fatherly, and a benign tyrant.

No, we must never blame other people for what happens, or blame ourselves either. I think the only thing to do is to try to understand things better, more generously, and then do what the angels tell us.

3.

In Stamford; I think Will and physical condition are the panacea. My mother's visit. Her death. My inner struggle: whether to be good or to be remarkable. It may be all right to discipline yourself, but never a child.

I COME NOW TO A PERIOD OF FIVE YEARS THAT HAD ITS PAR-ticular character. I moved from the little house on the· cob-blestones to a pretty clapboard one on Shippan Point sur-rounded by vacant fields of gorse, and I could see the light-house and hear the buoy that hooted and laughed in snow-storms, like a musical hyena.

Living there, my expenses were about five hundred dollars a month, with rent and coal and our maid, young Peggy Dwan, whose Irish voice was the softest I have ever heard. It was anxious business to make this money. An article took often a month to write and then one might not sell it. I was always just a jump ahead of the spears, in this free lance business.

At the end of the summer Gaby and I were in Minneapolis for a visit, and I remember being downtown with Julie a cold drizzling day in September, with a smell of winter in the air. "I have the coal heebeejeebees," I said, thinking of the hun-dreds of dollars' worth that I would have to buy for the win-ter. But when we came home I found that *The Ladies' Home Journal* had bought a story and *The Saturday Evening Post* an article. For both I got fourteen hundred dollars. It is a skyrocketing joy to sell things and I went back to Stamford and bought my coal with a flourish.

I worked every morning for four hours and then, bare-legged and exposed as much as possible, I walked or ran around the Point, perhaps six miles, in the rain and snow, or in the bright salt sunshine. For at this time I was trying to make myself perfect, an athlete, a beauty, an acrobat (I was working on handsprings, which I have never perfected), and a scholar. And I was going to do it all by my Will, which was nourished by a piecemeal reading of Nietzsche. And sometimes on my walk I would memorize Shakespeare and other poetry. I learned many long pages of Hamlet. This affected me and stimulated me very much. I always respond to the Renaissance idea of a fine, brave, proud human being, a swordsman and a poet at the same time.

I realize that this may sound as though I were very young, but I was thirty-six, which never once crossed my mind as being a less lively and comely age than twenty.

Jan. 15th, 1927. Me: "Why, I thought she was only my age! ... Just a kid of thirty-six." This makes Tookie laugh.

The queer part is that I feel that way now, and even more so, surprised (about once a year when somebody speaks of it) that age is supposed to be a handicap or a slowing-up process.

Nov. 15th, 1926. Work hard. Very depressed. Tomola lectures me. Christ versus Nietzsche. She is right. Self-assurance. Mushiness, soft, blandishing kindness, is awful. Anger is a blessing in spite of my arguments for intellectual detachment. My story back from the *Post*. I am sunk.

Nov. 18, 1926. No coffee since December 15th. Brilliant color. No more must let people put it over on me. *No more. Self-assurance* is what I need. To thunder with this unresisting charm.

Tomola says Faith, self-assurance must be rooted in oneself. Not a bluff.

Dec. 9th, 1926. Wonderful running around the point and the dogs all go with me, running when I run. I say to Tomola: "If it were not for the fact that I have on a teamster's union suit, it would be quite like Diana."

Dec. 13th, 1926. Ruin my perfect condition with cocktails.

December 14th. Lazy. Indecision. Boredom. Angry.

Dec. 16th. Read George Jean Nathan and H. L. Mencken on the train. I am in slough of melancholy and worry about work. *Vanity Fair* and *Mercury* full of venom and envy. Only two things expressed always: "I am smarter than this fool" and "How terrible America and the world is."

But then I read William James. The gentle impersonal kindness, wisdom, lack of ego of a scientist. I am full of good will again and compassion. One might as well feel benevolent toward every manifestation of life, stupidity, vulgarity, bad taste.

My mother came to New York that fall and she spent a few days with me. It was so nice to have her. Order and peace and life that was clear and interesting seemed to spread around her. She made all the waves still. The day she arrived she had been reading about Sir Ernest Rutherford's bombarding of atoms to make a transmutation of elements and told Gaby and me thoughtfully just how it was done and what happened, with lucent clearness. To her everything was worth understanding.

Oh, Mother was so darling. She made cocoa and buttered toast for me and Gaby on Sunday evening. I remember thinking: "Now if Mother could only live with me, then everything would be perfect." It was not that she ministered to us, but that she was so quietly independent, attending to her own important work in New York and Washington. There was not a touch of the pathetic about her. She was no more of a dependent and a filial responsibility than Sir Ernest Rutherford would be.

This was the last time I saw my mother.

December 26th, 1926. Get notice of my decree. 350 dollars for psych-analyst article. Tomola and I scrub house. I have one weakness . . . a worried uneasy mind if people are not happy and doing what they want to do.

Jan. 3rd, 1927. Fast all day. Feel punk. Going to get thin, 115 pounds and stay there. Two assignments from *Liberty*.

Jan. 13th. Letter from Mother. She broke her wrist. Arm in cast. Father has bad cold. Worries me. Mother says: "Your letters are so precious."

This last sentence, now in 1938, surprises me. Did they really think so? I have a gush of pleasure. "Why," I think, "perhaps I was not so bad, after all!"

At eight o'clock on the evening of March 1st, Tomola and I were in my house. There was a fire. Gaby was in bed. A telegraph boy came to the door and I read what he gave me.

Darling Mother killed instantly in automobile accident.
Sigurd.

What did I feel? I cannot tell. Incredulity, shock, and a blanket of calm level commonsense. I telephoned to Minneapolis and to Anne and Elsa, and made plans to go west. Whenever I woke up in the night it was a pain to become conscious and have the realization dawn on me.

On the train going west were Elsa and Anne. And Marguerite Wells of Minneapolis was there too. That was a relief. I was so glad to see her, because with her fine, clear-cut little nose, her beautiful clothes, she connoted so many things about Mother—her intelligence and gentle but tremendous ability. She had worked with Mother for woman suffrage, child labor, the League of Women Voters. She seemed so sensible. It was just a wonderful comfort. Elsa too was so wonderfully quiet, almost beaming with goodness and quiet. She said so sensibly: "Of course I have lived through this many times; it is not a shock to me." She explained how it was:

"If you dread a thing for a long, long time, for years, then when it comes, you can accept it." All this talk was a relief. Although poor Elsa suffered worse than any of us, for many years afterwards.

When we got to Minneapolis, to the house, the tall sliding doors to the library were closed. But if you went around to the sitting room, you could see in there. I knew that the coffin was there. Yes, it was. I could see it. I did not once go in and look. I was afraid to. It filled me with utter horror, the thought of it. This was fear of dead bodies plus my sorrow. Father that morning, as we all sat about the fire, talked about what had happened in a matter-of-fact sensible voice. He told us all about it and other matters, of what was to be done, the funeral arrangements and all. Dr. Frederick Eliot, the Unitarian minister in St. Paul, would give the service. And it was queer: it seemed cheerful and a relief for us to be talking so, in such ordinary voices, such as at a gathering when the children have come home for holidays. But at something, Father suddenly began to cry. His voice came in loud adult sobs, his chest heaving. But he stopped in just a minute, just a second or two. This made the most heart-breaking impression.

Thereafter he seemed to be very busily and efficiently doing all sorts of things, going through Mother's desk, fixing everything, and harrowing us with the most painful matter-of-fact questions about this and that. And it seems to me we did not want him to muss up things that way. "Honestly, we mustn't let Father do that," I can hear someone saying humorously. This was because he was so notoriously awkward with his hands, setting things on fire in lighting his cigarettes. He seemed callous. Then I remember Anne's saying upstairs, "But he is bleeding inside." I have never forgotten that phrase. I think of it often, often, and it seems just right.

I was frightened at night and had unforgettable nightmares. In one there was a gloomy plain under a low, lowering, darkling sky—a Gustave Doré gloom and dread. And over this plain comes a horse and rider. But the rider is an amorphous Thing, hideous as a corpse, with wet corrupt flesh and the legs horribly drawn out and elongated to the ground, as though the flesh had lost its ability to adhere, like dripping, stretching dough. This frightened me beyond words. As I remember it, for a long time I was afraid at night. These dreams thoroughly terrified me.

But all during these days, we would go over to Rolf's house, or Sigurd's or Arnulf's (they had all married and built houses in the pasture). Many drinks and sweet heavy liqueurs. A jolly feeling, a thorough-going cocktail party feeling. We told funny stories. We ate better and larger meals than usual and enjoyed them. This was really to make oneself obtuse and blunt. And it is right and natural that we should, because it was so hard, underneath.

The picture I got of what happened was this: Mother was walking home from the street car in the late afternoon. She had been to the State Capitol, then to Dr. Bulkley's, for she had sprained her wrist that spring. And how I have thought always, if only he had delayed her just thirty seconds, it would not have happened. That terrible concatenation of events, so that catastrophe comes in a certain split second!

She was crossing Richfield Road just below our driveway. There were icy ruts. A truck, a light one, was coming fast from Lake Calhoun. It seems she had a second of indecision and the driver did too, because he tried to get around in front of her, and struck a slim young elm tree. But his truck swerved and knocked her down and she struck the back of her head and was immediately unconscious. The young man was not to blame. I heard that he was nearly demented with distress about it.

At the funeral we sat in the separate room. Anne and Arnulf's eyes were streaming. They are "the children," I thought. Dr. Eliot read a beautiful Matthew Arnold poem. We were then told to do that barbarous thing—look at the body for the last time. I don't know why I did this. But I did. That was queer: I looked down at the waxen face, beautiful, clear and noble. But instantaneously I had a sense of relief. "Why, that is not Mother at all. They won't bury her, because she has left. This is just nothing. The cocoon. That is all it is."

And I was glad that I had looked at her. Fright and horror seemed to vanish with that look.

But for years after, what childishly distressed me was this thought: "Is she lonely?" Always when walking from our barn to the kitchen door, and looking up at the night sky, and the stars above the high bare branches of the elm trees, I thought: "But won't she be lonely? and it is so very cold. . . . But this is childish. If I only knew some metaphysics. . . ."

My mother had great political power in the state and when anyone ran for alderman or governor he came to persuade her to back him. And this amused us (we could see the man gravely talking to her, in the sunlight on the front porch) because she was so unlike a political boss. Instead of a cigar and conniving, there was naïve, clear, disinterested goodness. That is, if it were proposed to have a playground downtown that would cut the value of Father's court house lot in two, she would be very much interested in it. A playground. A good idea. Of course, this was a family joke, but it tells how she was.

There were memorial services for her at the State Capitol and, among others, Ole Sageng, a Norwegian farmer and member of the Legislature, spoke. And I am glad he did, because he was symbolic of everything wonderful in Minnesota—sturdy and spare and good and self-taught, one of those countless obscure but great men. He said how many people win fame for themselves, but then someone truly remarkable comes along "who forgets himself into immortality." Yes. That was a good way to put it.

Well, that is the story of my mother's death. But really the story went on, in all of us, for two or three years, a deep, subcutaneous, progressing wound and injury. But I guess the death of any loved parent is an incalculable lasting blow. Because no one ever loves you again like that. You have to grow up.

What seems to be characteristic of this five-year period in Stamford was a great deal of egocentricity. At this time I thought that Will and physical condition were the panacea. I was trying to become perfect. And the trouble was (as Tolstoy said, who did the same thing until he was forty or more) that the more one tries to make oneself perfect, the more uneasy one is in the presence of other people, and convinced that probably one is not so.

I understand this better now, after many years. The Ego and Will and self-discipline are fine and glorious, but we mix up the human ego with the divine one. But perhaps before the end of the book I will have been able to explain a little part of what I mean by this.

Anyway, there was still within me the struggle, on one hand, to be sweet and wonderfully good, and on the other, to be ruthlessly remarkable; the struggle between my mother and my father in me; between (as I described it) Christ and Nietzsche. What I think now is, that not one or the other should win, but they can become reconciled so that we are *both* strong and good, gentle and fierce, at the same time.

There is also, in this five-year period, something that I cannot tell about. All I can say is that I was wonderfully and completely loved by someone, in a way that I liked. And that I swam in that ocean of admiration with satisfaction and became selfish and weak. And also that I was often miserable because I was captured again. Not free.

But remember that nobody is to blame for these things. It is all a process of learning.

My diary shows a little bit, how I was:

April 11th, 1927. Too much to eat. Eyes have old-vulture look for several days.

April 12th. Eyes better today. Today I work hard. 1. Slim. 2. No coffee. 3. Work. 4. Hand stands, hand springs, cartwheels. 5. Benevolence and real good nature. Freedom of conscience.

    Am getting better every day from cutting down on coffee. It is true—the eyes look slipperier and clearer and more handsomely set.

May 24th, 1927. In the middle of the night I wake up for a couple of hours and castigate myself for all my omissions. No work done, procrastinating about money, just as always; no self-control; pretentious fool; bluff, poser.

June 1st, 1927. I have a mental struggle. I must stop being a hypocrite, as all people are, and a bluff. No more of that. Certainly I can stand up and tell the truth. I can and will and no more cowardice.... It is a weakness, a romantic weakness of mine that I want sympathy, admiration, passionate affection. A lot of nonsense and I can easy get over it.

June 4th. No more procrastinating. It is cowardice and so is irritation and bad blood, for it means one is so timid, cowardly as to let others thwart us. Don't allow this. Always do what you will, and be full of good-nature and affection. Yes.

My inner conflict seemed to be how to reconcile kindness and amiability with blunt truth-telling and heroics in general; between wanting to be a tender, graceful, unfathomably kind lady, and a jolly athlete and soldier.

June 30th. I discover that my flaw is that impulse to please, to charm and seduce with gentle kindness. There is something wrong in this, timid and placatory, for I am always ashamed of it. It is a way of suing for admiration and approval and popularity. Should never never do that. To be kind because you feel so is all right, but not to charm people. More robust I must be.

July 1st, 1927. I am all rage and annoyance today. Temper is an externalization of one's own shortcomings. One is a coward, sloth, and searches for someone else to blame and lay low with a righteous slug or uppercut.

July 12th. I walk and in my meditations realize my real interest has not been on work and money but on other things, such as the secret of absolute personal courage and truth. And yet the basis of all, ass that I am, is self-respect, and behind that is wresting a livelihood out of the world. And a good one. The disgrace of poverty and protection. When that exists how can I be this bold arrogant one that I aspire to be? And so now all my consummate guts goes into work, production. . . .

I should write at least two stories and make at least 1400 a month. Tomola says she can make 800 a week. Tells how when she made only 50 a week she suddenly thought, "I can make a hundred. Why not?" And did. And thereafter was always pushing it up.

November 30th, 1927. I work and walk in slanting cold drizzle. The gulls so beautiful and wild and they chose the wild, cold side of the point. There is nothing like walking alone in the wind for hours, and in the sun and air to give one equanimity, to make one jolly, spirited, hopeful and merry. It seems to make one again a fine animal; for my belief is that our guts, hearts, instincts—these are by nature free and good-natured, and full of Will, the Whatever-it-is that makes us struggle for a more abundant life, to surpass ourselves. It is our brains, intellects, that are queasy, nervous, jealous, malevolent, anxious, timid, pussy-footing, afraid of being grieved, hurt, overlooked, rebuffed. But when my heart is strong and untrammeled, then I am a god and a genius. Dionysus looks out of my eyes.

December 3rd, 1927. I walk in the high wind. A cold agate sea with jagged parallel white caps and I am at a loss. Passionate impersonalness. Perhaps that is the thing.

December 10th. Nietzsche. I fill myself with courage. I wish I could achieve perfect courage. Also achieve indifference to approbation. Yes. That is the secret of true strength.

Never crave, need, or work for approval. Never shrink

from criticism, dislike, hatred. Never, never put best foot forward. All is within, the source of all. All kindness, love is within. Never try to draw it from without. We should be *self*-improving only. The sad mistake of most is trying to improve *others* and one's surroundings—angry and vexed that they are not right. All is within.

Read Ibsen's "Brand." Must always be reading some great man, for just a sentence is a reminder of what puling pygmies we are. Low stature, etc.

I tell Tomola of my Dionysus theory, of the young god in me which is in the body, the instincts, and not in the Mind. The body developed as a device to *warn* of danger, the querulous, doubting, finicking pussyfooting mind, so crafty, so slavishly diplomatic and calculating.

Tomola says my kindness is nothing to stamp out though, but the God in me.

But my weakness (I thought it was my kindness and amiability) kept slipping out of bounds and I could not manage it at all, and keep it under. And then, in this rhythm, I would decide that it was goodness that was the key to life. "Because pugnacity and contempt make one gloomy and suspicious, and all encounters become hard and to be dreaded, instead of easy and welcome. Yes. For if one is truly full of good will, then one is free."

December 30th, 1927. Saw the beauteous and dazzling A....
That poor girl is mean, mean, and hates all and sundry....
The Blurr girls nice, but have language that embarrasses me: "chortle "
...But I am irritable. This comes from running people down. Too much clever critical analysis. Very bad to fill up your mind with this. To see through, comprehend peoples' manoeuvres, jealousies, etc., is all right, but do not pass judgment....I should have no editorial opinions (judging people). It is emotional and egotistical, not remote and intelligent and full of good will....This is not repentance, but I must be reborn.

And so gradually, I began to think that kindness, goodness, was perhaps all right.

Of course you must remember always that I may sound, in these diary excerpts, far too interesting and noble. Bear in mind that I was also often a cross, over-fed, commonplace, uninteresting-looking kind of a person.

But although I tried so hard to discipline myself, I never disciplined Gaby. Thank heaven for that. My motto for child-raising was: "Always be careful never to cross a child." And I never did. And from the very first I always bowed low to her and respected her wishes and her differences from myself. I always tried to do this: to tell her what I *thought,* but never assume or feel that I was necessarily *right.* She might feel differently. If so, fine. Then she must defy me, tell me to go to thunder. Of course it made it easier that she was the only child and there was even no father in the family to compete for my attention. And because there were no other children I had none of that policing to do.

At Christmas and on her birthday, thinking of the time when I had been disappointed, I bought an avalanche of presents.

"Gaby," I wrote to Mother, when she was five, "got her turquoise-studded watch, and was delighted with it. Christmas was a tremendous success: a tiny umbrella, a raincoat, a coat, books, a scooter, a fire engine, a doll, a doll's bed, a drum, and all the usual five-hundred-dollars' worth of stuffed animals, bears, kangaroos, and foxes, some with glasses on. When she saw her presents she made a great fuss over me, saying how nice I was to give her such things. This is surprising. Having never been disappointed, it is strange she should feel such affectionate gratitude. Why didn't she just say, as spoiled children are supposed to: 'Well, why didn't you get me the suit of armor?'"

I was always in debt after Christmas, but I was glad of it, and still am—that I should be so foolish, and I hope I continue to be so, only more so.

Once for a short time I had a tall, refined, splendidly edu-
cated French woman to take care of Gaby, a governess. But I
could not get rid of her quick enough. And I tremble with
indignation to think of it now, for she believed in "discipline," the usual firm, flute-voiced, relentless will-breaking
that is practiced all over the world by the most enlightened
people. With splendid firmness she forced Gaby to eat fish,
so that she threw up and cannot eat it ever since. When four-
year-old Gaby took a gum drop from a puppy and ate it, and
denied it, though the Mademoiselle distinctly saw it in her
mouth—well, when I came home at night the Mademoiselle
told me gravely how Gaby had "lied" to her, and what sort
of a serious treatment we should use to deal with that sort of
thing. But I cannot write about it without feeling within
me the running fire of a berserk right now. Yes, I would
throw all such people in the ocean. No, let them live. But let
them never come near any child in the whole world, every one
of whom must be free and a friend and an equal.

And I have always thought that there is nothing in the
world as bad as scolding. When you come to think of it, it
is the thing that we, as adults, most dread. I am not much
afraid of physical pain. But to be scolded, to exchange harsh
words, makes my flesh creep with fright and dreadful excitement. It seems so much more cruel than blows. Scolding
means there is a temporary spiritual state of dislike. And
dislike is so much worse than good-natured physical fighting.
So I thought that children should never be spoken to sharply.
And never expected to mind quickly. *We* are never expected
to mind quickly. If anyone orders *us* like that, we are apt to
murder them (if we are any good). I tried always to use
only good-natured force. If Gaby was too slow in going to
bed, I would at last carry her up and if she kicked and
screamed I remained as amiable and jokey as could be,
and would say: "I bet you can't cry five minutes more. If you
can I'll give you a cookie."

And if my violent temper came, as it does about once in six months, when I feel strong enough to pick up the piano and dash it on the floor, I would try to explain it to her, at intervals, throwing a child's rocking chair at a mirror and with frightful swearing. "Don't be scared, darling. This is just my temper. I don't mean it."

Yes, I know that parents who discipline (so-called) their children make them dull, break their spirits, extinguish their ideas, initiative, and creative energy, and are just getting them ready to be afraid of all the employers and bullies and mean husbands and wives of the future.

And I felt that a child of two even is wonderfully intelligent and always understands things clearly, if you express them well enough. Their understanding is as good as ours, perhaps better, but it is just that they have not the vocabulary or experience.

It was like this. On Christmas Day we were going to Carl Taylor's house in the country, at Westport. I had that maternal uneasiness that comes because a small child is not polite to strangers. That is, strangers beam and offer hands and ask questions and the child stares back with no response, a cold fishy look. There is the impulse to say: "Now what do you say, dear? Now say 'thank you,' dear, to Mrs. Q." But I never could. The words rose in my mouth and I could not let them out. Because it was humiliating for the child, perfunctory and forced if she *did* smile, embarrassing for the company. And embarrassing for Mama, who wants all to feel happy and at ease.

As we drove up to Carl Taylor's I talked to Gaby about this. She was four.

"You know there will be lots of people up there, Anne and Ken and others, and they will all be so glad to see you. But look, darling. This is something I want to talk to you about. You know grown-ups always feel fond of children and interested in them and make exclamations and smiles and ask questions. But children are apt to feel bashful. And this is what they do: they just look back like this." I then acted it out. "Here Elsie Arden will say, 'Hello, Gaby, blessèd baby, well, how *is* you, sweetness?' and she will smile and you will just do this": (I looked up at an imaginary Elsie, unsmiling and coldly.) "But I will tell you: if you possibly can, smile back and speak to them pleasantly. Or anyway, just smile. Because, you see, when you don't, it makes them feel you don't like them. And that hurts their feelings."

She listened to all this thoughtfully, and suggested some thoughts on the subject which I cannot recall, but I could see it had cleared up for her the whole reason for all politeness. When she got up to the Taylors', all pressed around. She smiled at everyone in the kindest, brightest way. She answered all questions sympathetically. She has had tenderhearted and good manners ever since.

4.

Fridtjof Nansen.

NOW I COME TO A LOVE STORY. IN 1928 MY FATHER WENT TO Norway and wanted me to go; but I was too anxious about making a living. He wanted to take care of all that, but there was my old complex about not being an expense, a nuisance. Besides, free-lancing is not like a salaried job. The work you do this month may not be paid for, for six months or two years, or ever. So I was dogged by conscientiousness. And all the time living expenses, rent and so on, went right on ticking off hundreds of dollars, like a kind of relentless gas meter.

So I would not go. But I saw Father off on the boat and felt sorry about it, and sorrier later, because on this boat he got to know well Fridtjof Nansen, the Arctic explorer. He was the great man of Norway. As well as an explorer, he was a famous scientist, a zoologist and oceanographer; he had been ambassador to London during the critical period of disunion from Sweden in 1905; and as the representative of Norway to the League of Nations, it was he who had repatriated millions of prisoners of war.

That winter Nansen came to this country. I read it in the newspaper. He was planning, it said, to go with Eckener in the Graf Zeppelin across the North Pole, and he had come to make arrangements with the United States Government, for mooring masts in Alaska.

I wrote him a note and asked for an interview. I did not really want the interview so much as to see him and talk to him. This was my hero-worship. I felt that he was really great. If I could just get near and see him and hear him talk a little. In answer, he wrote me that he must go west but after that, when he returned to New York in March, he would surely see me.

And then it turned out that in Minneapolis, where he had to go of course, because there were so many Norwegians there, he stayed at our house. Julie wrote and described him to me, and this is what she said: He was sixty-seven years old (I later found that he was born on the same day as my mother), a tall man with the most beautiful physique, a broad chest and lifted head, who was reluctant to sit down and stood up lightly, dwarfing everybody, and moved around like a quick young man. He arrived in Minneapolis the day after a blizzard, and this—the bright snow with the sun on it and the sub-zero cold—delighted him, and Julie said that he could not stay in the house, though many people were pressing to see him, but kept going out to the kitchen and on the back porch to breathe the snow and the air. And finding some old skis in the barn, old-fashioned child's skis without harness, he went hastening over the surface of Lake Calhoun without an overcoat and in his broad-brimmed black hat, followed by five floundering little boys.

In March he was in New York again. He wrote me a note that he would see me. He was staying at Mr. Henry Goddard Leach's house in the East Seventies, he said, and that I should come there.

The moment I saw him I thought: "Yes. He looks just as he should." He had bright color, a big nose, a wide white mustache slanting down like a viking's, a bald forehead and skull and under his perplexed, intent, slightly scowling brows, there were level searching blue eyes, full of passionate intelligence and search, and a kind of anxiety-of-life and sadness in them. But the chief thing about his eyes was this striving search, this questioning, questioning.

Now my father also was in New York just then, at Anne's house, and so at once I said to Nansen: Would he not like to go over there? My sister was so nice, etc.

"First," he said, "let's have the interview."

We sat facing each other by the window and he told me about the proposed trip in the airship across the Pole: the purpose of it, to make oceanographical discoveries about wind currents and ocean currents and zoological things. And he told why the trip was not a difficult nor a dangerous one, how there was little wind at the Pole, and so on.

I listened with interest, though knowing that I would probably never write it, except in my diary. I said that I would like to see him again. Yes, he said, he would let me know, as soon as he got back from seeing President Hoover in Washington.

And a week later he telephoned me; the Leaches, he said, invited me to tea. When I went in town to their house Anne and Father and others were there. I did not talk to Nansen, except that he said, just as I was leaving: "How did you get along with your interview?"

"Oh, fine," I said. I invited him politely to the country to

see me, if he could find time; he could see the water there
and hear the buoys; my father would be there in Stamford
for a day or two. And in the next few days he telephoned me
once or twice to Stamford, and his voice sounded placatory
and gentle, almost anxious and tender; a "please-like-me"
kind of voice. Would I come to town and have dinner with
him perhaps?

And here is my diary.

Then I go to see Nansen. I dread this, think it may be hard
work conversationally; am tired and stuffy from having too many
clothes on. Work up my will-to-endure-pain as hard as I can, in
preparation. To my amazement, when he comes in the room, he
grabs my hands with such cordiality, holding them, talks to me.
And so it is on the train (We went out to Stamford for dinner).
He keeps talking, so rapidly and eagerly, intermittently pressing
my hand and in a confiding friendly way, smoothing the fabric
of my coat over my knee, just the way I would if talking eagerly
to someone I am fond of, like Julie or Gertrude or Henrietta.

Says he had a strange feeling about me—because of my first
letter to him. He felt he must see me. Why should that be? he
doesn't know. Perhaps because I said I had a sister, who was very
nice, and that sentence proved that I was. He said that at the first
interview, when he put off going to the Taylors' house, where
Father was, that he was pretending he wanted to give me an interview so as to be alone with me. Very, very strange. I have
mixed feelings. I don't know whether it is that he is a man with
a great deal of temperament for women, or whether it is myself
personally. He tells me about his boy who died of brain tubercu-
losis and who said, "I have such extraordinarily interesting
thoughts"; and then he would tell his father that now he must
leave the room, because he was going to have one of his seizures,
and they were terribly painful. Nansen says he has never spoken
of that to anyone. And he tells how one day he came downstairs
and this child was crying. A governess had punished him for eating some grapes that his father said he could have. Nansen com-
ments on how children are not allowed to defend themselves. And
he says, with a wince of feeling, how he has always wished this
had never happened, how he should have turned out this disagreeable woman.

It is so queer. We talk like girls together. I speak and he listens so eagerly. "Yes, yes . . . Do you think so?"

My diary ends here. But these are some of the things he told me:

He had been a very vigorous wild strong boy, a skater and a skier, a sailor and a huntsman. His father wanted him to go into the army or navy, but this did not satisfy his intellectual cravings. Yet he could not bear city life, indoor life. (People in cities, he said with abhorrence, were like bugs running from box to box.) He decided to become a zoologist, for that would permit all kinds of exploring in the mountains and northern rims of Norway, and at sea too.

When he was twenty-two he crossed Greenland, which had never been done before. He decided that all the failures of the past were due to this: they tried to cross from west to east, so that they could always retreat to their base. But he would try it from east to west. With no line of retreat, they would have to go on. And this was one of the great principles of his life. "Burn your boats and demolish your bridges behind you. Then one loses no time in looking behind, when there is quite enough to do in looking ahead; then there is no chance for you or your men but *forward*. You have to do or die."

A few years later when he was thirty, he went on his Arctic expedition in the *Fram* (it means "forward"). Nansen had found, in his zoological studies and by other evidence, that there was a continuous drift of ice across the North Pole. In this ship, built to stand great ice pressure, they pushed as far north as possible, became frozen in for three years, so that they would very slowly be carried by the ice, and drift across regions very near to the Pole. At the nearest point, Nansen and one other man, Johansen, left the *Fram* with dogs and guns, and struggled toward the Pole on foot. They got to a point about a hundred and twenty-five miles from it. Then the Arctic winter caught them, and instead of the three months they were provisioned for, they had to live through fifteen months before they got out. Their dogs were eaten. They shot bear and walrus and for ten months tasted no other food.

But this adventure and escape were not just a happenstance. It was thought out with Nansen's extraordinary foresight so that they came through it all right.

"You may think it was hard," he has written in a little book called "Adventure," a rectorial address at St. Andrew's University, "but I assure you it was a happy time, for we had the spring and the homecoming to look forward to. In these plans I had most of the competent authorities of the world against me. However, I had the advantage of living a great deal alone in my life and had thus acquired the habit of making up my mind without asking the opinions of others. Not that every man who stands alone is strong. For a strong man there is a great danger in obstinacy and foolhardiness. It takes a superior man to allow himself to be convinced."

Well, I find myself so anxious to tell what a remarkable man Nansen was, but all this you can read. You want to know what he said to me.

He talked about Ibsen. He could recite whole pages of "Brand" by heart and in English. He told about his children, his wife who had died. He talked about my grandfather, Ole Gabriel Ueland. He described his house in Oslo and the tower that he worked in. He told how he had become surly and lonely after his wife's death. He told about his work in the League of Nations, repatriating prisoners of war and how it was exhausting and he would like to give it up, but he could not be supplanted, for governments and prime ministers would not act for a lesser man. He admired me for not smoking or drinking. He said that the reduced food rations in Europe during the war, had been hard on the children, but had improved adult health.

Gaby, who was ready for bed, appeared at the top of the stairs to say that she would like to be told a story. He went upstairs at once. He told her about the time in the Arctic that the kayak with guns and supplies in it had slipped off the ice ledge and was being blown lightly out to sea. He had to take off his clothes and swim for it, in that freezing water. It was the only thing to do. He had to go very fast too, and Johansen stood on shore and looked on in agony. Nansen caught the boat, but the hardest thing of all was to get in it, because he was so frozen and weak. Gaby liked the story. But she thought they should not have shot walrus or bears. That made her indignant.

The next day, when he was gone, I had the strangest experience. I felt the usual mild relief one has when a guest is gone. "Now that's over," with a mental dusting of my hands. The house was quiet and the sun was shining, and I could work again.

At one o'clock I went for my usual walk, far around to the other side of the Point, and before turning back I sat for a moment on the yellow sand in the sun. As suddenly as if I had been hit with a bludgeon I seemed to be in love with Nansen.

This is my diary, a few days later.

Friday, April 5th, 1929.

I go to town, arrive 4:40, and go to the Leaches'. Nansen there, but his son and daughter-in-law cannot come. We go to dinner. I am alternately all admiration and misgivings. A Norwegian accent always seems so gentle, almost womanish, so harmless, when he looks like a Northman on a ship about to kill a thousand Saxons. He should have a helmet with two tall wings on it. But then his sudden smile, softness and gentleness, is attractive and warms one towards him. He speaks of women who paint (they are all about us in the restaurant); speaks conventionally about this. I argue the point. I say it is all right to try to be handsome, though I don't like to try to be alluring, soft. But I try to be handsome with all my might. He laughs and says "It can't be hard." He also says "how dark your eyes are," and I do not explain how much I prefer light eyes.

Then we go back to the Leaches'. He tells me how when he returned from Washington he went straight to Anne's house, made a fuss about missing Father, but how it was myself he wanted to see. But, he said, from Anne he finds out all about me. Says how he pressed my hand, and how I returned it too, just once, very faintly. I cannot quite remember this.

He says I must have his pictures. And he gives me his books, a few of them in paper covers, and he sits down to the desk to write in them and I have misgivings. Am I in love with him? No, it seems so queer, so mysterious, too unfamiliar. . . . But when I look at some rolled papers on his desk, he says I may look at them if I like, and they are his drawings. And I think how modest he is about these, and I am overcome at their excellence and wonder that his very large thick hands have done them. And then I have the strongest feelings that he is a great great man and a viking and sincere and tender and strong and full of self-understanding and self-criticism and full of appreciation and delicacy and will and mightiness and nobility.

Earlier in the evening he said he needs someone to talk to, and speaks of "Faust" (cannot remember what he said) and I speak against marriage. But he says one cannot be alone; there is always a feeling of incompleteness in a man. We speak then of children, or morality. He listens to me with respect.

I take the eleven-thirty train to Stamford. He comes down there with me. (He was leaving for Norway the next day.) And when he says good-by to me and kisses my hand, I shall never forget his face and I know that he loves me, for there is the terrible look of the sense-of-eternity, or the sense-of-death in it. In the cab on the way to the train, he spoke one sentence of great sadness. "I wonder if I will ever again. . . ."

For a year we wrote to each other every week, until his death. We had a plan that when he came the next spring to go in the airship across the Pole, I would go with him. He would arrange it.

I was so much in love with him that it was hard to keep from writing to him all the time. I could easily spend five rapt, vanishing hours on a single letter. And a letter from him was the light of my days, and I have never in my life felt just this way at any time. The most disconnected things would sing through me like music, just looking out on a spring morning, toward the Sound, toward the poplar tree and the tangled ragged meadow of gorse. The words: "Whose name is writ in water" went across my mind, and such a strange and unconnected thought like that, but it struck me and sang through me and made gold harp wires of me. Those words and something vague about Keats would make tears of inexplicable rapture come into my eyes.

Of course when I think of my letters to him, I have my usual dislike for myself of yesterday, because they were so planned, so composed. I wrote them over and over, as though they were poems. That wish to be effective—I am always so afraid there is an insincerity in it. Yet I did love him unutterably and there has never been anything like it.

And all the time, you understand, it was a sort of dream love affair, a literary one. We never really believed we would see each other. And yet I know my letters were comforting and exciting to him. I can tell that from his. And I am so glad they were.

April 25th, 1929.

You cannot possibly understand what your letter means to me, it is as if a flood of strength suffuses my whole body and soul, and I feel that you are near. How very sweet of you to write so soon. I needed it badly, as I felt lonely. And what a letter! Just you, as I was sure you must be. . . . There is not a corner of my heart or soul which I do not wish you to look into—not because I think that there may not be so much which is ungraceful or offensive, but simply because it is all parts of my own self, and you have to know it. I have a feeling that I could talk to you about everything, as I have *never* before, and you would always understand.

. . . But you know nothing about me! It is equally strange that when I got your first letter, I already felt an inexplicable attraction towards you, and had a vague anticipation that I would like

you very much, and that perhaps you would like me too. And after
I had heard your father speak about you I was decided that I had
to meet you, and that we would understand each other, and had
much in common. . . . And I had that letter with me and your
second one too, on my journey west. And I read it again and re-
gretted more and more, that I had not made a special effort and
gone out of my way to meet you, already during those first few
days I had in New York. But anyhow, what a great thing it was
that we met at last. But distinctly I remember you the first time,
in that blue tight coat that suited you so well, trimmed with fur
. . . .

But we ought to be thankful for what we had, and I am, more
than I can say. Yes and how good and dear you are and how
beautiful. Though I miss you every moment, still how rich I
am. You see recollection is the only Paradise from which we cannot be turned out. . . .

How really absurd it is, so short is life, and still we cannot arrange it and these few flying years as we know would be great
and wonderful. . . . Your letter—I never received any letter like
it, never experienced such a revelation of personality that I could
give myself to without reserve.

From my diary I find this is what I wrote to him in one
letter:

May 16th, 1929. I wrote about the following to Nansen:
  1. About being in the public library and reading about him
  and feeling inferior to him.
  2. His letter changes me from an egotist to an altruist.
  3. About my asceticism, and how I never know whether to
  be a good-natured Negro or a stern Spartan.
  4. About my Faith: everything will come out all right.
  5. How people's shame causes others to be scandalized. For
  example, Lord Byron; so wicked yet not ashamed and the
  world admires him.
  6. How if we could only be together (*fused*) as he says,
  then I could have his blue eyes, legs, his nose, his brow like
  the infant Hercules, his skull like Socrates. He could have
  my black hair and brown skin.
  7. How people who loved each other, the bond might be so
  strong that, paradoxically, there would be freedom. "In loving bondage, free," said Nietzsche. Like that.

May 20th, 1929.

Dear Brenda,

I am in Berlin, tomorrow back in Norway. It is Whitsuntide, it is spring, it is sunshine, flowers, green beeches, glittering water, and there is a lady, very pretty, charming, we are good friends, and life ought to be smiling, but—it makes me feel still more lonely—why am I not with you? where are you, with whom are you, what are you doing? I long for you more than ever. I am leaving with the train tonight, will there be a letter from you when I get home? I hope it will be, I need it badly. But I feel happy nevertheless, I know that you think of me, that you love me—

Do you think I am silly to write such stupid letters? I wonder. I am continually in such a strange mood and cannot sit down quietly and collect my thoughts. I miss you perhaps too much. There is so much I want to tell you; but I cannot write it down on paper, then it seems banal and not very important. . . .

What have I accomplished on this journey? Very little. The accident with the Zeppelin in France is not good for our expedition. . . . And the refugee work for the Russian prisoners. Well, I have to continue with it, though without any wish or interest, simply a dull feeling of duty because I cannot be replaced. But it seems all of it is so very indifferent, both that, and expedition and the rest. What do I really wish for? Life seems so meaningless; we are marionets moved by something else, and still they want to go on forever. Why do I write when I am in such a depressed mood? It cannot be very cheering for you. But I miss you so badly.

Lysaker, 22nd May, 1929.

Darling Brenda, what happiness! your dear letter of April 27th was there when I came last night. New life, new vigor, new vitality. What wonderful witchcraft do you possess? . . . and the spring is there, more beautiful in Norway than anywhere on Earth. Here from my window in my tower I see the maidenly birches in their bridal veils against the dark pine wood; there is nothing like the birch in the spring. I do not exactly know why, but it is like you, to me you have the same maidenliness—and the sun is laughing, and the fjord out there is glittering and existence is beauty!

. . . And you wish to go with me on the North Pole expedition. Oh yes, I feel like you. And if we never came back, what would it matter. I wish we could remain there. . . .

What you say about your asceticism seems to show that you have it very much in the same way as I have often had it in my life, and the resemblance is really striking in some points, when you speak about the training of your body, sleep, etc. You have obviously a strong violent nature. . . . You could never be slave to any vice, if you think there is any danger or too much of a thing, you can stop, and so can I. But please be a little careful not to overdo things. You can overstrain your body and your brain, you know, and then it may take a long time to build it up again. I speak from sad experience. Be especially careful about sleep. . . . You ought certainly to have eight hours sound sleep, it makes you feel healthier and happier and you work much better, and are not too overtaxed and strained, which perhaps is a danger of American life. . . .

But my dear Brenda, I cannot tell you how deeply moved I am by all you say about my letters, and how much you like them. . . . I am sure you cannot like mine better than I like yours. Every one of yours simply works miracles, I feel another being when I read them, and then when I have finished them, a few hours have gone, I long for the next one, while I rehearse all you have said in the last one.

. . . You say that you know nothing about my life, but you "know how much temperament and passion I have and you can tell that I like women very much." Well I think I have already told you something about my feelings, but I wish to tell you everything, as I cannot bear the idea that you do not know every part of me. That I have temperament and passion is right I hope, at least some. That I like women very much may also be true, but it depends on how you understand it. I think a man really needs a woman to be complete, and the fact is that I have never had a male friend with whom I could speak much about myself, my feelings, my innermost self, etc., and to whom I could confide my most intimate emotions, but that I only could to a woman I really cared for, but I have met with very few such women in my life. The fact is that most of my time I have lived alone, ever from my youth a lonely man. And now, when I am here in my home, I never go out to parties or to friends, refuse all invitations (except to my daughter and son-in-law when they have no parties) and I live in my work, live really the life of a hermit, take just a short walk in the wood before dinner, or I may take a walk to the post office, about a mile, to mail a letter to you. There you have my life, it is not very exciting, but you have suddenly thrown a new fire into it.

July 7th, Evening.

I have a letter from Henry Leach, about my article "My Faith" for the Forum. He likes it and says it is just what they want. It reminds him, he says, "of the voice out of the whirlwind in the Book of Job. It is charged with starlight and woman's eyes." What woman's eyes, I wonder? there can only be one, do you know her? But he does not. The plan now, he says, is to publish my paper second in the series, Bertrand Russell in September and mine in October.

Then he writes in pencil, on March 7th, 1930. It was my last letter from him.

Dear Brenda, I am more sorry than I can say; I am tied to my bed and cannot write to you. I have quite unexpectedly and without any reason I know of, got an attack of phlebitis in one leg, which is badly swollen and have had to be in bed without moving. The doctor says it is all right if only I do not move. How long I shall have to lie here, I do not know, but it may take some weeks yet. I cannot write to you here, but will write as soon as I get up again. I am so troubled about it; as you cannot understand of course, why I do not write; but you will understand now, when you get this.

A thousand greetings. I wish you would be here, my dear dear girl. Your viking and your boy,

Fridtjof.

On May 13th, 1930, he died. The *New York Times* said that when Norway had separated from Sweden in 1905, they asked him to be king, but he would not. The English *Atheneum* said that he was "the greatest European" because he was a great scientist, a great explorer, a statesman and a humanitarian. He had also been skating and skiing champion of Norway as a young man, and was never beaten in either.

As for me, I have thought of him every day since then. He thought that we were extinct after death. I childishly think I shall see him again.

VII. HOME AGAIN

1.

The Depression drives me into retreat. My golden Julie with her wonderful frivolity. My work dwindles; financial help takes all the gumption out of me. More Minneapolis talk.

IN 1929 THERE WAS THE DEPRESSION. IT CAME ONE DAY IN October. The stock market went suddenly down. But I thought little about it, because I had no investments, and then as now, I was always putting off the time when I will have to understand a financial page. "Collateral," I think, "it's all collateral to me." Because when I took Economics B this was one of those mind-curling words I could not understand. Or rather I did not want to.

But just to show you the surprising prosperity of that time, which we all accepted as solid and everlasting. A dazzling red-haired girl I knew, with eyes like gray lamps and a gift for fashion, was making thirty-five thousand dollars a year, as a "stylist" for a Fifth Avenue department store, and for part-time work in an advertising company.

And because writing seemed an effortful way of making money, for a time I worked for Tomola. She sat in her sunshot yellow room and orders were telephoned in from magazines and department stores, for pages of fashion drawings, for newspaper advertisements, for store catalogues. Sometimes two hundred dollars was paid for a page.

Tomola said that if I helped her (she thought I drew fairly well, had a delicate line) and drew in the backgrounds and drew the diamonds in the wristwatches, we could make lots of money. And we did: about three thousand dollars a month. I gave it up presently though, because Mr. Costain of *The Saturday Evening Post* asked for more articles.

But by the spring of 1930, I began, mysteriously, to have trouble selling articles, even those that were ordered. At first I thought with fright that my own powers were failing. (It was curious how the seriousness of the depression did not get into our heads.) But it was just that the magazines were shrinking in size. There were not all those fat advertisements in the back.

I wrote three articles that spring, all besought, and none of them accepted. That meant three months' work was useless and about twenty-four hundred dollars was not earned. The first was the memoirs of a Moody and Sankey revivalist. *The Saturday Evening Post* said there was too much religion in it. "Of course I could have forced it down their necks," I wrote to Ray Gauger, "but did not, in my pride." (This was boasting. About money, I have never been able to show the faintest hint of combativeness.)

It was people like Ray Gauger, and Francesca, who had turned up again and was teaching violin in New York, who began to be comforting, because in depressed times, it is these fearless, smiling, poor people that we turn to—those of us who thought we wanted to be high-pressure financial bullies. They did not care about money and never earned more than barely enough. Ray Gauger was a smiling young man with a wide gallant mustache like a musketeer, and a wide smile underneath it. He never stood straight but relaxed on one hip and talked in the softest, most free, beautiful voice, like a colored man. He taught in a boy's school and made his savings do such remarkable things for him. He went around the world, playing all kinds of musical instruments, to get from one place to another. He even played a drum in a Chinese band. He bought a few rocky acres in Connecticut and built a house on it himself, and there he could live in the greatest happiness for fifteen dollars a month, and had much better food than we had, because he grew it in his garden and knew how to cook it better than any French woman. And he looked at the stars, and listened to the frogs, and worked outdoors, and wrote a symphony. And the queer thing was he could always give money to once-prosperous people, or support them for weeks at a time at his place, and send his sister to Columbia for a Ph.D. The thought of his happy philosophical Thoreau-like life was very comforting in times like this.

Then, under the fierce pressure exerted on myself by myself, I wrote two articles in two weeks. I did not hear if they were accepted for many days. Finally I telephoned to Mr. Costain, and he said they were buying them both.

I was on tenterhooks [I wrote to Ray] and too ladylike to insist on knowing what had happened. But it taught me a lesson: combativeness. That is the thing. Tomola tells me I must be harder —that good old advice.

Now my hair is all off, one inch all over the skull. I am sorry about it. Well, never mind. It will soon grow. But I am afraid I look like one of those cuff-shooting, sideways-handshaking women. Yes, I know what I look like: a ventriloquist's dummy. And suddenly shorn, I have a terrible cold.

My haircut has something to do with combativeness. Why is that? Contrariwise, rough he-men should improve themselves by wearing their hair fluffier. A chignon would tone them down just enough.

But I have some new clothes, a pink tweed coat and a blue suit. If only I could get my hair in ringlets again, I am going to dress cuter and more youthful. . . . I am learning pages of Hamlet.

April 7th.

Poor darling, it is too bad you have been sick. I am glad to hear your discovery about combativeness being the ticket. You, Cortez, would with your eagle eye. I have made no revolutionary moves, can't count any new continents. This light grippe has left no depression. "Like a bird in the wide air, has left no trace in the heaven of my face." How's that? Yes, Hamlet was a darling, a

poor darling like yourself, a butterfly caught in the rain.... I
send money today to Philadelphia for tap shoes....

I wish I could walk up and dump my talents on the table without quaking over personal feelings. You must teach me to do this.
It is hard to know whether I fear being disliked, or whether I am
afraid I don't know enough statistics. Ashamed not to be able to
answer all the questions. Wish for techniques I haven't any admiration for. Why should I want to stare down the ruffians or walk
across Carrie Kernochan's drawing room before the guests in a
kingly manner, no knees knocking?

God bless your editorial scars and make you Spartan.... Isn't
it great that I have a job this year? I will look after you at any
time. If you want to give Tomola a diamond bracelet I will pay
for it on installments. Must get a diamond bracelet for Avril too
... Perhaps I see things in false sunshine.

Little Boy Bluebird.

How is your raven hair? See you Friday night. I am always on
your side.

The only thing that made money anxiety painful was
having a child. Alone it would never have troubled me in the
least. And this is not reasonable or sensible at all, because I
do not believe in children being rich any more than anyone
else. But I had that foolish anguish about them. It was like
the Christmas presents; children must have opulence and
never one twinge of disappointment.

I remember a day I went to call for Gaby at school and it
was raining soddenly and steadily. She is so pleased to see
me and I can see she has great pride in me, shining in her
eyes, since the other children like me. On the way home she
asks me:

"Mama, do you feel rich yet?" and speaks of the manuscript that may have been lost in the mail. This makes me
feel badly. Oh, Lord, I can't have her anxious about me. I
immediately reassure her and say that soon I will be very rich,
never to worry about that. Gaby has such great admiration for
my prowess. One day I had walked ten miles and when we
had dinner together afterwards, I read Malory's *Morte*

d'Arthur to her, and she said sweetly: "Oh, Mama, if *you* had been there with all those knights of the Round Table, *you* would have been the one to take the sword out of the stone. I bet you would, Mama." When I felt so incompetent this talk seemed especially pathetic, and just squeezed my soul.

Yes, in all my anxieties, Gaby was poignantly involved. I could not pay much attention to her, because I had to work, and when I was not working, I had a long habit of anxious absent-mindedness about work. I was not nearly as much fun as I could have been. But she was a loving, much-thinking little girl. And such a beauty! so slim, so deft in her free run, and in all the footwork and her joyful balancing; a straight black mane piling around her perfect chin; her perfect nose, her perfect upper lip. An Italian contessa, I used to think.

We never talked about religion or such things, though whatever I was thinking I told her about that—if she cared to hear it. One night on the train going west, she asked me about praying and what it was. I explained what I knew about it. I gave a kind of Shavian explanation of it, I think.

"Well, let's pray," she said. "Let's do it tonight."

"All right. You do it first. You start," I said.

"God . . ." she began, writhing a little in concentrating, "make it rain or shine, whichever's the easiest."

That was so like Gaby. Such a considerate prayer. And perhaps God never got a better one. She was a Tolstoian and a Christian without being told about such things. One April afternoon we drove over to Croton-on-Hudson to see the Hodsons. This was Gertrude and William Hodson from Minneapolis. She was Henrietta's sister and he had worked with my mother in Minnesota for child labor legislation. They had a big white house in a green valley and three children, and they had such democratic, child-loving, work-respecting, middle western ideas.

April 5th, 1930. Oh, my, that wonderful Gertrude. Thinks she
is an intellectual stiff and is really prettier than Gilda Gray.
As soon as I see her everything is all right. We say how our
kids must go to coeducational schools. Then they'll make
honest, friendly, happy marriages; not like mine, broken
and confused.

Well, as Gaby and I drove over there, across the high back-
bone of Connecticut and into New York State, and went winding through the wilderness of Croton Dam, we talked about
punishment.

She said:

"If you or I saw a policeman chasing a man, we would help
the man get away, wouldn't we?"

"Yes, of course. Unless perhaps he had done something
very bad, hurt someone."

"Yes, but if the policeman caught him, and put him in
prison, that would make two bad things happen instead of
just one—two mean things in the world."

As it gets dark, she becomes sleepy and fixes herself a bed,
with my coat as a pillow, and she asks me to continue singing,
and gives my hand a gentle touch after an interval, that
touches my heart, and says:

"I just wanted you to know that I wasn't asleep." And I
think how in the afternoon she had leaned down and kissed
that old savage police dog that slept in the thicket, and that
had limped sadly away. And how I must do much, much for
her, fortify her against this world.

Yes, I was very anxious and low-spirited that spring and
summer.

But I am glad I had this experience, this fright and depression about money, because ever since then, I have felt so sorry
for men trying to support their families, and for poor people
who cannot. I, for example, was in no real danger at all. There
was always my father in the background. Yet, even so, when
I woke in the morning, a stone turned over in my chest of

depression and apprehension. It got to be so chronic that I would think "What is this weight?" because one felt slow and unsmiling from morning to night. "Oh, yes, it's the money situation."

And so I began to think of going home and living there. Father lived alone in our house on Lake Calhoun. He worked all day in his office, and at night sat alone in the large empty shell of a house, in his Morris chair, reading works on the Higher Criticism of the Bible.

He was lonely, I told myself (and I have one of those stabs of self-disgust as I write this, because I did not do half enough to dissipate that loneliness). Sigurd, Arnulf, and Rolf had all married and built pleasant houses in the pasture. I wanted to live near Julie and all of them. It would be fine for Gaby to have that life. Sandra and Jeanie, the twins, were just her age and her very favorites. There was the lake, a tennis court, dogs, cats, the Lake Harriet school, the huge Sunday dinners in Father's house, with everybody there.

There was Inga, who had worked for us for fifteen years and who was Norwegian and related to us, and looked something like my father and had his pride and energy. She still works in this house now, in 1938. She has a wide fresh face, a beautiful mouth and because of her figure and lopping coil of hair, looks like a Zorn drawing, and in her clear blue starched dress, she hurries upstairs and down, and through the house and out to the garden, always on the run in her heelless shoes, like a Bersaglieri, grabbing my clothes to wash them before I have worn them three hours.

At three o'clock when I have had a long walk and sit in our bright kitchen drinking milk, Inga comes up from the basement or down from the third floor to talk, to argue.

"Inga," I say, "in Björsen's poem about Ole Gabriel Ueland, he says in the last verse how the Valkyries carried him to Valhalla and there grandly led him toward the chief's high bench. And he says:

'There up rose many an old lord
And forward stepped to greet him;
And first of all King Sverre
With whom he was of kin.'

"That's what it says, Inga. So do you think we are descended from the kings of Norway?"

She wheels from the sink.

"Ya, that's true. Now that's true, Brenda. Don't laugh. Because it's true. Mr. Ueland had that kingy feeling, and Mrs. Taylor has it, and *I* have it!" she says fiercely, with a quick lift of the head and a scowl.

I know what she means. Father walked fast and wore his hat like a bravo. He had pleasant get-out-of-my-way truculence. And my sister Anne too. Very kingy indeed. But I think everybody should feel kingy. I think perhaps that is my life work, to make people see that they should all feel kingy.

But to go back to 1930. It was pleasant to think of living at home with Inga in the house, and also Tilly from North Dakota, also Norwegian and such a lovely person that when Gaby dreamed that I had died and half a dozen others in the family, it was all right, because Tilly adopted her.

I told myself that I could write much better at home.

Yes, I think I will come home [I wrote to Henrietta]. It occurs to me that I always think I must live in the East because it is so wonderful to meet all the fascinating types in New York. But what are the facts? Don't see anybody.

I have been carrying on a just-pals flirtation with an unhappily married man. (Don't tell anybody.) His wife leaves him half the year to go to Florida with her parents, and in twelve years, he says he has never kissed another girl and (from his inflection) "don't intend to." I like to tell him that when his wife comes back, I will telephone him and say in a strangling voice: "When are you coming over?" and how he will answer: "Well, I tell you, Jack, I don't believe we'll be able to fix up that carburetor, Jack, after all."

Well, we will come soon, Henny. What larks.

This book is depressing me more and more as I write it. My life stretches out as so foolish, useless, full of excuses and asininities and theories. And I will think now how that was a weakness and an excuse to come home, and the flirting disgusts me unspeakably. It is strange that to me the present and future are always so full of wisdom and brightness. "Good," I think. "I have learned that now. Why, I would not have missed knowing that for anything." As I sit here I feel so illuminated, intelligent, hopeful. As I look at my diaries, my letters, I think what an ass. Though once in a while I come upon a place where I seem to be tenderhearted, or honest, or good.

Well, we sent our soulful little spaniel in a crate by express. And Gaby and I came home to live in the white house and here we have been ever since.

My work slumped at once in the most surprising and interesting way. This was, of course, because now I had no rent to pay.

"The usual Minneapolis lassitude (mental) settled on me right away," I wrote to Anne. "I work on a story but find excuses to quit it after an hour and a half. I cannot explain it. Is it the removal of financial pressure? The presence of people on the tennis court? That wonderful Julie over in her pretty house? Or a regression to childhood? I don't know. Anyway, it begins to alarm me."

I went into what was so easy and pleasant for me—athletics and exercise. I would play for hours against the practice board on the tennis court, in silk underpants and a bared back, a white polo shirt tied around my neck and tucked in the belt. This was shocking then (although that a thing is shocking never really occurs to me for a long time, until I begin to hear in a roundabout way that people think it is so). But even then I don't care. Because I say to myself: "It is not I, but those people in corsets, dress shields, long stockings, garters and innumerable layers of homely clothes who are the foolish ones." Or when I am trotting along and a lady in a closed sedan car, with no air in her lungs, comes by suddenly and looks out at me in astonishment and I have a moment of sheepishness—I say to myself: "No, hanged if *she* isn't the foolish one."

Julie and I went downtown one day with our tanned bare legs and only socks on, and then, because it seemed to startle people so, we could not stand up against it, and got back into the car to hide them. This was only about seven years ago. Yes, I think we were true pioneers in this pleasant nakedness that has now made everybody prettier and healthier.

> July 10, 1930. I am a tiger woman again. Run 4000 steps. Feel like it, want to. Sweat. Milady should sweat. Work in the afternoon.
>
> Tennis. In footwork, it seems to me I learn that keeping one's feet close together, one's legs close, footsteps quick, a smaller base, means that one is quicker and regains balance more quickly with each new blow. I should practice this walking, running.
>
> I work a half hour on my story. Oh, heavens.

And then several days would pass and I could not work at all, or even think, and my diary would say: "The trouble with having so much muscular spring is that the imagination seems to be all dried up and it is also hard to sleep at night"; though it took me eight more years to become really convinced of this.

But there was wonderful fun in being home. And this is what it was like:

Gaby was immediately out of my anxious maternal consciousness. She was entirely happy. She had the lawns, the twins, the lake and the personalities that were in all the houses, maids and children and dogs and so on.

Julie's house was right across the driveway, beyond the grove of dark pines. This house was her own conception: a

French house, quite small but as dignified and graceful as if it were on a fine street in Paris and a consular flag were hanging out in front. There were slightly arched casement windows and an L-shaped angle that caught all the sun and looked across the common lawn to the lane, where the long parallel flower beds were that my mother had designed, and the barn with its sharp pinnacle on one gable, and then another long cathedral-dark grove of spruce trees against the western sky. The floor of this terrace she and I painted in big black and white checkers.

We sat in the sun here, taking off more and more clothes, even though it was painful for the postman, and Julie would gaze at the little espaliered apple tree against the house, and at a tiny weeping willow springing from the lawn, and a crab apple tree which had wondrous legendary red flowers on it for one week in the spring, and cried out about how utterly charming they were! smelling with such deep ecstatic breaths the smell of mowed lawn, or the lake, or of hyacinths, or Gothic lilies, or nicotiana—all those odors that came wandering on a soft breeze.

Julie's drawing room she had had painted green and there were yellow satin curtains at the French windows. It was so much fun there and so pretty that somebody, we heard, had said rather bitingly, that Julie Ueland seemed to think she had a regular salon. On Lake Street and Hennepin there was a beauty parlor above the ten-cent store, and the proprietor, to make sure that it was French enough, called it not just "Joe's Beauté Salon," but "Joe's Beauté Saloné." So that is what we called Julie's house: "Let's go over to the Beauté Saloné."

She would lie on her couch, her blond curls against the yellow satin curtains, her slippers on the floor, so charming, paintable, gay, and yell at you to "just *look* at that sunflower in that green vase!" or groan with a loud cry: "Oh, those velvet petunias! I just can't *stand* it, they're so adorable!"

She had the greatest gift for sociability that I have ever known. There were the same people always, members of the family, the Shearers, the Lewises, everybody who was familiar. "Oh, for some new faces! We've *got* to have a cocktail party and have at least *one* new face. We could ask Robert Pack, but would he come undisguised? If only there were somebody interesting in town like Mahatma Gandhi!" That was always her complaint, but even with the most familiar people in her house, it was so peculiarly exciting and entertaining.

This is how my day went:

In the morning I would wake up at eight. Tilly brought my breakfast. I read William James' "Variety of Religious Experience." Then after trying to work for a little while (I cannot remember now what I was writing) I would go over to Julie's at about eleven or half past. Julie at that time had had two or three heart attacks, and had to stay in bed in the morning. The danger was getting over tired. So I hastened over there (I could hardly wait) the moment it was time for her to wake up. We talked, talked and laughed in her bedroom, which had pink marble paper, and roses in the stiff curtains and blue glass bottles on her dressing table. She had diluted coffee, cups and cups of hot water which she drank, the cup resting on her chest, and some figs. Her curly blond hair was tangled over her eyes, and her voice, her laughter went shouting out. Intermittently long trains of children, the twins with their yellow-and-green striped hair, and Gaby and others and several low, small dogs, came weaving in and out, listening and climbing over and under the bed, until we presently gently eased them out again.

We talk about everything. I have been reading Dante and the Gospel of John ("Say, the Bible is pretty good. You ought to read it.") and Hugo's Preface to "Cromwell." "I want to be known as Brenda Harvard-Five-Foot-Shelf Ueland."

She has been reading Ernest Hemingway's "Farewell to

Arms," and says it is too staccato and one is not interested in the war part. The hero's feelings are so inexplicably blunt and simple. "All very fine and manly, but trying for the girl. Oh, these strong men! My idea of romance is someone who will come home and talk to you for fifteen minutes."

Then we talk about my love affairs, although there was no real love affair then, just some flattering nonsense. "You're my Daily Novelette," she says. We talk with the excitement with which most people usually argue, but we are always agreed. That is, whatever I say, she laughs and thinks it is fine and offers something on the other side; and then I cry out: "Yes. You bet," etc., etc. In the evening when Sigurd is there, reading Matthew Arnold or the "Life of John Marshall," and brushing his hair (we are all brushing our hair— good for the hair) once in a while he will look up to say: "Oh, Julie! What do you mean, that Brenda should flirt with Bobbie Blount? Just one damn fool encouraging another one." Or once in a while he would say: "Nix on the obstetrics." He probably was entertained though. Sigurd has a long, flexible upper lip, long and sober in repose. But we would watch his immobile face and at last, if he turned away and the faintest depression appeared in his cheek, it was a reward greater than a loud laugh from someone else.

And then Julie and I had much to say about health and our figures and complexions. (Too much, everybody else thought.) Was coffee bad? Yes, it makes people muddy. That lack-luster old vulture eye. (Look at Mrs. B. and Mrs. C. and Mrs. D., the stimulant people, compared to Mother Ueland, Julie said.) We read McCollum of Johns Hopkins on diet and the importance of dairy products and green vegetables, and Sir Arthur Keith, the physiologist, who said that because man did not chew, the muscles of his face and jaw were deteriorating. So we ate much too much salad, raw carrots, onions and garlic and chewed a very tough kind of spruce gum. (This was my idea.)

Then I would read her one of Ray Gauger's letters.

Suppose [Ray Gauger wrote] you were teaching addition and before you had added up ten lines of your four-place figures, some boy out of his head yelled the answer. What would you do? ...

Give my love to Gaby and Julie. Tell them they must get to tap dancing too. Spread your aesthetics, girls, with garlic, and nice chewing gum, that shines the teeth. Preach the gospel of raw cabbage. Which reminds me that I just sent my mother her grade card for 1931, giving her 98 for being a good mama but only 65 for tact.

I have kept her wide awake this year by raising hell with her, in a jovial way. It is my job to keep her swearing for her morning buckwheats. By making myself out a hellion, she is given a mission to perform. She rises in a thunder cloud and rumbles great warnings about sleazy underwear, economizing on rubbers, failure to put burial money aside, letting people impose on me, consorting with people who are not balanced, lending money to a cousin who will spend it on coca colas and sets a finer table than I'll ever have. "You'd better get in with Hamilton Fish, now that you have the chance." I work hard to keep up the mater's ire.

I had no news from you for so long, and I shall keep your letter out to be reminded of my starry Viking with her two feet on the ground and her thoughts in the stratosphere. I talked with you about many things and am never far from you in my thoughts. ... I would like to see Gaby and her beautiful mane and see what kinds of kids she drags home and the new airs and vocabulary. Maybe I will before long.... If you are in the East in the late summer, you must come up to Litchfield to see me. We will inaugurate a Hermaphroditic Council so that you can stay at my joint without explaining to the lady preacher who watches over all. Keep me in your bosom until we meet. You must write me this winter. What shall I do without you, darling Brenda. Lay down my head and cry.

And while we are talking there in Julie's bedroom, probably Ditty Shearer comes over, with her current dog (always a rather unattractive, beseeching mongrel female). Ditty is a limp, wonderfully pretty girl and funny and imaginative as so many limp people are. Alan had lost his job, and they have one small child, and she has been utterly dejected for weeks about washing dishes and their hopeless difficult time. "I have the Glandular Deficiency Blues," she says.

Julie had urged her to get a job, to go down to the *Minneapolis Star* and volunteer to work free for two weeks. "Talk to George Adams because it is so easy to break his heart. And you are so smart, Ditty, so extraordinary! so wonderful! so witty! something will certainly happen as a result of it. Really. Do it."

Ditty is very gloomy, dismal, (and as pretty as a shepherdess) at the prospect of going to work on the *Minneapolis Star* tomorrow. "They will probably on the first assignment send me over to the State Fair to report 'strides taken in Needlework' in the year 1930." She tells us how she got a permanent wave and how tomorrow she will be looking perfect, all dressed up. "But only for the first day." And how she bought some new shoes. "Yes, I went into a store without my keeper, my psychiatric attendant, and bought a pair of shoes and got a six, when I have always worn fives, all my life. And now I have to get up early, before dawn, to get them changed, even if I have to call up Mr. Makowitz tonight at his residence."

Later in the day, other people come to play tennis, and perhaps Henny and David and Addison and Dorothy Lewis stay for dinner. The Lewises have bought a house seventeen miles out in the country at Long Lake, and have four little girls. Dorothy is radiantly beautiful with a rose-petal face and eyes as clear as brown-topaz and she has prematurely white hair so that we think she looks like a Venetian marchesa of the eighteenth century.

We sit on Julie's lawn in the moonlight after dinner, and Dorothy begins to explain how the moon is frozen behind and sizzling hot in front. "You see, it is a million times as big as the earth." From there she goes on to say:

"Now why couldn't it be that we are just tiny parts of a huge body? Today I was watering the lawn and in a great gush of water, a hundred ants were carried away and I thought now why couldn't it be that a flood on the earth, was just some huge person watering the lawn."

From there she comes to reincarnation. "Yes, I think that must be so—that we were first ants and then pass into something better. Take for instance if you were a mongrel cur, you would have to pass into the wolf, but if you were a lovely high-class dog with a fine mind, you would probably pass into the horse without going through the wolf."

She says it rapidly and earnestly and then breaks down and laughs because we are all laughing so hard.

Then we go into Rolf's and Margaret's house, where Lewis and Hannah Daniel are. We get on the subject of Mind versus Medicine there. Hannah says she could so easily be a regular Yogi-pogi like her father, and could believe in ghosts, pixies, fairies, leprechauns, if she were not held down by Lewis, because he's a doctor. And I say, "Oh, don't let that groundling hold you back from it."

Rolf: "That pumpkin-kicker. That manure-heel."

Margaret is knitting sweaters for the children's bears, with glasses on, and she looks up when I begin on Plotinus and quote Christ, saying: "Do you know what that means?"

"Yes," they all cry, "do you?"

"Yes, I do."

Then Rolf says Plotinus was probably crazy, because he took a course about him at the University and Plotinus said, "One should fly from the Alone to the Alone." Margaret (she has taken post-graduate work in psychology) gets a skeptical psychiatrist look in her eye, as one who would say: "But the Eternal Righteousness is merely a subjective delusion of the psycho-neurotic personality."

"It's an instinctive . . ." she says.

"But what is an instinct?" I say excitedly, rebutting Margaret. "The psychologists don't know that either!"

"Yes, they make me sick!" Julie shouts. "What's behind the behind?"

Presently Julie begins planning a cocktail party. And it will be for me.

"Who will you have?" Rolf asks. "Just the usual White Trash?" By this he means the usual people—ourselves, the Shearers, Daniels and so on; or he sometimes calls them, the Linden Hills Back-Biters.

"No," says Julie in her clarion emphatic voice, "I am going to have..." and names her list. Then there is talk of what they will have to drink. It was during Prohibition and cocktails were of home-made gin, and people drank much more then at a party, than now. At least a cocktail party seemed quite different then (or perhaps it is I who have changed, though I never could drink much) because in no time you were stiff-lipped and anaesthetic to the frightful yelling and shut off from it, as if you had blinders on and could only see and hear your immediate vis-à-vis. "Ducking for olives in a tub of gin," David called it.

"What should we have to eat?"

"Poached calves' eyes on toast looking cross-eyed," Rolf says.

"Now Julie, you *can't drink*," Sigurd bursts out with cross emphasis, making himself heard. "And *you know it*."

"I won't," she says imploringly. "Lewis says I can have just one cocktail and one cigarette."

"*No!* Not *one!*" He is worried about her health, her getting tired.

"Oh, Sigurd pet. All right. But now, Sigurd, *promise* me to flirt. You've *got* to promise that you will drink and flirt, so people will have fun."

"I won't promise."

"Well, what will you be doing?"

"I suppose as usual, I'll be going around in the corners assessing the fire damage."

By that time it is midnight, and everybody is yawning and a little dull, and the Lewises say they must go home, when somebody (probably me) starts the talk on some phase of men versus women. Such as: how men are all emotionally arthritic because they extinguish all their emotions and natural poetry, and pin themselves down to logic, skepticism, and facts; and how they make such a virtue of it, but really it is self-murder. Or I will start up the old subject: why is it that women feel that life is dull just because they don't work in an office?

Immediately there is a roar of impassioned talk, argument and jokes.

Henny is getting serious and her blue eyes narrow with indignation and she talks in steady immovable sentences, seeing them through to the end. And finally David, dead silent most of the time, begins to speak. And everybody is silent because he speaks with a deliberate clearness and never wastes time and you cannot help listening. David says that he would like to make a graph of his married life, and through it would run "the line of brutality." Up to 1918, all would be above this line, but after that (solemnly and sadly) all below. Henny forgets her whole argument because she is always so entertained by him.

Then Addison will make some remark about how women do nothing really to earn their keep, not meaning it, though saying it almost with the emphasis of bad temper. Addison is a tall blond young man with glasses and very smooth hair, a low voice that is usually running along and making, half to himself, a string of almost inaudible jokes, and he has a way of turning his head very far around, to look at you. When he makes this statement about the uselessness of women Dorothy becomes tremendously exercised. "Why, how can you say that?" she cries, really angry. This talk of his always excites her and angers her and he lets it out for the sole purpose of stimulating her in this way. For Julie, Henny, Dorothy—all have a kind of chronic guilt about being useless, a burden, not earning money, not doing anything that is important or takes some courage and effort.

And in self-defense Dorothy speaks of the effort there is to run a house, the real work of it, and taking care of the children. She speaks of the Blands, who live near them in the country, in a twenty-eight room chateau. And Dorothy begins to argue that, doggone it, Mrs. Bland in her twenty-eight-room house has a hard time of it.

Julie and I argue back.

What nonsense! That is as irritating as when people say: "Think of that wonderful Mabel Brownlow with her twenty million dollars—she actually studied biology; think of it! went right to work at the University and studied it! How wonderful!"

And Sigurd says:

"I would like to make a speech giving Mrs. Bland a medal for her heroism:

" 'Mrs. Bland,' I would say, 'on this memorable occasion, I want to thank you for your remarkable courage, your heroism in managing your husband's twenty-eight-room house. You fearlessly, unflinchingly, have sent bills O.K.'d for payment to Mr. Bland's secretary.' "

Well, by that time it is one o'clock. The midsummer moon has set. We all go home.

2.

Francesca shows me something about music and God. Rolf and painting. Julie becomes sick.

IN SEPTEMBER I WENT BACK TO NEW YORK AND MOVED OUT OF my house in Stamford. And I got from *The Ladies' Home Journal* an assignment on "Why Marriage is Happy."

"And this is rather tough," I wrote to Julie, "as I do not feel in my heart that I am an authority. And it consists of a series of testimonials from imaginary husbands, telling how mean they have been to their wives. Spiritual meagerness is the main fault, lack of the power to make women expand, feel free and full of potentialities. And I have these husbands say that at last, thank God, they learned to be otherwise, and how their marriage is now nothing but a glorious white radiance with a gold-spiked nimbus over it. If it gets published, it ought to do a lot of good."

And in New York, this time, I see Francesca. I must tell about her, because she had such an effect on my life.

At Anne's house for dinner one evening, Francesca was there and the Hodsons and Torvald and Connie, his wife. (I have no time to tell about Connie, and "wife" is such an undescriptive word, and gives just the wrong impression. When I say "wife" I always see somebody rather pinched and anxious and strainedly smiling, who has used a curling iron on her hair, and is no longer pretty. Connie however is young, handsome, brown-eyed and has a wide happy smile full of affection.) "Tokie-pokes," Francesca called Torvald, as she did when he was eight, although he is huge now, and gracefully padding and lumbering around like a smiling intelligent bear.

At dinner we ask Francesca if she has any animals now. She always had an uncanny understanding of animals, a capacity to teach them that was extraordinary.

"No," she says. "I have only the macaw and the canaries, and the cats." And then after a pause. "We don't think we can take the chimpanzees." And it seems by the "chimpanzees" she means a mother and a father and a few young ones.

And somebody asks her teasingly:

"Francesca, what a shame you cannot have an elephant."

"Oh, an elephant," she cries with round bright eyes and perfectly seriously, "is very expensive! Why, an elephant costs a thousand dollars!" Then seeing that we are laughing at her, she laughs herself, in her characteristic way, until she wheezes. But then she adds with a radiant face: "But oh, elephants are so wonderful! Oh, you cannot know how wonderful they are!"

Well, a week before, Francesca, whom we had not seen for many years, had written Anne that she was coming to New York, and Anne was somewhat perplexed about it. "Of course," she said to me, much troubled, that day we were waiting for Francesca to arrive, "of course now Francesca will want Carlotta to take violin lessons. But I really don't see how she can. She has her piano lessons and school is quite difficult, and she is so insistent on her riding lessons. I will get Francesca pupils, of course, but I really don't see how Carlotta can take lessons. I will have to be firm. And Brenda, I just can't be going around the house in my stocking feet, doing Dalcroze."

We were in Anne's room on the second floor, and the maid opened the front door below, and someone was coming up the stairs. "Oh," we heard Francesca's voice crying out half-way up the stairs, before she was visible. "Oh, I have the most wonderful violin for Carlots! Only two hundred dollars! And it will do until she is twelve!"

Anne, as it turned out, never said one word about her doubts. Carlotta began lessons that day. Anne began working many hours at the piano herself. And she was doing Dalcroze in her stocking feet. And so were the Hodson children. And they were all playing day and night, Bach and Haydn, in ensemble. And it was a wonder to us, we would say, that Ken did not go out in a trance and sell his new microscope and buy a cello.

This letter that Anne wrote to me about a month later, describes what had happened:

I am in a manic state about Francesca and wonder when the great depression will set in. I feel so elated, hopeful, talented, handsome, healthy and good. Perfectly ridiculous really. I go to the library and take out volumes of music, am reading through all the Beethoven sonatas, all the Well-Tempered Clavichord. Thursday Francesca comes at lunch time and we play all afternoon, Haydn, Mozart, Handel, Brahms. When my eyes get so tired I cannot see the notes, any more, I walk off little rhythms. Of course I do it all very badly. But that doesn't seem to matter.

Francesca takes Carlotta (eight years old) and Punch Hodson (ten) to hear Kreisler. She sat on the stage close to him; the first time Carlotta has ever been to a theatre. Think of the effect of that immense crowd, the staying up late, the sense of awe and revelation that Francesca imparts. The great experience of her life.

Then at midnight I and Francesca start playing the Cesar Franck concerto. We keep on until two. It is terribly difficult, the Franck concerto, way beyond me, but I played just ten times as well as I really can. It was like being able to speak French when you are drunk. It seems to show that most of our inadequacy comes from timidity, or self-consciousness, or tightness, and what we need is release, frenzy, intoxication.

Elsa is studying piano and violin. Kate the piano. Francesca went down there to Philadelphia last Sunday and they worked seven hours. Elsa and Kate are coming here for a lesson this afternoon. Kate asked Francesca to look around for a second-hand piano for her and she found a very good one, at an auction, for 13 dollars. Before she gets through with us, Dagmar will be playing the flute, Esther the viola [these were maids who worked for Anne], Ken the cello and Madamoiselle [a governess] will be in opera.

Love to Julie. Tell her that if she doesn't write soon I know it is because I am in this state of euphoria, and consequently I will take a slump, talk suicide, and then I'll get letters every other day, and even gardenias.

Now back to Beethoven.

Love to you, nice little Brenda.

ANNE.

As for me, after seeing Francesca that first evening, my diary says this:

Francesca. A saint of music. We are all like faint radio bulbs and she is blazing light. All my dejection, induced by reading Aldous Huxley, is gone. He knows nothing, and can feel less. He never sees the core in anybody, and really it is in all, no matter how drab they may be. And Francesca knows that. And a violin becomes beautiful with playing; so do people when she gets them to use their feeling and freedom. "There are two kinds of people," she says to me, "those who live for their outsides and those who live for their insides."

Connie is going home to work on the piano, herself, with all her might. Francesca told us we should not just work on one piece, but read, read through all the Beethoven sonatas, the Mozart, and Bach. Read them as you read Shakespeare, to get to hear them and see what the composers are trying to say. Then you can go back and work on things separately. But it is like knowing the literature of a man, all of it, and getting to understand it.

Francesca says to me:

"You used to say that most people want others to be such and such a way, but we want them to be themselves. Do you remember?"

I say: "But I thought I discovered that last week."

"No. No one changes."

She says how at first she must give many lessons for several days in succession, because "children get so terribly discouraged." But how one must keep up their excitement by every means. It was up to the *teacher* to make it fascinating, not to the pupil to work and be grim. In the first lesson she makes them play some Mozart, at least a line, to show them how fast they learn. Of course. It would go fast. Wonderful music right away.

And she says one must always work without grimness, for then you are lost. The grimness, the grinding, grinding in to things, that is uncreative. That is, in giving a lesson, when one difficult thing dawns on your understanding, she makes you stop right there; go on to the next. She says you cover so much more ground this way. "Many teachers teach only the first position of the violin, for the first two years, and then the pupils are afraid to try anything but the first position, and get it stuck in their heads that all the other positions are so frightfully hard." But she teaches all the positions right away, soon; in the first three lessons.

Two days later I went up to have lunch with her. When I telephoned her, she said, delighted: "Aw!" (her Ohs were umlauted from living in Europe so much) "we can play!" "Who?" I cried, startled. "You!" and she laughs.

And so I go there and while she is getting a fine lunch with

her left hand so to speak, and hardly seeming to notice it, we talk;
and she will say things like this:

"Read Herodotus," she says, "he is wonderful to read. And
Eckermann's 'Conversations with Goethe!' "

"In German?"

"Yah."

"Oh, I can't read German."

"Why, Brenda!" she says, looking at me with round reproach-
ful eyes. And I think, oh, how ridiculous of me not to know
German and read it with ease! Of course I should know German
and French and Italian and Russian by this time. And I will. I
will begin at once.

She tells about the child who came to take lessons. He had had
lessons for two years, but they said he had no ear. He could not
keep in pitch. When he would sing, he was a whole note off. And
his teachers would have him bowing, bowing, and the muscles in
his neck were rigid, and he could not listen or hear the true note,
because of his anxiety, rigidity. And because he was afraid of
failure. But in seven months (and her eyes filled with tears, she
was so full of feeling about it) he played with perfect ear.

"Do you remember when we went to the Lake Harriet band
concerts, and I was fat?"

"No," she protests, "it is not so. You were very, very beautiful,
the most beautiful I have ever seen!" She means it, but it is just
as she thinks that the macaw and the canaries are remarkable and
tremendously intelligent. "And you were so wonderful, because
you had no sense of duty. . . . There was nothing you could not
understand." And she adds: "And I had to bring you up a little"
(I would have a fleeting picture of my sultry, logy self); "I would
say: 'Don't you think you ought to do this, a little more?' And
you would think, and then do it."

She suggested that I had sweet reasonableness anyway and that
pleased me and filled me with admiration for myself. And she
said that I read all the time and had read everything by the time I
was twelve that there was in the house—novels and history. And
that pleased me too, although I did not remember it at all.

Then she made me play with her, a Bach violin concerto and
then a Mozart sonata. I had not played the piano for years, and
never anything good. And when I would flag and balk, she would
shout "Go on!" and the mistakes made no difference, and with a

flushed face I did it and it sounded, I thought, very wonderful, lovely.

And from that moment I became inflamed about music.

We walked down to Anne's house, along Lexington Avenue in the noise and flying grit, the hot air arising from the subway gratings.

"Do you remember when you used to be a Christian Scientist?" I asked.

"But I am now!" she exclaims (though as I remembered it, she was so unorthodox she no longer would go to church.) "But it's all in John. Read John." (The Gospel of John, she meant.)

And from that time, more than ever, I began to love and respect religion, and try to find out what it was. But of course I had begun to understand it too in reading Dostoevski and Plotinus, William Blake and many others, but Francesca was such a wonderful living example of it.

But of course it was not just Francesca's powers to stimulate one that affected me, but this too: that I was always passionately searching for the answer to so many things, always experimenting and thinking I had discovered something, and failing and swinging violently to another entirely contrary effort. Trying to reconcile my ambition and conceit with something in me that was better. Trying to amount to something, to work better and to care about people more truly and steadily, with endless inward Hamletian arguments always, about what was good and bad, what was merely conventional and public opinion, and what was my true conscience. All that.

In her, there was such freedom and ardor. She was high and wonderfully above all obstacles like doubt, crossness, contentiousness; and above material obstacles, too. She went all over the world: to Japan for example, because she thought there too they should have violin lessons; and sure enough, the children began knocking on her door to be taught, at seven o'clock in the morning.

It was because she had some great secret like this, that I kept searching into her and asking her questions. Part of her secret was, obviously, playing and hearing great music. But playing more than hearing. You had to play it yourself, she said, really to feel what it was.

You see, this, I think, is what Francesca did for me: she began to show me that doubt, tension, grim resolution, are no good. It merely steels one into rigidity, and usually in defense against a pain or a difficulty, or an enemy that does not exist. She made me feel that life, gift, greatness is in all creatures, even animals, and that if we saw it and believed in it and generously loved and admired it and praised it in them, it grew. Yes, that is why we like praise: it is just a corroboration of what we are trying to do, and a sign that perhaps we are succeeding, so we can take heart and go on. She made me feel that it is a fine thing to free and release this gift in others, or oneself; that music was, in a way, the voice of God, for it brought about, more easily than many things, this release and freedom and elevation.

Of course much that I learned from her came gradually. It took many years. She came out the next summer and gave us all violin lessons. And she wrote me now and then. In a curious way, whenever I needed it badly, a letter came from Francesca. She would say in them, things like this:

Many of the Psalms are beautiful. The 91st healed me once when I was ill for a long time. But do get Parsifal and play it. Once when I had $4.50 on Thanksgiving Day, I went standing, to hear it. That cost 3 dollars and I was a bit afraid when I did it, but when I came out I was afraid of nothing and commenced an unexpected pupil that very night:...

The way you can help everyone most is to do your own work. ...You have compassion and that opens your eyes to all inner life....

I have the restless feeling that you are pouring yourself into others. You are always so generous. It is just that I would like to have you pouring yourself into some work of your own that would carry you up where you see that our needs are not so important....

About the only thing I know how to do is to give violin lessons, and having that, with the small vision of reforming the world's mode of teaching with my book, I have a kind of crazy freedom.

And one more thing that Francesca said that I shall never forget. That summer she came to our house in Minneapolis. One night we were in our kitchen. She always had some supper at midnight, after teaching all day and playing ensemble in the evening at Rolf's house, where the whole sitting room would be full of people—sawing away in excitement at Beethoven's Fifth Symphony perhaps; and I would be there too, having had one lesson, passionately playing the open A or G strings whenever it came to those notes.

After our midnight supper, I would go to bed. But Francesca always worked on her book until four in the morning. The kitten was in the kitchen too, and the neighbor's dog. He always was where Francesca was. Going from the ice box to the table, getting milk and butter, I said something absently about how women lawyers and doctors had such a hard time of it, and Francesca cried fiercely:

"They want it so easy! They have to have a good salary and go into some office, where everything is guaranteed. If they want to be doctors, why don't they go far in the country, where it is needed, and do what they can for people! Then they will be good doctors."

Yes, I still think of that. I think of it every day or so, and it never fails to make me cheerful. If we are not so mournfully, nasally, plaintively anxious about being paid all the time, but do our work generously, generously. Then everything will be all right with us, now and eternally.

Yes, 1931 was a lively nice year with a lot of aesthetics in it. We all began playing music, everybody in the family and all the neighbors and friends who had ever had a lesson on any kind of instrument. Rolf revived his violin. If you left his house at midnight and turned back again to get something, there he was walking up and down the pale rug in his sitting room, practicing finger exercises. In company he seemed to be listening to people but the fourth finger on his left hand would be quickly moving. Practicing again.

Nov. 9th, 1930. Rolf is so wonderful. Leonardo da Vinci. No, Archimedes.

Rolf was also a lawyer and worked in the office with my father and Sigurd—a tall young man with a face like a sad duke (or my idea of a duke), utterly immobile with almost never an expression fleeting across it. A big humped nose, dark mustache, a fearless resigned mouth and sunken light gray eyes. He had a measured way of talking in complete well-turned sentences, full of the most painstaking, discriminating slang. A cold exterior and inside (I think) an uncomfortable mess of boredom, scorn and raw kindness.

He was a fine draftsman and interested in painting. Charteristically, he went to the library and learned a tremendous amount about the chemistry of paints and what made them last. So, he said, anything he painted might not look like much, but one thing he was assured of: it would last five hundred years. That is, the paint would not fade or deteriorate.

I have some pedagogue in me that wants to encourage other people, to make them work. Part of this was that bad thing that is characteristically feminine and maternal, i.e., I really wanted to paint *myself,* so I projected this wish on others, without doing it *myself,* quietly working at it in my own way. (One should of course do both; but it is much more effective in getting other people, children, to work, to work oneself.) But thinking Rolf was so gifted, I got him to work on a portrait of me, and posed enduringly.

He had already painted one of Margaret and to his surprise Julie hung it in her living room. "Why, it's a Modigliani," she cried. "Better!"

Presently he painted another portrait of Margaret, a more exact one, with exact careful drawing—not like the first one, spectral and mysterious, with an ovoid head.

Frances Greenman, a fine portrait painter, who had one-man shows in New York and, like all artists, was so generously uncritical, came and saw it.

"Oh, Rolf, yes. Those feet! Drawn like Ingres. Those feet, those feet," as though to herself and with real admiration. "Have you anything more?" she asks.

"Nothing but atrocities," says Rolf in his thoughtful way.

"Now, Rolf, go and get them," Margaret and Julie and I cry. "He has too!"

He presently gets up, says, "I warn you, they're a couple of eyesores from hell"; and goes lightly up the stairs to get them.

When Anne and Ken and Elsa came in the summer, as well as the music, we would all go out in the country and paint for a whole day. "Why, girls, it's *good!*" Dorothy Lewis shouted after the first ten minutes of painting, the first time she ever painted in her life. Everybody feels just that way.

For me, there was endless talk with Julie. Among other things, we talked about Mahatma Gandhi. I had just read his life and it made a tremendous impression, because in my curious way I am always so suggestible when it comes to soldiers or saints. On one day we would decide that the way to be was a jolly rip, a heller; to thunder with anxious goodness. And the next day (after reading Tolstoy or Gandhi), here we would both see that non-resistance, love, crucifying the self, was the way to be. A saint. (Not that we ever succeeded in being either very bad or very good.)

One night after reading about Gandhi, I drove Father out to the Lewis house in the lovely evening, going west toward the fading sunset. The top of my car was down and Julie was in the rumble seat. She let out a ringing peal of laughter.

"What's the matter?" I asked.

"I caught myself singing 'Abide with Me.'" It was the Gandhi influence.

Now Julie had such exuberance and euphoria (they say that a bad heart often makes one this way) it was terribly hard for her to rest. If she went to a party, she was to have just one cigarette and one cocktail. But just the excitement, the laughter, the stimulation of ideas, would be hard on her.

On top of this, she abhorred any suggestion of valetudinarianism. It gave her such a pain, to be one of those women who must be careful. "Now, don't overdo, dear." She could not bear the idea of herself in this prudent, limp-woman invalid role.

Wednesday, February 27th, 1931.

Today I have one of my changes; my rhythms. And I turn again to long walks when I am gently starving and want contemplation again, and all those hours of thinking.

The ways of the spirit, soul, or whatever it is, are mysterious. Last night I read essays by Bagehot on Milton, one on Race and Language by Freeman, and one by Huxley on Scientific Education (all in the Harvard Classics). And I heard the clock strike three, and outside there was a wet March-like wind blowing and I had the strangest mood—as though a sad, but beautiful tender spectral lamp were lighted within me. Very strange. I thought of Julie talking this afternoon of the difficulties of resisting dissipation: "It is all right for you, but I must keep saying to myself that if I do not be careful, I will die next year and the children will have a stepmother, a horrid stepmother."

She said it so gaily, and the sad spectral lamp burned in me with feeling for her incomparable radiance and gallantry, and a glimpse of what a loss it would be if she were not hereabouts. And I thought of Gaby, whom I kiss every night before I go to bed—so perfect and smooth and healthy and satiny, and how she sometimes barely awakes and smiles at me and murmurs something droll and affectionate and how, poor darling, she will no doubt think of that when she has outlived me, and need it badly.

In late November, Julie had another heart attack. This one, for some reason, frightened her more than the others.

No, not frightened, but it made her feel so especially guilty, as though she were to blame, and that it was her carelessness for overdoing and not resting; and she felt so sorry for Sigurd for having to feel sorry for *her*, that she cried about it.

We decided that while she had to stay in bed, and have a nurse, she should come over to the big house, where it was quieter.

I was in my usual doldrums about not making enough money and the feebleness of my work. Free-lance work was perhaps impossible out in Minneapolis: it was too far from the editors and the source of material for articles, or so I told myself.

"But I suppose it is because I am the laziest living white woman," I said to Julie. "A soggy procrastinator. I suppose it is because in New York, when you have to see editors, it is as enlivening as a cowboy shooting at your heels." And I talked about how I knew that Father would gladly support me while I wrote a book. "But I don't like that. The presumption of genius gives me the pip, the absolute shut-eyed pip! And there is absolutely no evidence to prove that I could write a good book. It might very well be the most awful weasel vomit."

We were both reading then the Countess Tolstoy's diary. We both loved Tolstoy and were indignant about it, because it was full of complaints against poor great Tolstoy, particularly against his sensuality, when he was preaching chastity to everybody else.

"Perhaps *she* was to blame. For she takes on so waspishly against the horrors of male concupiscence. Perhaps this is what made him feel like a beast, when if his wife had been sensibly grateful for his passion, why, he would not have fought against it in himself, so miserably."

"Exactly. Her clamoring for attention. That caterwaul that his love wasn't spiritual!"

"Now we must never never be like that. Never never be tragic. Full of fun to the ending doom."

"You bet your life," said Julie.

December 6th, 1931.
I run twice around Lake Harriet. The incomparable sense of well-being. The sparkling blue-diamond day and my tennis shoes sloughing along and kicking up diamond clouds of snow. And the golden sunlight over all and the cold wind over the blue water, blowing my hair.

But the next day, Julie had a heart attack. Lewis Daniel, looking unhappy, said it was not bad, in his kind way. But the nurse said she was lividly pale and sweating and had a low low pulse. "I have never seen one," I try to tell myself. "Perhaps they are that way." When I see her she is full of dope from the doctor. As I stand by her bed she smiles so charmingly, with charming sudden feeling, pulls at the crease in my sailor pants and says: "You are so cute," in an affectionate smiling way.

Dec. 30th, 1931.
This afternoon I sleep from two until 4:30. Julie calls me. She is sitting up and having difficulty breathing.

"Now sit here and tell me this is nonsense." She tries to talk, showing me Helen Fiske's letter about Bertrand Russell who visited her in Iowa. I don't know what to do. Talk to her? But she answers then. Finally I say, holding her hand:

"Now don't talk, don't think." Her two flannel jackets are dripping. I put my white sweat shirt on her. And then Lewis comes. I am worried, so perturbed. I know how discouraging this must be to her. When Lewis comes in she says: "I have been misbehaving again." She always blames herself. Sigurd comes in. She says the same to him. I cannot bear his face. Or do I imagine this? because Julie always says she cannot bear his face when he is frightened—and she has to see it so often. Again blaming herself for her crazy heart.

When I go in later she seems to be sleeping propped up, head turned to one side. But she says wearily smiling: "What a wonderful night out."

I say, I don't know why, perhaps because it is true and I can't bear to have her say it is a wild howling night: "No, it is warm and muggy, really summerlike."

Father is lying on the couch downstairs and Sandra is reading the evening paper by his chair, one light on by the stairway. And Father says about Julie: "It looks serious," and I try to gesture him not to speak because of Sandra. "She has been in bed six weeks," he says.

I then got him to stop talking. Sandra does not look up but continues to read. But oh, these children. They know these things, know everything, everything of course. After dinner I go over to see Sandra and Jeanie, each sitting on a bed with a dim lamp between them, drawing. "Where is Sigurd?" "Out to dinner."

Then, and now in 1938, this cuts me to the heart.

3.

Julie is very sick. I like to think I have a mystical experience. Father on religion; his loneliness. At the University. Dr. David Swenson and Plato. My father's death.

FATHER BECAME SICK TOO AND HAD TO HAVE AN OPERATION. He was seventy-nine. But he came out of it wonderfully well; and I think he was altogether surprised at how fond of him his children seem to be, for Anne and Elsa came west at once. I know that he was elated and comforted at this, and by the concern of us all. He told me so. He did not expect it in the least. We are none of us sentimentally demonstrative, and he less than any of us. As for the operation, he was an offhand stoical Roman about it. "All right, bring on your operation. To de *devil* with delay!"

Feb. 21, 1932. I go to see Father, who is in a happy, tender mood. He wants to go home and there is feeling in his voice: "to that place where I have spent so much of my life and where mother's life was spent."

It was his 79th birthday and he said to Anne that day, "Eighty is old enough to live, for anyone." He was to die when he was eighty. I am sure it was because inwardly he thought it was time.

But Julie got no better. Presently she wanted to leave this

big house and go back to her own. But her room, which was exposed on three sides, had thin drafts through the pretty arched windows, and a sub-zero blizzard came down from North Dakota. She caught cold. This was hard on her. It was decided that she too should go to the Swedish hospital. We all said: "She will be much more comfortable there, and will get well much quicker. She will really have some rest. She won't be stimulated by everything that happens in the house."

I went to the hospital to see her every day.

March 25th, 1932.

See my darling Julie. She has had a bad night, a bad day. I hold her hand. She says simply: "I wish I could get out of this, pass out. The kids are so wonderful it would not matter if they had a stepmother."

"You cannot," I say.

"I know it."

"You cannot on my account."

She talks to me of suicide. "How sensible, how reasonable. So weary of all this." Oh, Julie, my poor golden girl! She tells me what a dear her nurse is, Miss Halvorsen, and Miss Tollefson. Really these little Scandinavian nurses prove something about the children of poor people. And Julie says the only thing she likes to read, to hear about, is wonderful country, landscape, humming summer days, farms. This is her need.

Margaret Webster was there talking to Julie. She tells me outside how she told Julie she wishes she had a God (Margaret is a Catholic) to lean on. But I think just now: why should we always have something to lean on? (Julie should, of course, so that she can rest.) But I am always leaning, leaning, relaxing on something: my friends' admiration, sympathy, on Father's financial backing. Just this suggestion of faith, of not worrying, of leaning, makes me uneasy, for I know it is tempting. But again in me, it is the old whipsawing between the safe womb and exploration; home and adventure; peace and war; gentleness and fierceness.

April 10th, 1932.

Julie has a fine rose-petal color. Sits up. "I feel so good-natured." The first thing I come in the room she says: "Take off your hat." She has remembered that I was to have a permanent wave. Again she says how bangs are the only thing.

Her eyes are shut. Curling lashes. She says how wonderful Sigurd is. "I really think he likes me, don't you? And when I tell him what a darling he is to me, he nearly bawls and wants to come back in the evening. . . . I am a little tired but I feel wonderful."

"I must go so you can sleep. I'll come back."

"Yes, do. You are a pet. Now don't paw me, pat me," and to her nurse, "She always pats me and I don't like it because she never does other times."

When I first go in to see her, I am full of gloom—about myself, my work, and tell her so, using all the invective I can think of against myself. Her chin drops limply on her chest and she laughs. I feel much better. But going out and walking home in a lively, inspirited way, I begin to think: "Oh, Lord, think of going to that poor girl to get cheered up!"

It's a cold sunny day. Again I am troubled by thoughts of Christ versus Nietzsche. There is no fight in me, no struggle, and the religion business begins to persuade me. Why fight, why struggle? they say. Let God take care of you. But all my instincts feel that relaxation is wrong. Even Francesca thinks it is wrong. So what do they mean by it? I can't make out. For she is all for ardor, interest, frenzy. Hates apathy and resignation. The trouble is that when I become stern with myself I am so with other people. Yet I must remember that to the complex, all is confusion; but it is much better to be confused than simple, for it is more highly evolved to be complex. Strange how I am always looking for a rule, a simple, single rule. And there is no such thing. Of course not. When I think I find a rule (i.e., let God do it), the other force becomes restive presently and emotion, anger, passion want to assert themselves; or if fierceness has been my rule, and fight, why then compassion, gentleness, ease and gaiety demand their own use for a while. And so it goes. Tolstoy had made himself sweetness and light, but he had enough egotism, passion and anger to start with. I haven't.

May 2nd, 1932. Wednesday.

My darling black-haired Gaby with her beautiful face and straight legs. She comes and puts a calendar, a diet calendar, for herself and for me on my bureau. Each day that we eat between meals or have sugar, we do not get a star.

I go to see Julie but they won't let me see her. She is resting. All I can do is write her a note.

Get no work done. Depressed. Owe 165 dollars at Young-Quinlan's. I walked down to see Julie, but take the street car home because Inga telephones that Gaby was disappointed about not going to Lewis's. And there she comes through the woods on her bicycle, with the others; straight black hair to her shoulders, pink coat and brown legs. What a beauty. What a tender darling. At dinner she tells me how Margaret said that Jock (our dog) bit people, and cries out with indignation at this injustice, this terrible calumny. I must do more, more for her.

When I come home, she follows me to the bathroom, and I am churning with anxiety inwardly. She tells me how her bicycle and Anne Cooley's are old; how all the others have new ones. I tell her how I have no money to get a new one, how I have spent that twelve hundred dollars that R. had been sending and that we had been slowly accumulating. She cries. My heart is gored. What an improvident fool I am! What a sieve about money, sense, foresight. All slip away. Feel guilty and apprehensive. Tell her I gave X, who is very poor now, about eight hundred dollars, and Gaby smiles and says: "I am glad you did." What a lamb she is, a generous tender-hearted lambkin. Bless her. I tell her how I will get a job, go to the University perhaps and get a degree. Then I could teach. She is radiant. "Oh, Mama, you would be a *wonderful* teacher. I wish you were *my* teacher. I wish you were my teacher and went along with me in every grade." I should teach her music. Yes, I should. And I will. . . .

I am so anaesthetic to Julie. How strange this is. Only in long sharp thrusts does it pierce me, at strange times. At two in the morning, on waking up suddenly, my imagination is clear and encompassing and I see the loss, the horror, my love for her, my unbearable sense of loss. Yes, she is facing the forlornness of death. I love her more than anybody in the world. She is my alter-ego, my backer-up, one with whom I am myself to the nth power. Her radiance has warmed me more than anyone's. In all discouragement I have turned to her, as though her yellow aureole of hair were the sun. It is, to me.

Thursday, May 3rd.

I prayed last night to the Everlasting.

I must save. I must get a farm. I must spend nothing on myself. The very minimum. Yes, in all money things I have failed. Father gives me a check for 200 dollars. I accept it in pain, and could bite my tongue and roll my eyes out of sight like an epileptic, in my guilt and discomfort. Nervous about Julie whom I have not seen. Despair and sadness over her. At Sigurd's house, the rug, the beautiful handsome Sigurd with his motionless face—everything suggests Julie. All conversation points that way and I experience woe on my own account and doubly because of Sigurd, for I know what he is experiencing and oh, how much worse! Two or three times I speak of something, some person "whom Julie and I talked to." A stab because I have said her name. And gathering Inga's dishes in their kitchen, the knives and forks, every now and then I must pick up some dish that Julie chose, a Wedgwood coffee cup or saucer, and painfully think, with what life! what exuberance she chose it.

Julie died early in the morning of May 18th.

In the afternoon, I took the twins and Gaby over to the Rices' house, far beyond Mendota. You can see all the Minnesota River valley from there for ten miles, and in the afternoon, the sun shoots down rays like the spokes of a gigantic wheel on the far-away western meadows and the meandering shining water and marshes.

Virginia Rice, who quietly understands everything in the world and squints up her blue eyes in her smile, and says blunt surprising things, had told us to come over. The children could see the colts and puppies and have chocolate cake and milk. Gaby chattered and curveted, rolled her eyes, and I thought with misgivings: "Dear me, have I such a jabbering child!" That night when she went to bed we talked a little about Julie and she said:

"Oh, Mama, those twins are so brave. . . . Whenever they are quiet, I talk as fast as I can, so they won't think about it." She had been doing this at the Rices', starting nonsense which they would join in gladly but had not the force to start themselves.

May 19th, 1932. Oh, Julie, she must live eternally. Not in our hearts. Damn that measly immortality. She must live eternally, herself, herself. Her frivolous frizzle of wild blond hair, her long tanned legs, her green eyes, her golden eyebrows, the way her eyes streamed tears when she laughed. The way she sat with her long shanks crossed; and her pretty perfect bare feet, the upper one pointed toward the greensward; her enchanting hats; her elegance; her polished gold tanned shoulders in summer; the lovely sloppiness of her bedroom with its slatternly bureau drawers, gauze stockings and jewelery hanging out; her to-hell-with-the-details way in everything; her scorn for budgeting; her telephoning, yelling, telling Inga what to have; her laughing at her maid's jokes with a shriek. That wonderful frivolity! and all the time there was her clear hastening intelligence, looking at everything and seeing right through it. Oh, yes, she could have easily been a true scholar; and she was as lofty in her soul as anyone could be. You could see that from her admiration of what is distinguished, scholarly, intransigent and good in Sigurd. Yes, that wonderful frivolity in a clear lucent thinking soul!

I think to myself: I must write a book. I then think: why a book? No Julie to read it. No one else would see in it what I want to be seen. Strange what influence the dead have on us. After my mother's death, I seem to be in her place in a curious way, even to sitting at the dining-room table, the only one who has not had cocktails (I used to be among the rest who would tease her about Prohibition) and does not smoke. And now, I feel that I must make this place pretty and gay; must have people come and expand and talk and drink wine, and I must see their new dresses and hear their stories and laugh as Julie did, and give off some of that wonderful frivolity. It is as though she had entered into me.

Two weeks after her death I had what I like to think was a mystical experience. The Shearers and Lewises and Sigurd and I drove down to Iowa Falls to spend the week-end with Helen Fiske. I had been reading Van Gogh's letters, and was very much affected by them. It was my old suggestibility to those two things, a saint or a soldier, i.e., to one who loves very much, or to one who fights. Van Gogh had such remarkable passionate love for things outside himself, for human beings, and for the meaning and beauty in whatever he saw, —the sky, a flower, a thawing field, a lamp post in the watery twilight. This love, I could see, was the source of the creative fountain within him.

I was digging dandelions, my back bare to the sun, on Helen Fiske's western lawn, one of those small town lawns with huge rank dandelions in sparse grass under oak trees and pines. The others were in the sitting room, being very jolly, talking and drinking highballs. Sigurd had gone down to the creek in the meadow to sleep. It was in the afternoon.

"Yes, Van Gogh thinks," I said to myself, "that love is the creative thing. Why, look: even in physical things—you love a man and you want to create him, i.e., reproduce him, have a child. Van Gogh loves the sky and has to paint it. We love beauty, qualities, then we will create them in music, painting, or in ourselves. Francesca said hate is a kind of love reversed, for we become what we hate. I can see that: you are a pacifist and you hate war ferociously, and there you are fighting yourself, and wanting to exterminate people. . . . Therefore, if one loves great things, perhaps one can acquire them. I wish it were so. I see now why Francesca passes over things she might well hate and does not dwell on them. Van Gogh was that way. He even rebukes his brother for saying certain painters were mediocre, because the mediocre are on the way some place. Van Gogh had no scorn for mediocrity. He just saw (loved) what was good in it and knew it was working toward perfection. But I, and so many of us, we are so snobbish about mediocrities, and therefore we do no work, for we are afraid we will be mediocre ourselves; and we certainly will be, as long as we take all that time out to hate, so pleasurably, mediocrity. . . . Artists are lovers, and critics are haters. Artists see the bright imagined thing to do, the vision to love, and so do it. Critics are correcting and picking apart what was done *yesterday;* and that is why critics are always scolding, and artists generously praising. But never think much of yesterday and dissecting and correcting that. Always keep your face toward what is greater and lovelier and admire that, and move toward it, and do that."

And digging dandelions in Helen Fiske's lawn and thinking these things, my bare shoulders warmly sunburning, I have an extraordinary feeling: "Why, Julie is here talking about this to me." Her presence was definitely there, five feet in front of me and on the left, and she was so clear and alive and incomparably jolly. "Brenda, now you have it! This is it. Now what we talked of before" (all those endless conversations about love, fidelity, sex, Tolstoy, Gandhi, gossip, malevolence, children) . . . "that was fine, but this is really it. Now you have hit on it. Stick to that. As for this death business," she seemed to be saying: "It is so ridiculously simple, easy. A cinch. If you only knew how simple and easy everything is. Wait until you see." And she also seemed to say: "Have a glorious time, all of you. That is right. You cannot be gay enough. No one ever can."

Well, I would not perhaps have thought much about this (although the thoughts I had had about Van Gogh affected my life more and more) ; and also I have never been able to feel the presence of any absent person in that vivid luminous extraordinary way. But I told Dorothy Lewis about it while we were dressing for dinner. Then at dinner, in the midst of our drinking, joking, laughing, Henrietta suddenly said to me across the table, from the other end of it, with a kind of sharp soberness.

"What were you thinking out there on the lawn?"

Dorothy and I were surprised. I did not tell Henny then, but before we went to bed she came and asked to know, again. I told her. She said that she had looked out at me digging dandelions and had suddenly wondered, "What is she thinking?" It was a very strong feeling, and she wanted to go out and ask me. But then she had an equally strong feeling: "I must not, because it will interrupt something. It is important."

I tell this not to prove anything, or to fill anybody with awe, but just because it happened. Besides, remember that I have an incorrigible wish that there are Presences in the world, archangels, beings, saints, that we cannot see, and they sometimes pull us by the sleeve, saying, "Come; you can really do this;" or put a kind hand on us to help us.

June 30th, 1932. I am limp and tired and go to bed at 8:30. Gaby is on the porch and has a fever because of the mumps, but is contented and does not mind. Father reading downstairs, and his loneliness (he is always reading; no sympathy, no communication for anybody) fills the house with loneliness and me with sadness and unutterable self-reproach. Why cannot I surround him with more warmth, more kind voices, interest? I must, must.

But the next day is a beautiful clear day, with a bright yellow sun shining. Father reads cheerfully out in the sun. I walk, stop at the sandy beach and try handsprings and do them better than before, even getting to my feet. This is good.

Father too, although he had recovered from his operation, had not been entirely well. And I felt he was lonely. He was deep in the loneliness of old age, and another generation. No bridge can cross it.

I would walk around Lake Harriet with him on beautiful afternoons. He talked about religion and would go slower and slower until he stopped entirely and turned and faced me and talked. "Yes, I see, I see," I said. Sometimes I listened and sometimes I was far away. I can still see him, looking askance at him as he absorbedly talks. It is a late afternoon, a cold lovely day, but sunny and warm in the north stretch by the lake. I walk a little slower than if alone, to keep even with him. But not much. I make myself listen. Feel restive. But want to make him happy. And I am interested too. "I should know all this. Now listen," I say to myself. But there is a feeling of hopelessness because he cannot hear what *I* say about it. There is no alternating current. When I speak he does not want it, drawing his preoccupied soul into its shell, shutting the door, not hearing.

He spoke remarkably well, in long lucid paragraphs a page long, and the thread of thought and logic carried through them to perfection to the end, with wonderful delicacy, with exquisite discriminating transitions . . . " . . . inasmuch as . . ."

But some of it, I had heard and he could not hear me. I was an audience. When I answered, I found myself shouting, as one does to a foreigner, but unconsciously it was to break through his self-absorption. The most blessed gift (and so many fine people, men especially, lose it; and this is something I have to remember myself) is the ability to listen, to hear others, to be chemically affected by what they say. This means that talk is always regenerated and interesting and love is alive between you, and sympathy.

He is talking of Higher Criticism. He tells of Luther, who held with the Roman Catholics on Transubstantiation, against Zwingli, who held out for Consubstantiation. He tells me (I had not ever known the slightest thing about it) the Christian idea of redemption, and so on.

That is: Man fell in the Garden of Eden. God, in order to forgive or redeem man, could not do it Himself because he was a righteous God. So He had to send His Son to suffer, to be crucified, to atone for Man's fall, so that Man could be redeemed. Now some held that there was no such thing as Free Will—Calvin, for example, and the Presbyterians— that Man could not redeem himself, for this (as I understand it) would reflect on the mightiness of God and make Man not lowly enough. Thus, the Calvinists had the idea of predestination. As Father talked of these things, in the most precise, scholarly way, he would show how illogical so much of it was and nonsensical. Faith, for example. That strange concept— faith! "Faith is believing something that you know isn't so," said the boy. All of it seems just unbelievably foolish to him; and yet he is so fascinated by it. "Oh, Lordy, Lordy, we know so little!" he used to be always saying.

A beautiful evening. The lake is a shield, a blue-gray shield of refulgent light with small hurrying waves on its surface, their planes shining steel and silver, their little crests pale blue, and they make a sighing, hurrying, unrhythmic lapping on the shore. Beyond on the west shore, the woods are a black silhouette.

"Justification ... Faith ... Grace ..." He goes on to tell of those curious nonsensical words. But just the same, to me, who knew not one thing about theology and had never even been christened, they seemed unutterably beautiful. They were not just words but poet-words, words that have a meaning and open a door into some translucent golden universe of understanding, seen dimly because *we* are dim and can see hardly anything. They express an experience that is in all men some time, perhaps only when they are young and alive and have not pinned all understanding down into words. After a while the idea gets stereotyped, so we discard the word as a name for humbug—that is, if we are not poets, but scientists and lawyers or pedants or definers—and we give the experience another name, perhaps a dry boring word out of psychology.

But Father talked of these words as facts, hard facts, and therefore they were foolishness to him and a superstition and a notion to be discarded. I walked and listened and tried to talk up occasionally, but he could not understand, and so when I talked, it was hard going. I heard myself shouting in an effortful feeling akin to despair inside, that he would not hear or be interested to see what I was striving to say. So all I could do was to attack, gently, his arguments. He would like that, for it drew him on and on.

We walked slowly way around the lake. I think it was spring, for I seem to smell that day and remember that we stepped around soft muddy places occasionally, as though there was still some frost being thawed from the ground. We went to the outlet on the far side, and beyond that to the path that leaves the road and follows the lake along a thicket. Then back. Just in that space, he was talking of astronomy, about Sir James Jeans, about what man had discovered about the universe (I felt such respect for how much he knew) and I cannot remember just how, but he led around from that to the possibility that we live after death. I knew then he wanted to live after death. I felt a lot of pain. I didn't want him ever to die. I wanted him to live after death and wanted him to know that he would. When we came back a beautiful round moon, thin as pale gold foil, sailed into the pellucid green azure of the eastern sky, a large thin, gold disc like the halo of a saint.

For years afterwards, now more than ever, I think of how my father was undoubtedly lonely. On another golden spring day like it I remember I knew that he was lonely, and I wanted to be free. But I walked around Lake Harriet with him, and then I thought I had worked off my duty, and he would be at peace. But he was not. He gently hinted: What was I doing that evening? (I have such a terrible pang when I think of this.) He was afraid of the evening, of the emptiness, and wanted to do something. And I resisted for a moment, though just inwardly, hoping to get him settled and reading in his Morris chair, so that I could go out and have a livelier time with other people. But he was so lonely that I could really feel it, and I said: "We might go to that Swedish movie," and we did. He seized on that.

And this memory (it comes very often) makes me feel very badly, particularly about my reluctance, my mean reluctance, when I know so well myself what that loneliness is, and how it feels—like a sword in the chest, like foxes in the bosom. Yes, whenever I think of Father that evening, I can always easily shed tears.

The stories I was writing were no good and sold only occasionally. Then, that summer the editor of a magazine wrote and asked me to go to Chicago and write an article for him about taxi-dancers. And I did. But when he saw the article he decided that taxi-dancers were too near the underworld for his magazine, and did not buy it. I became thoroughly discouraged with free-lance writing. They got you to work for three or four weeks, and spend lots of money on a trip, and then did not pay for it.

So that fall, I decided to go to the University to work for a master's degree. This would at least be steady hard work. After that, perhaps I could teach. And I thought how all the writing in the world that I really admired, was a by-product, and not done primarily for money. Why, look at them!—I told myself with my usual grandiloquence—the great professor-writers like William James. And there was Chekhov. His writing too was an avocation, for he was a doctor.

"If I could only get into a steady ten-hour-a-day profession. That is why I think of the University," I wrote to Gertrude. "Why, I might become a kind of female William James, you know; or Hegel or Kant. They were all mousy professors who took daily constitutionals like me. Never be downhearted, for what is the sense of it, when one might as well be gay and hopeful. So much better for the metabolism for one thing."

It was so long ago that I had been in college, that I had to write to Barnard to ask them what had been my major subject. History, they told me. So now I took history and philosophy.

And in going to school again after such a long time, I found this: that I was much brighter than nineteen years before. It was easier to learn. In fact it was delightful and I had a kind of running passionate hunger to learn everything I possibly could. I found that it was an incalculable relief and frolic to study compared to writing those money-aimed stories.

In fact I felt guilty when I was studying. "Why, I am just reading! This is so easy. I am loafing!" I would think all the time uneasily, until I could persuade myself, again and again, that this was work, this was what I was supposed to do. The troubles with my infirm will disappeared like magic. Now it was no longer *my* will, but the routine that carried me, and I was doing what Dr. Swenson and Dr. Krey *told* me to do, and there was nothing to it, it was so easy. I worked early and late, once for twenty-six hours, in writing a long paper.

Moreover, I found that because I was older and had had some troubles and perplexities, everything that Socrates said about "the soul's tendance of the body" and being and non-being (though there was much about this that I could not understand of course) was excitingly interesting; and so was everything in history, whether it was the education of Erasmus, or the stupidity of Joffre and Haig in the World War, or the starvation of Germany by the Allies during the peace conference (things that never appeared in the newspapers). My only regret was that I could not study, with this new surprising grown-up intelligence, physics and mathematics, and geology and astronomy, as well as aeronautics and navigation, music and fighting with the broadsword.

And I felt such gratitude and admiration for the professors, and this was so different from my ridiculous obtusely young attitude at Wells College. They all seemed so remarkably distinguished, noble, gentle. Their disinterested search for what is *true* seemed so different from the attitude of businessmen, newspapermen and all the rest of us in the outside world, all propagandists for our own self-interest, and milling around and contending and battling for things about which we are half-informed. I was teacher's pet. I used to think, going into Dr. Swenson's class: "Yes, this feeling I have for Dr. Swenson: this is unalloyed love."

By my presence, I may have helped the professors too. At least compared to me (I thought) the others, the young ones, the undergraduates, were like mutton-faced potatoes with glasses on, and sent out no gratitude or imagination and appreciation at all. Nothing makes a good teacher so much as lively pupil and vice versa. Yes, in teaching, as in psychoanalysis, the transference must take place. That is, there must be love between them. It is too bad that teachers don't know this. I used to say that if ever I taught school I would be careful to be the most dashing, fashionable kind of person. That is, if you wanted to be successful at love affairs, it might be all right and make no difference if you look like a cold, literal-minded dyspeptic. But if you are a school teacher, you must look like Greta Garbo. They must admire you, inside and out, in order to learn much.

June 8th, 1933. Friday.

Studied history all day and went to hear Swenson's last lecture on Plato. I sit in the front row and am abashed to look at him at this near distance, as though our glances had electric charges and we cannot bear the significant current of sympathy that volts between us. I observe that strange man. He is tall, has fresh color and thick, lifted, blond-gray hair, and he is so deaf that a complicated little machine has to be rolled in and attached to his earphone, so that he can hear the questions. He has sensitive hands with fingers that bend backwards, fine eyes and small square teeth characteristic of Scandinavians. Then a slightly receding chin. As in all great men, there is the gentle woman in him, the maternal tenderness. He is rawly sensitive, like radio antennae; I think perhaps he is tortured in the quick by such minute things. In this lecture he says how Plato is out-of-date as a scientist, an astronomer, and even somewhat as a logician. But his ethics are not out of date. And the fact that every man must learn virtue from the beginning, by himself, that makes the unity of mankind, the brotherhood of man. It helps us to read what the saints learned, but to achieve it, one must search and fight oneself. "To learn love, one must begin at the very beginning."

He says how Plato, unlike many philosophers, thought philosophy was a life, a thing to be lived, a harmony, a unit of the intelligence and soul and body. "Many moderns do not think that," he says. "You hear people say of a leading politician: 'Oh, you must not object to his *personality*; it is his *ideas* that are important, not his personality.'" And Swenson laughs: "But there is nothing of any importance but the personality. That is the whole thing. Great ideas can only come out of a great personality.... Plato and Socrates were the great exponent of this idea: that one should use all the reasoning intellect in search for the good, and then live so.

Not impulse alone is enough, not headlong faith, but all the faculties forever painfully working ... Socrates was perhaps the greatest intellect of all time, but don't think he wasn't emotional. He was tremendously emotional, one of the most emotional men that ever lived. Socratic irony was this: that those who *think* they know something, probably do not. But Socrates was not a dry skeptic. His great emotion lay in this: in the *search* to know. That was to be passionately loved. *That* was his enthusiasm." ...

He speaks of the Danish philosopher, Kierkegaard (to him Ibsen owed his character, Brand, in the drama of that name) and quotes him. I don't understand just what he means by it, as I do when he speaks of love, the creative force.

" 'Life is love,' said Plato. But he did not go this far—" says Swenson, "and there was one more step for him to make: i.e., there is no happiness in the world for *me alone;* it must be shared, it must be possible to have it shared by all or it is not a justifiable happiness." And I don't quite understand this. (But I do now, in 1938.)

After the lecture, I go up to speak to him. He has sat down. The pupils are all moving out of the room. He has suddenly in his face a flushed hurt look. "My lecture was no good today," he says to me with distress. He has told me before how he has depressions that last many months, and that he is in one of them now. And a characteristic of them is that when he lectures he feels that he is empty and arid, that he is saying not what he thinks *now*, but what he remembers he *used* to think. That is, he is thinking *about* a thing (uncreatively, mere memory) and not *in* it.

I leaned forward and absolutely shouted, yelled: "That is not so! Your lecture was unspeakably wonderful, great, just wonderful! Remember that. I shall never forget it! I shall never have an experience like it! You must not say that! It was a wonderful lecture!"

I could just see the impact of this compliment (and I meant every word of it), a slow startled deep flush. I don't suppose anyone had ever before said such a thing to him, or even hinted that a lecture was good. No, we do not thank people nearly enough.

Father was supposed to have some teeth out; there might be some infection from them. Characteristically he went at once down to the dentist's, and said:

"Take them out, today. I have a lawsuit tomorrow."

"I will take one or two at a time," says our nice dentist, who looks like an albino Abe Lincoln, and always blushes.

"To *de devil* with dat! Take them all out!"

After a week or so he did not feel well. Tired. Could not eat. He went to the office, drove down in the morning with the boys. But in spite of himself, he had to lie on the daybed in his office. Miss Goldsbury told him to.

Elsa wrote him a long, long letter which made him feel happy.

"But I don't feel right in my body," he said to me that evening. He had slept better though, at night. I put my hand on his knee and say: "You must be more patient," and he says gently: "Maybe so."

January 10th, 1933.

Home and reading for history. The great Renaissance teacher, Vittorino da Feltre, described his day: "Rose at seven, scourged myself and went to work." Yes, must scourge ourselves a little every day.

Father comes upstairs, stumbling very weakly at five o'clock. Has been to the office. Lies down on his bed, asks me to take off his shoes. His pride, pride. He will not be sick, and smokes and moves about as always (though so very slow, weak; such difficulty in getting his left leg around the corner of the couch.) He lies down. We have given him my bed which is wide, softer than his. I go in and sit beside him, with an arm across him. His blue eyes, half closed, looking at me searchingly. Wisdom in them and I know not what loneliness, sadness. There is nothing I can do but pat him and talk cheerfully. In my imagination it is loneliness and the longing to be loved, enclosed, that is the greatest need. Perhaps I am wrong. Perhaps just because I have felt it so often.

February 2nd.

At the University looking up the ninety-two cardinals of the year 1490. Have not smoked for two weeks. It took the usual six weeks to stop. Oh, the horrible asphyxiation of central heating and thirty cigarettes a day! Rolf says one feels as though one has leprosy, slow poisoning, gangrene and Hutchinson's teeth. And the perspiration is a sticky ichor. I have now a third more energy.

Feel purer, fresh-mouthed, water-sluiced and pure. Pinker. [I have never smoked since then, and never will.]

March 14th.

When I came home Father says he wants to see me. Holds my very cold hand. I explain how he has been sleeping so much or I would have seen him before.

March 15th.

Said passionate prayers last night; for my father, for Sigurd, whose darling little dog Mike is sick and probably won't live, who carried that poor little Mrs. Clark's case way to the U. S. Supreme Court, with everybody against him and trying her in the newspapers, and he has now no incomparable Julie to be with him. Must do more for Sigurd, Gaby and the children. For Father. Must be more industrious, work, work; less self-indulgent.

Father had to give me another check. I had been skimping along and refusing money in my usual unbusinesslike way. Every so often he would ask me anxiously and kindly if I didn't need money. "Now, Brenda, I want to give you money . . ." I evaded and lied to avoid it and finally he would get angry. I remember one day he came up to my work-room on the third floor, to speak of two things: about how Connie had not written. And then the other thing: Money. He then begins to be the haranguing Judge Ueland, nostrils squared, mouth wide, arm sawing the air and ending each sentence in almost a shriek of eloquence.

"I want you to let me know *when you need money*. I don't want you to be *vexed!*"

Darling father, he was so good, so good. It was like him to be furious when I wouldn't let him help me. But to go back to this March day when he was ill and fast getting worse. He had a trained nurse, but as long as he had an ounce of strength he fought her off, to dress and go down to the office.

March 23rd, 1933.

My darling father gives me a check. Wandering in his head, and this takes the form of a confused anxiety about securities, or

some legal paper that has been lost. But as soon as I remind him
that I need money, at once he shows such strength and responsibility. He remembers how we have spoken of this before. He
writes the check, but with difficulty. November? No, March. A
strange combination of vigor and dreaminess. I feel such alternate
cowardliness, love, strength, evasion, callous mental diversion and
Weltschmerz and horror and religion.

Sunday April 10th, 1933.
   Sore throat, feel weak. Study in the morning, but listlessly. Sit
in Father's bedroom. No walk; a repellent cold February day.
Marion Mills for dinner and talks to me while I lengthen the skirt
of my admiral suit.
   For a week have deserved a star; eaten little and sensibly. Yesterday terribly hungry though.
   Father in pain in the evening. I go in, hold his hand, and he is
flushed and trembling. It is the catheter. And he talks rapidly and
holds my hand tightly and keeps saying: "We must fight. Yes, that
is the only thing to do. But if we fight.... Yah-yah, that is the
way I figure it out." And then he will make a grimace and laugh
with such gallantry and bravery. And then he repeats this struggle,
describing in strange disconnected words, as though he were speaking in French or some unknown language, a state of mind, a
monumental struggle and heartbreaking gallant battle. And then
the nurse gives him morphine and he keeps it up. In his words he
uses the names of *cards* now to describe the battle, as though it
were one of his exuberant fighting bridge games, when he likes
to slam down his cards with a shout and make the other players
bite the dust. But now, these words mean his battle with pain, his
fierce fighting. "We'll play the king.... Take *that!* That will
hold them. Now if we get out their jack and with one more heart!
We'll hold them!" looking at me always intently, through half-
shut eyes, with his ungiving fighty joy.
   And at last the morphine begins to work and he shuts his eyes
and there is now only a perplexed frown on his face. And he is
so brave, so beautiful, so gallant and I touch his forehead and try
to smooth away the beautiful perplexed frown. His face makes me
think of little Eric [Rolf's child] trying to understand, to know,
to pierce some puzzling mystery. I kiss his hand many times and
press his forehead, his face, and look at him earnestly and answer
firmly all he says, as though it were the greatest sense. Oh, that

incomparably brave and droll and humorous laugh in the midst of this dreadful battle. I have seen a great man. If I have only inherited a little, a very little of this valor.

Monday, July 31st, 1933.

Yesterday, Sunday, my father died. I sat in my room writing to Dr. Owre, and could hear Gladys (the nurse) feeding him breakfast in his room. She is altogether a darling and a wonder. But he did not want to eat. She forced him with that inexorable, sweet, insincere, disgusting professional-nurse pressure. He of course is simply a poor emaciated body and no intelligence is left, only just a faint reflection of it shows now and then, but for no longer than a word or two, in many days. And this seemed so harrowing to me, so dreadful, that they should make him eat when for so long he had wanted to die by starving himself, as anyone would. Nature is so kind and dignified and kills us with a noble quick blow. But the doctors and the nurses won't have it. They will not even let us quietly starve and fade away. I don't say this resentfully but it seems an odd and barbarous paradox.

Went for a walk between twelve and one o'clock and am surprised to see Margaret in her car. "Your father is very bad." He had been out on the lawn as usual. His heart, pulse had gone up. Gladys and Inga carried him upstairs, and Gladys thought he was dying. When I saw him he was unconscious and working hard for breath. (This morning I went in to see him, kissed him many times but he had I think perhaps almost no recognition in his eyes. He made a motion under the sheet with his hand, but on second thought I thought it was not, perhaps, to reach mine.)

Lewis Daniel is here. And Harry Ulrich is coming. Going upstairs, I see Gladys and Lewis by his bed. Gladys in the bathroom crying: "It is all over." I hover around in the nurses' room, see her and Lewis standing over him, on either side of the bed, watching his chest? His pulse? I wander off; come back again and see him there dead, all alone. It is so familiar to see him there. Death is such a commonplace, I am struck with astonishment, and such an appalling mystery and drama at the same time. He looks much as when he sleeps. He has looked too much like this too many nights, when I have looked at him through the nurse's door. But now that ruddy sunburn is paler, yellower. I sit down on the nurses' bed and cry. Inexorable Time. His bravery, gallantry, swagger, truculence, vigor; his beauty, his humor, irony, fight, his integrity. Never in his life did he say anything he didn't mean. George Morgan spoke of this. He knew him as a lawyer in many bank meetings. This was his remarkable distinction: his bold simple vigorous honesty. Nothing was hidden in him. There was not a trace of craft, of lawyer-subtlety, of indirection. So much I have had from him: his physique, his walk. If I am less honest than he, at least himself in me makes me ashamed of it.

I am drawn nearer to his body. It does not horrify me at all. I kiss him. His hands look so clean, so beautiful. Not in the slightest are they an old man's hands. He never was an old man for a minute. His hands, skin, neck, were never those of an old man, nor his eyes. I kiss his face, forehead and cry a little bit and bless his brave spirit, which must be free now and unencumbered. Whence the feeling comes I know not, but like a primitive or a Catholic or an orthodox Christian, I feel certain he has escaped into another more vigorous and better plane of existence, and there his identical personality is exerting itself exuberantly, as it always did. So many nice people are dead and I think they are together in a fine company—my mother, Julie, Helen Baxter's father, Dr. Bendeke, Nansen. How comfortable and interesting and without loneliness it must be.

A year later, looking through something, I came upon some of Father's things, pocket books, railroad passes, spectacle cases. I put them away, valueless as they are, in a closet drawer. A pang of tenderness and love. I say half out loud "precious ... darling ..." and feel just that—as though he were my child. I wish so poignantly that he were here and that I could show him this feeling. And yet when he was here, I had that childish shame, dread, my complex about money, my sense of guilt about being supported, or balked in any way, made a barrier. Too bad. A childish fear stood between him and myself all my life. How badly he would have felt about it.

But he knew before he died, how much we admired him and cared about him and how grateful we were. And I think, I hope that he knows it now.

4.

On learning not to scold people. All mothers should try to be some fun. Working in the garden. Twenty below zero. A hot summer and the house is full of pianos; Seroff.

I HAD GOT ENOUGH CREDITS AT THE UNIVERSITY FOR A Master's degree, but I did not write the thesis and polish off that degree after all. But this was not all due to laziness and evasion. I said to myself: "I will do this instead: I will continue taking work at the University until I at last have enough credits for a Ph.D., and *that* thesis I will really write."

The reason was that I decided I did not want to teach after all, but to write again; because now, after studying, I felt I would really have something to say when I wrote. Besides, there was again a sense of haste and uneasiness about making a living.

March 5th, 1934. Go to the University and study on William of Tyre, reading pages of mediaeval Latin. An agony to be doing this when I should be working, trying to make a living. It is like taking a piccolo lesson when the Titanic is sinking. It makes my head hurt so . . . so mentally pierced.

Now the first thing I wrote was this: Dr. Krey had said that the paper I had written for him, which was to be the basis of my master's thesis, was good. It was on Renaissance education. I thought: "I will make it into an article and sell it to one of the more literary magazines." I was ardent about it. I thought the whole world should know what my ideas on Renaissance education were (and still do) and know how important they are for all.

But it did not sell. And now I know one of the reasons why (though perhaps one of the less important ones), and that was that I railed too much. I scolded. Just think! I have learned at last not to scold people, even in writing. This is a great, great lesson. Everybody, it seems to me, is scolding (except perhaps the professors in their classrooms)—the journalists, the popular philosophers, the ministers, the leftists, the right-ests, the pacifists, the humanitarians, the militarists. A loud or subtle scolding. "Now you should do *this* and I know it!" they are all saying.

But this is wrong. The scolding only adds to the conflict already in people and the world, and the anxiety and the re-sistance to what is true and good. For either people resist your scolding with indignation (as they should, because no one really knows what is good for someone else), or if they heed your scolding, as children do, and suggestible and un-happy people, they try to do exactly what you tell them to, but automatically and externally, without true inner convic-tion and understanding. And this means bleak, dry, anxious, guilt-corroded duty, and unintelligent nervously compulsive forced work, without either enthusiasm or sincerity in it. I am sure that this kind of duty, the feeling that you *ought* to do something because somebody else says so, when it may not be what your own conscience or inner gift tells you to do at all, is all wrong and does so much harm everywhere, both outside in the world, filling it with ugly and unnecessary things, and in people's souls.

No, I have learned at last not to scold people and rail at them, because it is better just to love them and do your own work. For example, when I tell children what I think is true, I have at last learned never to let myself even *think* at the same time: "Now you *ought* to do this, children, because mama knows best; and mama has had years and years of experi-ence"; when the facts are that the children may be entirely different from mama and should not behave as mama behaves at all, any more than the lion should behave like the lamb. Children are so afraid of us because they know we may try to keep them from making their biggest and most important mistakes. And mistakes are often so terribly important, and our only way of learning and progressing.

But I think it is all right to tell people what you believe is true, if there is no forcing or scolding in it. You see people around you having a hard time, trying to work out their destiny, to get free, to be better. Well, we can tell them *our* truth, if we think they want it. That is, we can quietly give them a tool, in their tragic struggle: "You might try this. This may do some good."

But to go back to what I learned about Renaissance education that was so important. During the Renaissance there were so phenomenally many great personalities in the world. It was because of four things.

1. The passion for learning.

2. The belief that the end of education was to make a great personality, one who was complete; i.e., physically fine, intellectually remarkable and also full of feeling; that is, an athlete, a scholar and an artist all in one.

3. And it was because all the children of kings and noblemen were early put into the care of a teacher who was a great man; that is, a good example. Vittorio da Feltre was responsible for three generations of wonderful people in the Duchy of Urbino. And

4. Because in Renaissance education, instead of learning only the theory of things, they got actual practice in it. That is, instead of going to lectures on ethics and the theory of courage, say, they had a great deal of laboratory work in courage, i.e., fighting and danger. And instead of studying just the theory of religion, of charity and benevolence, they had, each person, laboratory work in it, hours of fasting and prayer and giving up comfort so that others might have it instead. And instead of lectures on Art, such as we have in our colleges, in which one learns to identify a thousand photographs of the work of great painters and sculptors, they painted themselves. And instead of just attending concerts,

and poetry courses, they played the lute, composed music, and wrote poetry, all of them.

All this led me to the following ideas: that I want to play the piano myself, and make drawings myself too; and I want to go through physical ordeals and not just read about them. And whatever I can understand with my mind, I want to do and act out with my body. In order to be a good teacher to my child, I want to be a good example first of all. That is, instead of plaintively telling the children to practice their piano lessons, it will do much more good and be more effective if I practice myself very hard, and like music. And instead of being physically limp and weak as so many women let themselves be, I think I cannot be any good in my soul, unless I am light and strong and physically enterprising and courageous, not only throughout youth and middle age, but until I am dead.

And that, in turn, has led me to this thought: if only women, mothers could get this notion of being good examples to their children not only morally but in every way, in one generation, the world would be filled with the most wonderful children. Because in the genealogies of remarkable people they must trace greatness not so much from father to son, as from mother to child, and from teacher to pupil. For example, there was that great teacher-pupil generation in the direct line: Anaxagoras - Socrates - Plato - Aristotle - Alexander the Great. And because mothers are teachers in the most important years of our life, that is why it is now recognized (I have been told this by an historian) that a great man is explained not by his father, as they used to think, but by his mother, who was so much closer to him. Yes, he had an obscure great mother who taught him and was his good example.

But again the above sounds as though I did so much for my child and Julie's children. Oh no. That is another thing I feel sad about, because I could have done so much more. But at least we had fun and talked about many things. And at least I did all I could to bolster up their freedom and belief in themselves. For instance, I believe in letting children see all the time that they are beautiful and wondrously smart in every way. I like to lift from them the strain that makes them feel they must always be trying so anxiously to be good. It just fills them with fear of making mistakes, when the whole secret of a good life is making bold jolly mistakes. For how do you know what is a sin or a mistake until you have committed it? Besides, what is usually called naughtiness in children is something very glorious, enterprising, bold, ebullient and imaginative. And so I have always told the children that I know that I would give a gold diamond-studded naughtiness cup to the one who could be naughtiest for a whole year. "But no half-way naughtiness goes," I said. "You have to be a devil." This of course shows them at once how instinctively, deeply, naturally good they all are at heart, and makes them feel freer and happier and full of ideas.

One day a servant girl was scolding the little Shearer boys.

"You kids ought to live with me," I said, "because of the naughtiness cup."

A half hour later, when I was leaving Pat, who was five, came up and said:

"Brenda, I think I ought to get that naughtiness cup."

"Why, what did you do?"

"Do you know what I said to Roddy? I said 'Damn your backsides, you big pooh-pooh.' "

I shook my head sadly.

"Not half bad enough, Pat. You will have to do better than that." This was an interesting shock to him.

But to show you what we talked about, Gaby and Jeanie and Sandra and I, here is some diary:

March 29th, 1934.

I have to study Latin all morning. Dr. White is so gentle, leisurely and naïvely helpful, and yet so large and regally fine looking. In the class is Miss A. with her pale beautiful highbred face and her enormously bad figure and childlike smile of white oval teeth. She dresses in the most wretched confusion of maroon wool and bits of rat fur with a tinsel hat on her heavy drooping hair, that looks like a pot scraper, and there is the acrid odor of sweaty woolen cloth.

I drive her to St. Paul. She tells me so sweetly, naïvely of her life. For four years she has had to get up at a quarter to six and work until twelve at night; and she walked homeward, zero nights, always to the city limits to get the street car for Lake Phelan, sixteen miles away. This saved her fifteen cents a day. "What about lunch?" I asked.

"I bring it usually."

"Where do you eat it? In Shevlin Hall?"

"No," she says hesitantly. "I eat it anywhere.... In the women's toilet. Oh, anywhere." She is ashamed, she says then, to be seen eating lunch "because so few bring their lunch."

"Never, never be ashamed of being poor," I tell her.

Her mother, she says, is thin, nervous, though all her family have big legs. Just as she has. She tells about what they say at the health service about her overweight. She has been dieting, eating raw carrots and so on.

"I get my breakfast and my mother eats after I go because it makes her nervous to see me eat so little. She thinks I am hungry, though I am not." She says then, that for her four years in the University, she would be going to bed at twelve and getting up at five. "I got only five hours' sleep. But it is funny, I didn't lose weight."

And then I let her out in St. Paul, on a cold dark corner, to wait for her street car for Lake Phelan, her arms full of books, a foot and a half pile. And she is so sweet and so gay and grateful, and it never occurs to her to complain—such a child, and I feel like crying. To think of my having felt scorn....

In the evening in Gaby's room, Jeanie and Sandra are there and the three children are making paper clothes for some play. I tell them the story of Miss A.

"And so," I say, "you can't tell about people ever. You may think how awful they are, how dumb and icky, but you don't know what is underneath, ever. So we shouldn't judge people, I guess, but think of the wonderful courage of the poor, it is just unbelievable. And so there is a lecture for you."

"And a good one, too," says Sandra, and Gaby chimes in: "Yes, it is."

"How many here think they are geniuses, hold up your hands," I say. All four of us lift our hands.

April 6th, 1934.

As I come out of the bathroom today I hear the children, the twins and Gaby, coming upstairs. I crouch down and then spring through the air at them with a terrible pounce, with a willy-wah-woo! the cry of the North Dakota coyote. They laugh, shout and Gaby cries out: "Oh, Mama, how *cute* you did that!" How kids like us weary adults to have a little fun and bounce in us, to be a little rowdy. Of course. More rowdyism for grown-ups, shall be my motto.

Jeanie and Sandra come over to dinner, and we talk about fortune tellers. "Well," I say, "people may really be clairvoyant. I am, for instance. Because I can tell what is going to happen to you."

I grunt a little and then begin to predict, and they are utterly fascinated, breathless, and I can see how they believe every word of it.

Gaby, I say, is to marry a big man named Donovan, a Senator, "the cowboy Senator from Wyoming," they call him, and he wears his hair a little long around the ears and a huge Stetson hat, in Congress. He is Catholic and they have a child named Eileen. She cries out with true sharp pain, because she doesn't like the name Eileen at all.

Sandra, I say, will go to Vassar and not care much for boys, but be a wonder at basketball and biology (it is only too true, she feels, with suffering; yes, that is how it will be.) But later, I say, she will be simply adored by a New York architect named Sebastian Brown, and they will have twins. She is pleased at the architect, dubious about the twins.

Jeanie, I say (Jeanie is a funny, lively charming-looking gawk of a little girl, and has not yet the chic of Gaby and Sandra, so I must make her fortune romantic and good)—Jeanie will marry a French army officer, Captain Pierre de la Chaise, a fascinating man with a black mustache who looks exactly like Ronald Colman. (She is radiant and blushes with flustration and happiness.)

The next night, the twins came rushing over at the same time, when Gaby and I are in the dining room, to go on with the clairvoyance.

"Well," I say, half shutting my eyes, making them go into neutral, a mysterious unfocused gaze, "and so Gaby goes to Bryn Mawr, and everybody thinks she will be married first, because of her success with the boys at the Lake Harriet school, and she does get engaged to Phil Horn of Cornell, who asks her there for the Alpha Delt house party and the Junior Prom. But this engagement is broken. Why? Well, Gaby at that time is a little selfish." (This hurts her feelings and to prove otherwise, she cries out how at the Zoo, she gave five ice-cream cones to the bears, and the twins corroborate this, and it is to demonstrate her amazing generosity and unselfishness.)

I fumble around with Phil Horn and then tell how Gaby goes on the stage, and the trouble is, she does not work very hard and doesn't progress fast; she does not realize at first that to be a great actress, you must not only be a beauty, as she certainly is, but you must know all literature, also French, German and Italian, all about phonetics, and fencing and dancing, music and philosophy. ("Now you are being Socratesish," she says.) But after a couple of years (I say) she buckles down. She is playing the Nurse in "Romeo and Juliet." (Roars of laughter.) They have just seen Katharine Cornell in the play, and Gaby throws a butter knife at me, and her eyes are wet with a confusion of laughter and hurt feelings, for this emotion always stirs in her when she is the butt of a joke. Pew!! That *awful* nurse! (Sandra and Jean flop on the table with their long arms and flat big hands; lovely openmouthed Franz Hals mirth.) "But of course you get the leading part right away," I say hastily.

I then turn to Jeanie. (This is because her prospects are so bright with her Ronald Colman, that Gaby and Sandra feel I have been unjust.) And I tell her how she goes to Leland Stanford and (to make her future less perfect) I tell how after a year in college, she gets so terribly interested in Y.W.C.A. work that Sigurd is worried. (Great laughter from Gaby and Sandra; Y.W.C.A. work, how dumb!) But she does then really marry the French officer (she blushes with happiness and hardly knows where to look) and lives in Paris. (Paris! that's good!) But for most of the time, because he is an archeologist, in the Holy Land (and this makes the other two rock with amusement: that awful Holy Land!)—until he actually digs up and finds himself an undiscovered report written on stone, of the daily life of Jesus in those unknown years of his life, between the ages of about twelve and thirty. "You can imagine how famous that made Captain de la Chaise, and his perfectly beautiful wife."

Sandra and Gaby are looking wistful.

Well (I say), within a year Gaby gets to be a remarkable actress, the greatest in the world, which surprised the people in Europe particularly, especially the crowned heads; for while they admit an American woman might be good-looking, one can certainly never, never be a true artist, for every American woman has really, au fond, the soul of a bridge-player. Well, it is while you are acting that famous gala night at the Paris Opera, that a telegram comes from the President of the United States, President Worthington, who is the youngest and handsomest president there has ever been.

"America's proud of you," the telegram reads. "Stop. I am engaged to Sandra."

April 15th, 1934.

Gaby and friend Polly come in and are rancorous and anxiously embittered because the twins and two other kids are mad at them and have been snubbing them all afternoon (they have these divisions every so often); and I say: "Do this to them," and put my hands fan-shaped, end on end to my nose, and stick out my tongue and cavort around with the most insolent defiant antics I can work up. They grin and are tremendously relieved. How cheering it is to assume that attitude toward what oppresses you. Bernard Shaw: this is his symbol.

May 1st, 1934.

Polly is here at dinner with us. Gaby tells how she had told Inga that Anne Colley was at the twins', so that she could come here. "Never lie to anyone, darling; not even to your mother," I say. This amuses them very much. Polly especially. I lecture them good-humoredly. When they don't want to tell their mothers anything they should say: "My dear woman, I cannot tell you that." I, as an adult, I say, have no right to pry into their private affairs. Then we have a discussion: "Which would you rather be, a coward or a liar." "But they are the same thing," says Gaby. Then the twins come over and we get to talking about Russia. Miss Ray, their teacher, has been telling of the horrors there, and I try to open their minds, to the other side too, to the good things about communism. Very alert and interested they are. They are smart, lively, vital. I speak of the women in Russia. They can be generals and admirals. All discriminations against them are wiped out.

Gaby says: "Well, I don't want to be a general. What could be worse?"

That is true, and good for her. She is more tender and maternal than I am. I have a longing, an admiration for fighting, of some kind. The word "fight" enkindles me. Though I hate murder and hunting and war. Very queer.

Gaby is so gay, exuberant today. Later, she tells me how darling Jeanie is, the most generous person in the whole world; how she would really give everything away. And how beautiful she thinks Jeanie is. "Her big mouth. I like it, don't you? It is so stylish, and her eyelashes curling back and green eyes. Oh, I think she is just a beauty. And you can't imagine really how generous she is, Mama. Anything you do for her, any tiny little thing and maybe nothing at all, she will give you a nickel."

Gaby then complains that just now one trouble with Sandra is that she is often posing, fixing her face, lips, profile. And so she is no fun, "because if you have to have your lips arranged a certain way to talk, you can't say anything interesting." And I tell Gaby how she has me and Inga paying attention to her, telling her how pretty, beautiful, etc., she is, and we keep her beautifully dressed. Sandra and Jeanie have no one to admire them this way.

"When I think of Julie and if she knew how they were now, it just makes me feel like crying. And Julie always had them the most burnished, stylish, brushed, charming elegant children in the world—among all the children the most chic and spruce, like the children of a French countess rolling hoops in the Bois de Boulogne ... And so," I said, "it is up to us, to you and me, to make them know they are beautiful and to do everything in our power."

To all this Gaby listened in dead silence. "You see," I went on, "you know that you are beautiful because I tell you so, and so you can forget about it." She takes it all in, and is moved, I think.

Yes. Vanity can come from too little praise perhaps more often than from a surfeit of it. Perhaps it is always so. That vanity means a starvation of praise and appreciation. I tell her of the most beautiful girl I ever knew in New York. "And perhaps here again," I say, "there was no assurance of the fact that she was beautiful, because her mother and a sister, whom she hated, were very critical, and this made her insatiable for admiration, a terrible dearth, so that she never never had enough of it to make her feel at peace. Why, that beautiful D. would be afraid to go to musical comedies, for fear she would see some pretty chorus girl, even a twentieth as beautiful as herself, because it would put her in a funk of despair for days."

And Ditty, I went on (talking far too much), told me of her youngest brother, William, who is so nice because he was so terribly spoiled. Her father said to her mother: "Now I don't care what you say, but I am going to rock this one." And so William was always rocked and a lollipop slipped into his mouth and pulled in wagons. He turned out to be just a darling.

"Yes," said Gaby, when at last I had finished all this, "I think that is true. I think you are really right." And of course I was.

Then Sigurd married Harriet Fiske, who in a curious way looked something like me, enough so that the clerks in stores downtown got us mixed up. And Harriet had warmth and something that I can only described as "grandeur," perhaps because she had that wonderful ability to love people, and yet never, never to press them. And gradually that family, Jean and Sandra and Harriet's little boy Timothy, became cheerful and jolly, and I did not have to be so anxious about the twins any more.

June 12th, 1935.

Today the three children graduated from the Lake Harriet School. The exercises were at 9 o'clock in the morning. I went perfunctorily and as a duty, and to my surprise, was sadly moved. The boys in their first white long pants, the girls in dresses they had made themselves in sewing class, with flowers pinned to the shoulders and a rosette of the Lake Harriet school colors, satin ribbons of lavender and green.

And the program: there was a trumpet solo (very beautiful) from Clyde Ostrander: "The Lost Chord" by Sir Arthur Sullivan. The trumpet is long and shining and brass and the lifted face and the angle of it, is so archangelic. And Sandra and Jean and two others play Schubert's Serenade; Sandra the cello, Jean the violin, and the piece is so quaveringly interminable, shaky and feeble, but so pretty. Then the speeches. A child would get up (a stiff, straight, little black-eyed girl), and speak on "Leisure Time," saying how one should practice music in leisure time and spend it on worth while things, like reading good books, and not go to trashy movies, for it is such things that were apt to lead one into the criminal classes in later life; and how stamp collecting was a fine hobby for leisure time, because it taught us to love our foreign friends. Character development, that was what leisure time was for. (Thus outraging all her natural instincts.)

Incidentally the program was devoted to internationalism, to pacifism.

A boy then spoke on music: "There was the German Beethoven," he said, "the Italian Verdi, the Frenchman Gounod. In this we learn of the greatness of other lands." Then a poem by Robert Schauffler in which four children get up and each recites about some foreigner. "From Genoa, Columbus..." "Then Jesus, the Jew..." and ending up with the American melting pot.

Well, it was so moving that to my surprise I turned on the waterworks throughout, and was not only crying but sneezing, a general snuffling and sloshing about of all the lymph and tear ducts in my head.

But, as for Gaby, she was not pathetic at all. In fact she was all self-confidence, general derision and smiles. When the class earnestly sang the "Volga Boatman" (they touchingly had devoted their study to Russia this year—they were so full of praise for Russia! it was really extraordinary, considering the politics of the present) she stood in the midst of them and sang not one note, but wigwagged and signalled and smiled at everybody in the audience.

Then there was the giving of the awards, athletic letters and so on. There was the Dean Shaw reward for leadership. The American Legion award to the president of the class, Chester Knutson. (When I ask Gaby about him later: "Is he so wonderful?" "Not specially. He is the kind grown-ups think is wonderful, but not children, so much.") One award was a C (made of green flannel felt outlined with lavender) and these C's stood for Character and Conduct and went to all children who had perfect marks in Conduct and Thrift, and like virtues. Only two boys got it and a vast proportion of girls who wore glasses or were too fat or too thin. A dubious honor. Gaby was so relieved she did not get it, and far from it, thank God! she said. Apparently she was quite a rascal in school. Much more than I was (I am glad to say)

who had not the courage to stand up against the teacher's disap-
proval—not in her rollicking way.

Sigurd and Harriet were there to see the twins, and I suppose
were also secretly sobbing. Sigurd afterwards was so amused. "Do
you remember your graduation?" He said it was downtown in
the old auditorium, but all he remembered was giving the Lake
Harriet school yell on the street car.

After that Gaby went to West High School where I had gone.
And there she is now.

That spring was the first time that I had a garden and the
last one. It is too dangerous, an opiate. It was too tempting,
like playing the piano. All one's time and thoughts and energy were bled away into that garden.

There is a long strip of vegetable garden which runs along
the western lawn. The western lawn is a lovely place. The
lake is on the north and the white barn on the south of it, and
there are charming small trees there, a choke cherry that is
so perfect it is like a tree in a legend. Inga watches this
choke cherry tree out of the kitchen window and she cannot
bear even to have its lower branches bumped into by small
children. And if the man who mows the lawn comes too
close to it, she will run out and give him the dickens. There
are also horse chestnut trees here, with their straight candles.
It is a fine protected sunny place for tea or cocktails.

In this spring of 1934, Pete, whom my mother had so
gravely called Mr. Gunderson, left, and because he was a
mean, smiling ruffian, we were all much happier. We would
take care of the vegetable garden ourselves. And so we divided the strip into four sections and each family would work
its own plot.

April 22nd, 1934.

We all dig in the vegetable garden, spading it up. "I have a
feeling," I say, "that Rolf's and Margaret's will be the best."
Rolf hearing it, a smile breaks through his sad, immobile, preoccupied face. "You said it."

Harriet and Sigurd were there and all the children and dogs and
cats and all the neighbors' dogs, and beyond, by the section by

the lake, were Arnulf and Louise. The Sigurd family and I are the dishevelled ones. I am in white sailor pants, and barefooted, and my hair is in my eyes. Harriet is sitting in the dirt and her hands are black and she works slowly and contentedly, stopping for cigarettes and wine; and all her tools are strewn about. Rolf works in a quick deft way, and his garden has the order of jewelry, and his hands are entirely clean. Margaret is silently working with the most exact knowledge, which she has got out of books. She has really thought about gardening and though her arms and legs are bare, she somehow looks chic, as though in a cocktail lounge. Beyond are Arnulf and Louise; Louise, tall with slightly gray hair and a childlike wonderfully pretty face, a little-girl face. And Arnulf handsome and romantic looking, with sunburned skin and a dark mustache. Louise wears gardening gloves and slacks and looks as though she were playing tennis at a lawn party. And Arnulf too.

We are all happy in the sun and sweating. Harriet and Sigurd get tired first and go home to their terrace to smoke and drink wine. Rolf remarks about the tools they have left strewn about: "How much do you bet they will still be lying around two weeks from now?"

May 19th, 1935.
Seduced again by the garden. Work all day from nine to six-thirty. I should have been working on my "Miss Swanson" story. Dirty, bare back boiled, gently sweating, nearly naked. I transplant zinnias and plant onions, tomatoes. Also bachelor buttons. Now a little square place is left for Sweet Williams, and I am through.

Working in the garden I am contented and happy, digging in the dirt, mulching with my hands in it to the elbows. But I have not a thought all day, not a thought. Abeyance of will, like an amoeba. It is a state like dozing. This placid well-being is all very well (it is not deep; underneath one's conscience gnaws at the placid torpor), but many use it as an opiate, to hush all the striving intellect. There must be both.

I plant the tiny Sweet Williams. It is jeweler's work. Little plants. "Little Plant." That is what Francesca called Julie. And I feel so tenderly about them and think while doing so, how I really should not even be a vegetarian. I feel really so touched, mournful when a tiny one out of the hot-bed must be discarded and so die. I think of this humorously, but I am glad I have enough imagination to feel so, however faintly.

I am thinking in the garden, sitting there in white under-pants and grubbing, how grateful we should be to feel hate, blood-thirstiness, envy, malice, all those feelings, for that is the only way we can have insight into murderers, evil-doers, sour people, and be forgiving . . .

At four o'clock, Henny telephones and asks how I am. "Fine. Well, pretty good. Fair. Gloomy. I mean suicidal. Come on over."

Inga brings out tea to us on the big silver tray (it's her idea) and a fresh cake with jelly between the layers and powdered sugar on top. It is so sparkling and elegant, this tray, and Inga with her fresh face, her swift rotund body in a starched green dress and white apron. I am dirty from bare angles to hair, and sunburned, in a loin cloth practically.

Then Henny and I play tennis. Suddenly I know how to hit the ball, with a free catapulting wallop—hit it just right. Perhaps no other woman knows as well how to do it: a loose shoulder and fist gripping the racket like a hammer. Yes. And I am really going to become a good player? If I had the time now . . .

The next winter, 1936, was the most wonderfully cold one. For six weeks it was more than fifteen below zero, and once, I think, it was thirty-eight below. And there were high piles of white blinding snow with paths cut through them, so that they rose above your head like a giant lemon pie.

I walked just the same. When I do not have air and exercise, I get what I call my "Mrs. Gummidge mood." You remember Mrs. Gummidge in "David Copperfield," who huddled indoors by the fire all day and complained dismally how she was nothing but a "lone lorn pore female critter" whom nobody cared about and who suffered a great deal, in her snuffling way? Well, this Mrs. Gummidge mood seems to be in all us women, a substrata of grievance, plaintiveness, a subtle and indefinable mood, which I do not show much externally. But it vanishes like a phantasmagoria in thin air, when I exercise out of doors, breathe and sweat, and lo! I am free and easy, kind of cheerful. Yes, I think the Mrs. Gummidge in women is due to the lack of circulation, a stale body and the cozy asphyxiation of central heating and too much

to eat. That is what makes us so atrabilious. Remember that.
So I walked every day, just the same.

February 6th, 1936.

This noon I went around Lake Harriet and two miles farther.
It is more than 18 below zero. But I am warm. I wear as always
my burglar suit, and under it two layers of wool underwear, and
two layers of truck driver's mittens under horsehide, a Norwegian
ski cap with a visor. I am warm in this cold, though the air is a
sword in the lungs. It is very beautiful. The sun is a blare of gold
in the pure blue sky and everything is so still, golden, pallidly
golden. No one is out except an occasional snow plow or milk
truck. The drivers stare at me, smiling through their closed-in
glass cabs. Two dogs come out barking at me, but overjoyed to
have a human being out and walking, and they frolic around me,
their joy overcoming their hostility and their barking indignation.
They nuzzle my glozes, hold my hand in their mouths as I walk
along.

Mrs. Gummidge leaves me and at once, with this air, I become
good-natured, fresh-faced. A roysterer. I must always always exercise....

Saturday we skied: me, David Shearer, D. Spencer and the
little boys. My horrible indoor face which looked yellowish, gets
red. There is nothing more wonderful than this skiing; the ex-
hilaration, the beauty of the world, the interest in trying! I do
what David and Hank Norton and D. Spencer do, except that (I
am ashamed to say), on that icy bald hill, when they fixed sticks
to go around, I did not try it. I tried it from a lower angle, but
not from the top. This was the girlishness . . . And on the other
hill, through the woods, I did not go down. I looked at it but did
not plunge. Again this is womanish—not to attempt the difficult
and the alarming. But I did go down it later, stemming well, and
D. Spencer shows me how to make a left turn—a hitch from
the knees and an easy turn with the swinging sticks, a kick out
of the left heel. I feel it a little. I try it many many times.

I ski home from beyond Kenwood. There is heavy going because there are no tracks across the lakes. On Lake of the Isles,
there was that sunset. The sun is a rose-colored ball of quiet fire,
and the low ceiling of clouds is lead gray, and broken softly like
sheep, and each leaden scallop of dark gray is limned with rose-
colored fire.

When I am on Lake Calhoun it grows darkling. The middle of the lake gives me a feeling of Siberia, the desert, of God-filled quiet. And I work along sweating and breathing hard, practicing long strokes and running. The silence and the cold winter air and the beauty of winter. I think of Nansen, of my feeling when I read his book on Siberia, and how I wanted to be there with him. The glorious loneliness. And I think of the times I walked over this lake: twenty-five years ago, when I walked home from the *Tribune*. And when I walked along it, when I was married to R.—one day particularly when it was rough and cold and the jagged waves were green and I, married, felt caught—felt I must surely escape. The thoughts in my mind then were of Paris, Moscow, China.

Then I stop skiing just for a little while. I think: "Yes, I must stop and hear what is said to me in this moment." We are always striving forward so that we do not stop enough and listen. I stand still. At first there is longing, the hollow feeling that I cannot take in this beauty, and there is a sense of flatness and non-ability. "This is not the poetic fervor one reads of in literature." But presently it comes, and I don't fret about details, and I begin to feel it so poignantly. The ghostly masts of ice boats are fifty yards from me. They are caught in the drifts of snow. How silent is this fading light! What depth there is in space, the mysterious space between me and the masts, their guy ropes! How beautiful they are, twenty of them, in this luminous, cold, lowering twilight. The street lights, far away around the boulevard, are yellow now and big four-pointed rectangles, because it is early and not black night yet. The blackness makes them shrink to white stars ... Yes, in such moments I suppose we are what they call "living eternally."

Then I go home, read the newspaper, write a letter of complaint to the gas company, have meat loaf for dinner, and go reluctantly to a meeting of the Parent-Teachers' Association, making a few remarks when called on. Oh, lordy! why does my voice sound so queerly hearty, like a middle-aged clergyman at a young peoples' get-together? I thought I had kicked my sweet-goody-goodiness in the pants.

For the next three months, from February until June, I wrote every day some news for the radio, and I did it very well and made some money. But toward summer I felt low-spirited and quite downhearted for a reason that I cannot tell

about. And when this is so, I have this longing to go far
away, to be disconnected from any base, and to move through
some vast distance, endless space—perhaps on the Trans-
Siberian railroad.

Anne in New York was taking piano lessons from Seroff,
whom she considered an extraordinary pianist, a genius, a
wonderful person. She thought it would be good for Seroff
and all of us if he came out here for the summer and lived in
our house and we all took lessons. And I thought: "Fine. If I
can't go to Siberia, why, Siberia and the Caucasus and Vienna
and Paris can come here in the person of Seroff. And that
will be the next best thing."

Harriet, Margaret, Dorothy Lewis and I and all the children took lessons. There was a Steinway concert piano as
long as a locomotive in the sitting room, and another one for
playing double pianos; and our old family piano was hoisted
upstairs in my room, so that music, the sound of practicing,
now came floating out of all four houses, and even from the
upstairs windows, all day long.

Seroff was Russian, young and black-haired with small
slant eyes and a cowlick in his eyebrows and darkly, tragically
handsome, especially when he was gloomy and contemptuous.
But although cold and haughty to strangers, he was funny,
twinkly, humble, off-hand and affectionate to everyone he knew
well. In his short Tyrolean pants and red suspenders and loose
dark-blue linen shirt, he would go slapping up and downstairs in his slippers, and in and out of the kitchen and down
to sit in the lake, with the water to his waist, while he read
the newspaper. For as the winter had been cold, the summer
was the hottest one there had ever been. "Today you are Papa
Bach," I would say to Seroff, when he was so *gemütlich* and
entertaining and wanting company and (I think) almost
afraid to be alone.

But in giving lessons he was fierce and contemptuous—
or, it may have been, just to me. He was terribly scornful of

the measliness of effort that he would get out of us. Of course I had to astonish him. I wasn't going to have *that*. I worked like the devil with my very limited knowledge and technique.

"All right, if you think you're so much," he would say to me, when several people were at Rolf's house, "play your piece for them. The Moussorgsky."

"Sure I will. You bet your life." And I would go to the piano and tackle it, hammer away as best I could.

"All right, Indian, if you think you're such a pirate. Play the Schumann Fantasia."

"O. K."

The first day he came he seized upon a word I use very much: "namby-pamby." Thereafter he said that about almost everybody. "Ahk! *she* play the Appassionata? Never! too pansy-wamsy!" Or if you said that you have been practicing for three and a half hours: "Practicing! I heard you. You were just lullabying yourself!" And at a lesson, when you started to play for him, a Mozart concerto, say, he shouted and tore your hands from the keys. *"No!"* And then he would shriek. "Put something into it! When a Russian makes love they *crush the bones!*"

That was a lovely summer. Seroff would practice for four or five hours every morning, such wonderful music, like Beethoven's greatest sonata, No. 111. And you cannot imagine what an effect that has on you, to hear that music again and again and again, as though you were absorbing some kind of blessèd, blessèd mysterious sunlight. One Sunday morning Sandra consented to pose for us, so out under the elm trees, we all drew her with pastels—Anne and Ken and Elsa too, for they were home then. And Seroff's music came floating out of the sitting room window. That was one of the best days of my life; that unspeakably beautiful music floating about us and touching us all with gold, and the summer day, and all those nice people. And my drawing of Sandra was just wonderful.

VIII. THE PRESENT

1.

I have to say some things above love. Gaby wants to talk to me about it. My symbolic dream: William Blake talks to me in the thunder.

WHEN IT IS ANNOUNCED THAT YOU ARE WRITING AN AUTO-biography, people think, with a kind of delicious disgust, that now you are going to tell all about your love affairs. And certainly it is true that being in love is about eighty-five per cent of our lives, and the great river of energy, hope, bewilderment, and thinking pours into that. So it has been with me, I am glad to say, and always will be.

But, as I said, I cannot tell about it specifically because it always involves somebody else and I have no right to pontificate upon what is in the soul of anybody else, because I don't know. I may be entirely wrong. No, the others must tell their own story.

And so, on the subject of love, you will have to put up with generalizations, which always conceal very much (and will make me out much nicer than I am), but I will try to make them as truthfully as I can.

After I was separated from R., for quite a long time I did not have any love affairs. I did not want to be married again. It was queer that before I left R. I had flirtations; but I think this was due just to that competitive protest: "All right, *you* are such a man of the world! I guess *I* am not so unattractive either." So many young marriages can be a kind of mutual watch-dogism: "All right, if *you* have fun, I guess *I* will have some fun too; and see how you like *that."* As though one should not be absolutely overjoyed when someone we love has fun and a lively time! But it takes a long time to see this, and then years and years to be able actually to live it. Perhaps I cannot, even yet.

But in a curious way, as soon as R. was out of my life, then I dropped my flirtations immediately. Or am I lying? No, I think this is literally true.

But after quite a long time, I fell in love again, and that state has been almost chronic ever since then. But by some chance, whenever I have fallen in love, it is with people I cannot marry; that is, either they have lived in Europe, or in Seattle, or where I do not, or are married already. Could this be because unconsciously I do not want to be married, and am afraid of it? This is a possibility, though in my conscious thoughts marriage seems to me the most distinguished, lovely, wonderful state, and I am always wishing that I were married, and thinking how nice I would be then, and how generous, and full of fun, and how, after all my experience, I could make the person I was married to feel both loved and free, and not smothered, and how I would be no expense to speak of. Well, it is too bad. And why didn't this happen?

This may be an explanation: because, as I have shown you, for a long time I felt that falling *out* of love was the great, stimulating, and enviable experience. That was because of my discovering that repudiation, being cast out and alone, always means an extraordinary and vivid life, even though a sadder and more uncomfortable one. There are things in my diary like this, that seem to prove it:

December 10th, 1929.
And then I think, coming home in the car—and I say to Margaret: "Perhaps we should be fiery and strong enough not to get attached. All this love nonsense, all the thought expended on it, and the aura of sentimentality. Ridiculous. And, look, how when you become fixated, all the future is shut down, all the

mysterious, exploring, adventurous future. That is, just as soon as you fall *out* of love, you think of being in China, Tartary, Patagonia—seeing and learning all things yes."

April 29th, 1930.

A sunny day. But there is little resilience in me lately. Julie is at Westport with the Taylors.

We talk of marriage, sex, the Minneapolis necking. It is most undistinguished, low-brow, she insists, and I agree. Then we argue about love, because I say I would never lose my integrity, my proud solitude, never surrender and merge myself in the loathsome cozy way into the other person. (This is boasting; I haven't accomplished it, but I maintain that I aim to.) For from this proud solitude one is never timid, anxious, afraid to tell the truth, and accept the truth as it is.

Julie says that perhaps my cool armor is lack of feeling. But I don't think so. I had that horrible experience of jealousy for six or seven years, and so I learned how to overcome it. Will never have it again for long, for a thick self-protective cicatrice is now formed.

But how I talk in these diary excerpts! It is most of it boasting and how I would *like* to be, for I have never been able to maintain this fine Nietzchean hauteur for more than a week, if for three days even. Unless I had a tremendous amount of love and admiration from other people—friends, family, men—I experienced to a point that was unbearable that peculiar loneliness: "foxes in the breast" as Robert Jones calls it. Yes, the North Dakota coyotes of loneliness are howling in the soul. "Loneliness on fire," Ray Gauger used to call it. But I was always ashamed of feeling this painful weakness, which of course made it all the worse.

May 1st, 1930.

I tell Julie about the loneliness of not having anyone in love with me. Infantile need, etc. And oh, gosh, I have it! and isn't that a fright? And yet, I say, I think how lonely X.'s life was, and Z.'s, because children and friends do no good in those moments. But it is some sort of complement, a true steady love that one craves. And yet, I say, how uncomplaining X was. And Julie laughs and says:

"Well, what about you? You don't think you are complaining, I hope."

But at the same time there was another reason why I did not marry anybody, and it was much less imposing and fine than the proud-solitude one. Because my diary says: "I tell Julie how I discover that so much of my life is directed to getting that delicious thing, admiration, to *charming* people. That is why I am afraid of "getting tied down by a love affair." Because thereby I must forego that delightful thing —arousing hopes in others.

And so you see I wanted to be free because it was a dangerous and living state, and so that I could continue to have other men like me, not just one.

But now I think of it, this is something of a libel, for I never was completely selfish; and now I know I am hardly selfish at all. And of course there is another possibility: that nobody came along whom I could completely and truly love and marry.

Well, all this was eight or nine years ago. But not even yet have I achieved the proud-solitude state. No, I am always inextricably attached to somebody, or thinking with semi-romantic interest of two or three people, or trying to get free from them, or trying to be much better and kinder to them. And my diary, to my surprise (for I had not known it until I began to study it, for this book) continues to be, eighty-five per cent of it, a record of emotional backing-and-filling, and I-said-and-then-he-said, an endless search into this love business, and what in thunder is it?

And this may be one reason for it: Ever since that proud-solitude period, I have been growing less and less egocentric, and more and more kind and warm. And now I have so much of that quality, which women have a great deal of (and men less, though all of them should cultivate it and pray for it), i.e., that power to encourage, foster, praise, appreciate others, and make them feel beloved, happy, and strong and full of life. Why, sometimes I think I can permeate people with it, as with a golden cloud, a kind of interpenetrating blessing, although this of course, may be my illusion, my superstition. And now that I know what it is, I think I shall always have it, even if I live to be ninety, and men will like me then too.

For what is so often mistakenly called "sex attraction," is warmth and generosity, a spiritual thing entirely and not a physical one. It is centrifugal (generous) and not centripetal (greedy). Of course it charges one's physical body with some beauty too, that is, it probably gives you a good complexion and a fine eye and a small waist, but it does not spring from the physical self at all. That is the mistake, I find, that so many men make in their notions about love. They neglect their imagination and feeling, i.e., the spirit, to pride themselves on their virility, when the first are the only things that make men lovable or even virile. At least all the first-rate women I have ever known seem to feel that this is so.

But now about my love affairs ("love affairs" sounds so cold-hearted and frivolous and I have never felt that way about anyone), I must really be more specific.

There was a long, truncated, sad love affair which lasted many years. It was a mistake, I have thought. All loss. I mean it was such a loss of psychic force, such a leak in my energies and integrity. And it was wrong and hard for him too, because he could not feel clear and good about it. One thing I am glad of is that there was never any lying in it.

Here is an example of my mental writhings over it, from my diary. You might think from it that I am violent, but that is because my vocabulary is violent and varied. My actions are hardly ever violent.

April 7th, 1935.
In this love business, I must stop this cavilling, self-pitying and belly-aching (most of which is internal, and may not show). Alone, alone! I need *no* one. Remember that and make a note of it. Only then will I have strength so that I can be of some use to

my friends. All love, romance (so much, much of it!) is a wish
to be cozy, safe, a return to the water-tight womb; a mutual-
admiration society. So much of it is that way, and that is why it is
bad for people ... the deterioration of marriage. And then they
stir each other up [I am always trying to raise his friendship-
affection temperature] with disgusting fallings-out in order to re-
unite in a delicious coziness. [Now, in 1938, I think perhaps you
never do this if you really love somebody.]

Oh, yes, some love is glorious. I think it is so when you admire
each other. But I mean admire each other with great passionate
feeling; I don't mean just fishy intellectual admiration: "Yes, indeed, I esteem you for a number of good qualities and particularly
for your splendid stand on the Pact of Munich." No, it is like
this: Say he has courage and I have kindheartedness. Why, by admiring (passionately loving) his courage I will get some of it, it
will be added unto me, and in the same way he will get from me
whatever it is that is worth having. Then you are really doing each
other good, i.e., becoming like each other. But how can you admire
each other much, where there is a comfortable compromise? and
you are making no sacrifice anywhere, not one? How can women
do men any good when they are nothing but a pillow? ... I suppose I have real true love for Bach, Beethoven, Michelangelo,
William Blake, and God. And of course for five hundred others.

My diary, as I said, is full of this—crammed with long
discourses and wrestlings on this subject. It is full of my
feeling of vexation and emptiness, and then my feeling *guilty*
about my vexation and emptiness, because he was so good,
such a dear. Oh, all that. And now I read these things and
groan over their useless interminable length. Because perhaps
this was the simple truth: that we did not love each other.
Where there is a tremendous amount of talk and wind in that
way, this is almost certain to be the case.

I have an idea that if it is really love, either you do not
forever fret and rage against a compromise, or there cannot
be any, and you just have to be together throughout life no
matter what happens, and that is all there is to it. But at least
I discovered that in my case, if it is just a kind of mutual
comfort, then it is no good. Because a thousand times I would

tell myself: "This is fine. This is consoling. Think how we help each other and make life pleasanter!" No good. I just would again sink into an abyss, and feel corrupted and weakened by it. I think it is because a compromise like that is so uncreative. You cannot build anything together or do each other any real good. You cannot make each other more full of life—only more dull (because all compromise is dulling) and comfortable. And in spite of yourself, instead of making love important and serious, you are reducing it (as thousands of people do in order to be more comfortable, and they are so sadly mistaken!) to a peanut butter sandwich. I hate that idea that one reads about in French novels, where people seem to think of love, which is so great and important, as a delicious little dinner with wine. It may be all right for some, but I don't like it.

But you may begin to feel that I think, as rather prudish women with congenital low vitality do, that the physical part of love is perfectly horrid, and it should instead be unctuously "spiritual." Oh, I should say not! The stronger the physical feeling the better. No, to me "spiritual" means only this: that the feelings, the heart, must be involved, the strongest and most passionate affections, and not just the intellect and the body (the only abhorrent sensuality is that of cold intellectual people). That is, one must be able really to feel with violence and complete sincerity: "Oh, this person is a darling, and his whole life is very important to me!" That is all it is.

So I now think that true love means this: that you are able to give your life to this tremendous generous feeling. And that is why I can see at last, after thirty years, why marriage is a sacrament and a religious thing, i.e., you try with all your spirit and imagination to do each other good.

Yes, even weddings, which seemed to me so obnoxious when I was sixteen, may be all right, though I hope I will still be able to hold out to the very bitter end against ever being engaged.

But to go back to my changing from an effort to be proudly alone, to a wish to be kind and generous. My loving-kindness, for a long time, was very hard on me because whoever was fond of me took so much of my time and emotion. Again I got no work done and made not half enough money. I struggled against this kindness, or weakness, whatever it was, and saw all the flaws in it.

I am glad you turned down that foolish woman [I wrote to a man I knew]. You and I are too kind (weak). I have been thinking about it. It is a mess and a kind of inverted egotism. It is not bracing or good for people to be kind to them. Really it is feeding one's own sense of power. *Heraus* with that stuff! It is like the slimy kindness of some cooing little women who want to keep everybody in their power; and like those maniac nurses who feed their patients arsenic to have the pleasure of alternately murdering them and saving them. It is much better to make people stand up and take an account of themselves and not lead them on and make them happy in their maudlin ways.

Yes, sir. We are quite a lot alike, but I am much worse than you, rascal and pet lambkin and nice young man that you are. So know that I am haranguing myself. Yes.

But now I have struggled so hard against it and without one trace of result, I think I will continue to be as kind (or weak, whatever it is) as I possibly can be, and accept it as I do my eyes and nose. Perhaps it is both the weakness and the great noble thing about women. And perhaps it explains one of the difficulties of love between men and women. Women perhaps are more generous with their admiration and their feelings, and then presently they get a little resentful because men do not show that same wonderful generosity to them.

Joe and Dagmar Beach and I were talking of the difference between men and women in love, of the yearnings of women and the boredom of men with that. Dagmar spoke of Byron's remark (always so trying to first-rate women): "Love is for men a thing apart, 'tis woman's whole existence."

Afterwards I thought of this and this may be the explanation: We are all looking for a mother, i.e., one who gives praise, backing, unflagging admiration, belief in us, fostering, tenderness. Men find it in women, who if they are any good never fail to respond to this yearning, to the I-want, I-need sadness. But women cannot find this everlasting mother in men, or very rarely. And so women are always a little en-hungered. I think this must be so, because one of the loveliest women I have ever known, so undemanding, so beloved by men, once said to me: "You never get love when you need it most, from men." I don't think anything sadder was ever said.

Men—we *like* to have them need us, while it puzzles and perplexes them when we need them. They do not praise or encourage us much, except to encourage us to be more encour-aging to themselves. (I know a very brilliant young man who is most pleased with his wife when she has cooked up a batch of cookies for his dinner. Well, cookies are fine, but imagine if we only spoke and praised men for their cookies!) But remember always that I love both men and women. I just think that they should borrow some of each other's virtues.

As for Gaby and love, I have never held anything back from her that I have thought—that is, if she cared to talk about it—and whatever sins or mistakes I have made, she can know them too; and often I have asked her advice and got good sound answers.

This is one reason, I think, that she is casual and free about telling me any of her emotional turmoils, jealousies, jiltings, and passions, for of course she has many of these things, now that she is a very popular seventeen and can shag and truck and Charleston to beat the band, and is so pretty that really I think she is Miss Western Hemisphere.

One night last summer I was playing the piano and Gaby was upstairs in her room reading. She came down.

"Mummy, will you come up and talk to me. I am not lonely at all. But I have been reading an article in *The Reader's Digest* called 'A Plea for Chastity,' and it makes me feel awful . . . I don't know, it seems so awful, and I want you to talk to me about it."

We go up.

"Don't read it aloud. Just read it and then we will talk."

I do. The article is all true factually—statistics, psychologists, doctors, and so on—but there is in it only the vulgar truth of all generalizations on such subjects, when the only truth is individual and within, not external. The writer says that to a shocking degree the younger generation all are having sexual intercourse, in cars, etc., and before marriage; that it is bad for them physiologically; there are abortions; that it tends to make them promiscuous in their habits; that men after marriage don't like to find their wives are not virgins.

I say to Gaby:

"Well, darling, I will tell you. Now I don't know at all what your experience is and I will never ask. I once pried into your life a year ago, wondered, snooped to find out if you were spooning with boys, and so on. I saw from your face that I was doing what all adults do, with their adult ideas and habits, so revolting to the young who are idealistic and romantic."

I then find out from Gaby, at once, that this is so.

I go on to say:

"About love, I can't tell you what to do. You must do what you feel is right, and you will know, and of course your ideas of what is right will change all the time, and they should. And you can talk about anything you want to with me. Sometimes I think this: I rather hope you will not have a real love affair or get married for a long time, well, at least until you are twenty-three. Then you will know more people and you will have had some fine adventures and a chance to support yourself and be independent for a while. A love affair is a terrific bond, almost a slavery. It is all right and fine and poetic, but it is a terrible bond.

"And everybody is different," I said reading on into the article more statistics about the gigantic sale of contraceptives. "There are over-sexed people, but they are good people too. I know a girl, one of my best friends, whose sexual life began at thirteen. Well, I like her, I love her. Perhaps it is too bad, but anyway she did, and perhaps she couldn't help it, and she is different from me and many others.

"As for me, I was a rebel, and perhaps you don't have to be. But I rebelled against the injustice of the attitude toward women, and the mercenariness of the women's attitude. That is, they said if you don't behave and stay a virgin, then you won't get a husband and be supported throughout life. I wouldn't have that. And also I felt that it was cowardly of girls to be afraid of what prudish people thought, and calculating of them—not noble and pure at all. That is, it isn't very noble to refrain from certain actions because then you will not be able to inveigle someone into marrying you.

"The thing is, if you fall in love with someone, try never to lie to anyone else, and least of all to yourself, and second, always take it seriously and feel responsible for the other person, and feel it is important and hope that it will be forever. Then whatever happens it will be all right. It is not the physical outer behavior that is bad, but what is inside. The contempt for your partner, instead of love and admiration, that is the worst thing.

"And remember this: in Dostoevski's 'Crime and Punishment' there is a little prostitute, fourteen years old, who is one of the greatest noblest souls that ever was on earth. And don't forget that. She had to be one to support her family. No, it isn't what you do that is important, but the inner feeling."

Well, I think what I say to Gaby must be all right, because she is so nice: neither coquettish nor arrogant nor prim, but wise, tenderhearted, and full of fun.

As for me and what the future will be like for me emotionally (it is just nonsense, the notion of the young that people have no romantic feelings and impassioned love after forty or sixty or seventy), it ought to be much happier and more important than before, because after this long puzzling search and experience, at last I think I shall know both how to be alone, integral, and how to love people at the same time.

I hope so. At least one night last spring, when I was troubled and confused by these things, I had a wonderful symbolic dream.

May 20th, 1938.
What an extraordinary, amazing day! Exploding with inner joy. I bent over and laugh—such a bubbling in my chest and thorax, it makes me silly. Last night I had one of those sickish nightmarish nights. There was wonderful thunder, rolling and bombing big guns, from St. Paul to Linden Hills and back again, with never a silence. It was William Blake talking to me. I dream uneasily. I am half awake part of the time, and uneasily aware of Mabel's Teachers in the room (Mabel is my friend, a little Swedish clairvoyant, and these are the radiant beings that she sees in her visions). Anxious and afraid. Half awake, I turn on the light and it must have burned brightly most of the night. But Blake kept thundering. Then there was a dream. I did not understand this dream until I began to write it down. I was writing a book and it was all confused, a confusion and a jumble. Then as a great clarifying thought, the idea came to me: "Why, yes! Call it Tanagra" (it was not this word exactly) and I felt all was cleared up. Why, of course. And this Tanagra (there was in it an Hungarian idea) was a wild lonely galloping horse or horseman, and that was the subject of the book, and what all the book was about.

Well, as soon as I tried to express all this, in a letter to Anne, I saw at once that Blake was thundering to me to be a wild lonely galloping horse, compact in myself, in my life and my work; not to be just a tenderly loving woman, being bled of anxious love by others and encouraging and nursing them, particularly men who like me. No, I must be compact in myself, in my own thundering, exploding, blazing work.

I tell Helen Baxter about it, this rainy noon—all about this dream and the feeling back of it. Yes. One can only have power and do good for others, if one is an integral center of power one-self, not by being just a ministering angel. That is the trouble with women—they are so generous and good and it is so easy for them to be good to others and bleed their lives away in it; and I feel so sorry for them, because they have no concept of work, of action, of violence and striving. And if they are lonely and un-happy, and their husbands cannot see at all what is in them, and they love someone who cannot return it, or be with them, they just diddle and wash out their underwear and yearn. Oh, I am so glad I am a wild thundering horseman, a Valkyrie, that I have this idea of myself!

2.

A writing class; the pupils teach me many things. Walking; I find that physical condition is not the panacea, but the Imagination. Am I too much like my Uncle Fred? I look forward to everything, including eternity. I shall always be growing better.

NOW I AM COMING TO THE END OF MY BOOK. I MUST SAY A few things about writing, walking and religion.

I always thought I disliked writing, until recently. When I was in New York trying to sell things it was always such up-hill work, so hard, so boring, something that your mind flew from and had to be dragged back. And underlying it all there was a kind of shame, a feeling that it was an ignoble and conceited thing to do.

April 9th, 1938.

I ought to work myself up to a real enthusiasm for writing, in-stead of being ashamed of it and half-hearted. I have this attitude: that I really hate writing, especially fiction, and think all current writers are fools and show-offs. This is very bad.

But at the Hodsons', that wonderful Bill defends writers against me. "Why, nothing, nothing is so wonderful as a great book!" he says. This cheers me up. He tries to explain away my feeling that it is show-offism and a wish to get money out of people by being a mountebank.

But nevertheless, for years afterwards writing continued to be hard, mind-wounding work, except for diaries and letters which could be poured out at the rate of three or four thousand words a day. Of course I loved great writing—Tolstoy and Dostoevski and Chekhov and Shakespeare and Euripedes and Ibsen. But who could be like that? Not me. Hardly, if you were "slanting your stuff," as the horrible phrase is, for the *Woman's Home Companion*.

December 19th, 1935.
My literary agent sent back some of my unsalable stories. I am shocked at how bad they are. This is terrible—to have the time and money to think up such repulsive flubdubbery. Olaf's (the hired man) work is honorable and decent.
A letter from Elsie Arden saying that Y.'s last book is good, beautifully done, but lacking in feeling. And I write: "I know what you mean. It seems to me true of almost all literary people, except the Titans. They write so exquisitely about life, but do not let the true life that is in themselves ever show in it. I sometimes think it would be better to be a dog-catcher."

But gradually I seemed to discover the philosophy and meaning of expressing what is in us, whether we are great or small, in writing or in anything else, in music, in carpentry perhaps; and how we must do it, for in our own tiny way we are all prophets and poets and minstrels like Isaiah and Homer and Bach. And I saw how expression is a generosity, not a conceited self-indulgence. That is, you just tell sincerely what is inside and give it to people, if they want to hear it. But you do not try to fool them or astonish them into thinking how wonderful you are.

Then three years ago I began to teach a class in writing at the Y.W.C.A., and these inexperienced people—stenographers, housewives, and even a few very simple and ignorant people—taught me more about writing than I had ever known. For from their scratched diaries and letters I saw this: that all writing (and I mean *all*) is alive and interesting if it comes out freely and truly. What makes it dead and tiresome is the so-called "literary effort," a kind of striving to be effective, instead of just opening your mouth and telling what you have to say. I saw that if a person does that, speaks from himself like a prophet, the words will not make any difference, or the spelling, or the arrangement, or the style. The life in the words lies in the truth and freedom with which they are spoken.

Well, this changed my whole life, and I got to love and respect writing. And even if I never make any money at it, and have to go to work in a ten-cent-store basement, I will continue to write what is within me. Because writing is the action of thinking, just as drawing is the action of seeing and composing music is the action of hearing. And all that is inward must be expressed in action, for that is the true life of the spirit and the only way we can be continually discarding our dead and mistaken (sinful) selves and progressing and knowing more.

That is why now I like writing this book. And I have not the slightest sense of apology because I am writing about myself, because here is one of the things I have learned from my class: that *everybody* should write about himself; that whenever people write from their true selves (not from their bogus literary selves) it is interesting and one is pulled along into it; and it does me good to read it, and it does them good to write it; it makes them freer and bolder in every way.

There are others in the class who cannot write about themselves (sometimes it takes months to give them a swashbuckling, free, to-hell-with-teacher feeling), and they hide behind dry travelogues (because they think it is more dignified to write something you can find in any guide book) or behind mechanical little stories, or in an ambush of elaborate adjectival humor, so that their raw souls will never be seen or known. This is usually called "modesty" and is drilled into people when they are young. But whatever it is, it is all wrong. And of course these modest, hiding people are gifted too. But as long as they hide, what they write is not interesting, because they are dissembling. In writing as in conversation, unless you mean what you say, it is not interesting to others and only an up-hill grind for yourself.

This is what has led me to the belief that there is too much hiding in the world, too much splendid reticence; not enough transparence. For say that you hold back one thing, for years and years, such as the fact that your father was a mean man, presently you will be hiding the fact that you love your wife, so that not only will she be miserable and bleak and bored, but actually the power in you to love somebody will dwindle and die away. No, the spirit, I think, is a stream, a fountain, and must be continually poured out, for only if it is poured out will more and clearer streams come. Where do we get this idea that it is only reserve and self-hiding that are noble and worthy? I think it is just as much hypocrisy to show the world a cold, matter-of-fact exterior when you have a warm violent inside, as to show a warm gushing outside and be cold within.

August 23rd, 1937.
Miss Quinlan has us for lunch downtown to meet Elizabeth Fraser, a journalist. She is stout, looks Scotch, with dark red hair, turned up nose and hazel brown-green eyes, and even her hair is in a little pug behind under her tricorne, like a laird's. A nice woman and tells of knowing Borah and Senator Glass, etc., and the inside dope on everything in the world, and all is told very impressively. When they ask me about my writing, I say my plan is to win the Nobel Prize in 1943 and to be canonized in 1947.

Now there is one more thing to tell about: my religious feeling. I have a theory that it came about through this chain: I was fat; that led me to walking a great deal; that led me to thinking and searching; that led me to being religious.

Walking meant being alone for an hour or two every day, when I cannot read or talk. And being alone, and even wretchedly bored, and limited to my own consciousness, to the sky, and the wind—this has given me all that I have in my soul now, all my thoughts, my consciousness of what life is for, my optimism. And being outdoors and in motion is now to me the secret of all cheerfulness and courage. Fine, bright, pure ideas come into me from some place, from the sky; I think perhaps from God.

If I had not been fat, what would have happened? Well, perhaps I should never have got to walking, and consequently to searching and puzzling inwardly. Probably I would be now a happily married prosperous, stoutish woman, with a mink coat, with several nice children; well-dressed, extroverted, active, aggressive, quite a know-it-all, though in a very nice way; very civic, a crack on foreign affairs, insistently cheerful, saying to disheartened people: "Nonsense! Don't think so much about yourself.... Mrs. Peebles, will you serve on the new budgeting committee?"

I would probably have certain disabilities that I have not now, that is, I would have to wear glasses (my eagle eye, I think, is due to the fact that I look at distances for a long time every day), and I would not have such good feet, as solid as tripods and smooth and plump and without tension, like paws. That is because I walk and wear very broad shoes and have good foot action and toe in. And I probably would, by this time, have had a couple of operations, because I am naturally gluttonous and I would always be eating too much if I did not have so much prolonged motion. Yes, I think it has given me more physical exuberance than most women.

August 25th, 1937.

Anne has come. Oh, my! I am so glad to see her. She tells of the dreadful New York and Connecticut weather. Enough to make you throw stones at your grandmother. Gertrude is here and we play tennis in the gemlike pellucid *Minnesota* weather—sapphire lake, sparkling green dragonflies, golden rod, two-gallon stars hung low in the romantic night.

I play a peculiar game of tennis. I never seem to win a point (with a fairly good player); that is, for each point we are rallying for ten or fifteen minutes and then they win it. But their knees are buckling at the end. Not mine. I walk off with an earth-spurning tread.

April 10th, 1938.

Oh, this spring day! The sandpipers looking inquisitively into the icy blue water, wading knee-deep. So sweet they are. The little ducks offshore. The two loons have arrived again, in their evening suits. What soloists! You try singing as high as a loon and you see they are an octave higher and it is still as sweet as music. Only birds really enjoy the weather in all its variety and see it all, every dawn and every twilight, and all kinds of clouds and the jagged agate waves in November and midsummer nights.

I walk for two hours and then go and meet Henny. "Say, let's walk around Cedar Lake and play on the boxcars," I say. But she won't.

For there is some romantic overtone that makes me like walking on railroad tracks and across country. I like the idea of being a runaway, an escaped convict, or David Balfour sleeping on the moors in his plaid. Last summer I walked in the country for twenty miles, and when I rested in the sun, a slow freight train came through a cut in the barren field. How easy for me to have got on it! The tramps all waved in a friendly way. Because I had been alone and out-of-doors all day, I liked and understood them and trusted them much more than if they had been school teachers. Such a sense of freedom and fearlessness comes to me if out-of-doors long enough. I could hardly keep from gently swinging on that freight train and winding on down to Milwaukee. I could find a piece of bread in a garbage pail for supper. Why, that would be all right. One's body, if there is enough sun and motion, does not require neat dinners and doilies and all. A few years ago Sigurd's twins said to Gaby: "Brenda looks like a robber." It was probably because my hair was shaggy and in Shetland pony bangs. I was so pleased with this description. What a compliment! I still am. But why I don't know. I cannot at all explain why I am more pleased to look like a robber than a pretty lady. There is no sense to it.

But to get back to what I was thinking about when I was walking. At first there was just an effort to get physical perfection and I guess I overdid it at times, for I experienced some times of exquisite mental suffering.

September 20th, 1931.

I do not smoke. I am tempted to, often. I feel morose and acutely melancholy most of the time. And there are compensations in mental acuteness and oh! the extraordinary fascinated delicacy of my perceptions.

To Zelles' for music. We all play Haydn ensemble. (Tootle-de-toot, tootle-de-toot!) Want so much to be liked, feel forlorn, and yet ashamed of the impulse struggling in me, which watches to see if people respond to me. It is terribly uncomfortable. A real funk of loneliness; afraid of Time and Death, and to be alone.

But in this state I must remember there is such wonderful sensitiveness—an alert, brilliant, clear perception. That is why I am miserable. Because I can think so fast, can see so many sides, see all the facets of my striving personality, my vanity, etc. It is a passionately ambitious state, as though I will burst if I die without amounting to something. Ego, yes, but thank God for this egotism. A table has it not, nor a chair. It is not a striving just for admiration, but to be *worthy* of admiration, to deserve it. There is such thirst for life, for beauty in it. And so I must endure it.

And I think how, if I am this way (and continue so because of this severe physical effort), it is this misery of loneliness, this struggle against puerile vanity, that will drive my forces into something *outside* myself. And so I begin to hear the music better. (We all play the Fifth Symphony.)

Yes, this is a hyper-imaginative state, because at night I will think with such terrifying vividness of the day in Stamford when the telegram came about my mother's death. It is too clear, too clear, glass-clear, brilliant! and I turn from it in fright, blot it out quickly. But it is better, better to be so than a clod.

I write a passionately hurried and energetic letter to Anne at six o'clock. And tell her a little of the above ... how walking around the lake I see the moon and am filled with horror and wonder that there *is* a moon, and what is it?

"Remember to live," was Goethe's motto. *Memento vivere.*

Then when walking I began thinking of the things that Francesca said.

I understand all you say in your letter, darling Francesca. [I wrote to her] although I would like to have it all elaborated, just as in reading the New Testament, I wish that Jesus had been more explicit. . . . Soon I would like to get to work on something I like. But I would like to have it useful and for the glory of God. Not self-expression.

Yes, you say things that set the ideas exploding in one successively, like those beautiful skyrockets that you think have gone out, and behold there is another burst of stars. Such as a thing you said to me about "getting inside yourself" and writing what is there. I don't think I have ever been at the center. So much is acting and performance. If one could only find the center, what force! what unflinching bold freedom there would be!

And now there began an effort to love other people. Why should I feel that I should? That is unexplained. I wish I could see the books of the Recording Angel on that. I think it was that I saw that in the presence of good, unself-centered people who can truly love something outside themselves— well, at once you know they are extraordinary and better than the rest of us, that they are arch-especial for some mysterious reason. A mystical warming power seems to come from them, so that you feel better immediately. I used to feel that as soon as I saw Kreisler, even before he played.

It was entertaining to dislike people and jeer at them, but it began to make me more and more uneasy. But still, I would say to myself, people certainly are lemons, fools and dolts. Why in thunder not say so? But in the midst of my conviction that it was all right to be cold and jeering, I would read something, perhaps from Van Gogh's letters: "The more I feel there is nothing more truly artistic than to love people." Or: "If one only bewares of becoming a prim, self-righteous prig, one may be even as good as one likes." Or the Bible:

"Who cannot love his brother whom he hath seen, cannot love God whom he hath not seen."

Reading these, at once I would know: "Yes, it is true." But what is love? "Love your neighbor. . . . Love your enemy." But how can you? You can resolve to do it and act it, but at once you hear your own voice and you become a sickening hypocrite and goody-goody. Is love a feeling? If so, I haven't it, I would think, studying my sensations of the moment. "No, I don't seem to have any particular feeling."

But I felt more and more uneasy about disliking people and deriding them.

September 21, 1935.
Troubled by M. She is such a knocker. That bad habit of finding everybody trying, limited, imperfect, with the result that all affection and admiration are snuffed out, a progressive sterility of feeling until the heart is a tiny cinder.

October 29th.
The saints, it is interesting to note, consider the greatest sin, gossip and depression. Cheerfulness is the rule.

November 6th.
Mrs. Baxter says cross talk about those who have vexed you is just an antic of your personality that is not you at all.

Must, must not talk versus people ever. Be like Hobhouse, Byron's friend, who told people their own faults but never told them anybody else's.

Yes, we are lost on this planet and where are we going? Some few people are lost but have fulfilled themselves, like Bernard Shaw, El Greco, Fritz Kreisler. But the rest of us—millions that have something pure and radiant in them, are lost, wasted, clogged, misdirected, tripped, discouraged.

And I have thought lately, how strange it is that we dislike people for their faults, are angry at them and shut them out of our sympathy. And yet nobody wants to have their faults, their meanness, their physical unattractiveness. They want to be beloved, golden-haired and beautiful gods. Of course. Really the meaner people are, the more compassion we should have for them. One could if they were children. If only one could be fond of them steadily, they would not mind if we told them what was true. It is only because the truth is told in moments of hostility that they harden and the battle is on. I wish I could say some time, and it would be so: "But I do not dislike or hate people for their faults." [I have come to this: 1938.]

I have really looked pretty lately. Limber and gentle. I have felt like a kind-hearted lovely kind of a lady. But a masculine spell is beginning. I can't keep my mind on using lipstick, can't remember to put on jewelry. I have a new coat. A soldier coat. It is green lined with red, with postilion flaps behind. Napoleon's coat for his trip to Moscow. Isn't it funny? when I am a pacifist. I wouldn't even fight the D.A.R.

"But what is love?" I went on puzzling and examining myself. "Do I love people enough? I cannot say that I feel an overwhelming love for anybody," I would think with self-reproach.

But then one night I had a very comforting dream. I dreamed that Rolf and David Shearer and I were skating on a river, and we stopped to look at a wide hole in the ice where the gray, dark water flowed along; and suddenly the ice that Rolf was on gave way, and he went under, disappeared out of sight beneath the cold, moving water. I had in my dream, as never in my conscious life, a rush of the most overwhelming love. I cannot describe it. I have never felt anything like it. "I will get him out, right away. I will pull him out this minute," I thought and dived in without one second's hesitation. There was not one split second's doubt or fright about it. I would just get him out, that was all.

This dream was tremendously consoling to me, because I saw that love, courage, are subconscious and very deep, but they are there all the time though we don't know it. So I stopped trying so hard to have conscious love and blaming myself if I did not. "Don't think much about it. Just do what you can for people."

Then at last I got a new concept of understanding people that was above my former intellectual one, of comparing, criticizing, and measuring. And this seemed to resolve that problem: how can you love somebody who you see clearly with your intellect is dull and disagreeable?

It is this way: with our intellect, we say of John J. that he has on the one hand some good qualities such as his undoubted devotion to his family, his accuracy in keeping accounts, though on the other hand he has a certain peevishness and is undeniably not as clever as Edward E. and has less perseverance, as shown by his tendency to go on relief. And so you pin him all out on the slab and divide minutely and name each part. But not true at all. Because every analysis is an autopsy, and as soon as you dissect and divide up, the truth, the life, has fled.

But there is something higher than the intellect. Blake called it the Imagination, and some call it the spiritual self. Anyway, it is the thing that sees and understands John J. as a whole—sees and feels the whole truth, inner and outer, sees his limitations, his struggles, his starved potentialities, his course in the universe, in this life and the life hereafter. So Christ is right: you have to love him because he deserves it and because it is the only thing that helps him and makes him expand.

And now I have come so mystically far that I think love is an actual thing—not just an emotion, a pleasant warm feeling in my chest, but a stream of power that you can send out to people without speaking and across great distances; that it is an imagined (but real) translucent stream of pure golden power which turns every molecule of the person you send it to (whether it is Thomas Mann or Hitler, and I send it to both of them, and they both need it badly, as we all do) into a two-hundred-watt electric light bulb. Or as I write to Gertrude: "I send telepathic love, and whenever you give a little involuntary skip of joy—well, that is it."

I am joking, but I also mean every word of it.

Well, it was this concept of using something higher than

my reasoning intellect, that seemed to make it possible for me to reconcile my two warring selves, my doubleness, the thing that I describe as the struggle between my mother in me and my father, between self-forgetting and belief in myself, between humbleness and arrogance. This means my energy can pour out better.

Because both are good. Why, you cannot have enough of both. And what is evil then? Why, evil I think is opaqueness and muddiness, the primordial mud out of which we are struggling. We are always falling back into it, but that is nothing to be worried about so long as we get clearer again. Evil is just hindrance—hindrance of others and ourselves, that is, of our shining evolving selves. And therefore what was good in us yesterday will be evil tomorrow, when we have passed on to a clearer understanding. But we must never be afraid of moving forward boldly and making new and greater mistakes.

And this is what I try to do now, when I walk: I try to use this Imagination which is high above my arguing intellect. Some think that my walking is calisthenics. But if I walk only for exercise, then after three days I become just meaty and muscular and want to drink and eat a great deal and tell people where to get off, and I am scattered and indecisive and there is no impassioned interest in me for anything, that is, I find that my ears prick up only at some slightly malicious gossip.

But I no longer have these violent revulsions from one side to the other of my character, as though I were a ship with loose ballast in it. And I am no longer so hard on myself, such a flagellant about my slumps. I just take a longer and more tranquil walk and try to see with my imagination how I really want to be.

The most important thing I have learned is to reconcile selflessness with a tremendous belief in myself. And this is the way I have done it:

I think people confuse the Human ego with the Divine one. But you cannot have enough of the latter. The Human ego is conceit and obtuseness to others and it is static: "Look at me, and see how remarkable I am!" The Divine ego is a liquid eternally-moving-onward stream which says: "I have a god in me and this is what I think and believe and care about, and tomorrow it will be something different and better I hope. And now tell me what is in *you* for that will help me to understand everything better."

And that is why those gloomy, homely, hideous Christians who go down into the catacombs instead of coming up into the sweet air, depress me—and once, even that great Tolstoy, who has explained so many things to me. Last winter I had influenza and I read again almost all of Tolstoy and, as always when I read him, I wanted to give all I have to the poor, wind straw around my legs with criss-crossed clothesline, and live on a frozen raw carrot a day. But this time his insistence on our loving *others* only and ourselves not at all, began to be terribly depressing.

His power and his greatness [I wrote in my diary] but his snobbishness about what is good, i.e., that all is bad but his particular ever-loving peasant. "The Kreutzer Sonata" is not a great story, for it is impossible that two people could live together and have children (five) and feel so to each other: no laughter, no helpfulness ever. And I am suggestible and shudder just the same. Feel upset about me and my life.

And look! Here I have been reading volumes of Tolstoy for many days. But that reading a thing, a great thing, that intellectually *taking in* a thing has no effect on oneself at all. I see that I remain cantankerous and vile all the time. This is because I don't say my *own* prayers and I am not alone and walking for hours. It is like X—he accepts and understands great ideas, but they do not become his, or a part of him because he does not pray.

I walk west in this brilliant light. It is perhaps five above zero. Pale blue sky. Not a breath of wind. Pale thin sunlight. How long it takes my imagination and will to come to life again! But it does after an hour or so. I think of the Sun god, Baldur, that shining young man, and I will slough off this dry cocoon of a stupid, middle-aged, fretful, disagreeable person. I see that dry shell falling off and the clear, aristocratic, radiant being emerging. I think of Tolstoy and how wrong he is to say how we should all be dirty moujiks in hideous clothes (that is what it would amount to, if we kept scorning and degrading ourselves forever, to be good to others) without the slightest personal glory or radiance or pride or sense of beauty. What good would we do each other then? The more glorious I am personally the more good I can do to other people, the more weight my good will to them has.

I stop in to see Helen Baxter, so funny, wonderful, and blue-eyed. What would I do without her? I tell her how Tolstoy depressed me. And then I say gloomily:

"What if Tolstoy were coming tonight to spend a month—say I had a telegram that he was arriving on the Hiawatha. . . ."

Helen cries out:

"Oh, no! Wire him at once. 'No thank you! Stop. Bridge lunch Minnekahda Club. Regrets. Stop! Unavoidable.'"

We laugh then, thinking how if he should come we would have to change our plans. Inga's wonderful lunch of popovers, rolled lamb chops, salad with artichoke hearts, would have to be hidden, and Inga would have to rush out to the garbage can and see if that old hunk of bran bread, as hard as rock, that had been thrown away, was old enough to use.

I feel better. Walking home I see that the palest sun comes through and is shed into the air gently, and the snow falls thinly and softly in the air, and with a turn of the flakes in this sunlight there is a diamond sparkle. And I think that Tolstoy's feeling that others, *others*, are the only important thing, is not right at all. Why, that is the whole trouble with us poor namby-pamby, excuse-making, child-chauffeuring, nose-wiping, shopping, ribbon-matching, doily-carrying, recipe-collecting, ministering-angel women, becoming more worthless, empty and plaintive because we tell ourselves it is so unselfish. No, *ourselves* are important too. The power inside.

Now this is my religious belief, and there is a kind of logic in it. It is simple and childish. But I will put it down just the same. And just when I shrink to think how intellectually unsound it is, how without the slightest proof or

foundation in fact, as they say, how superstitious, I begin
to think perhaps Whitehead and Eddington and Sir James
Jeans, with all their tremendous structures, have not worked
out anything more likely to be true. But I don't think I am
superstitious. Superstition means that one has a fixity of
belief, as though it were a charm. But my belief is never
fixed, but a kind of moving open-mindedness.

"The only thing displeasing to God is unbelief," says
William Blake, and I seem to know what he means. And he
says:

> If the Sun & Moon should doubt
> They'd immediately go out.

What do I believe then? That we live forever. Some people
are less good than others because they are, so to speak, still
in the third grade. This is an explanation that makes it easy
for me to forgive them, even if they are murderers, for I
would like to help them pass to the next grade. I believe
perfection is implicit in all, but it takes time for it to evolve.
But why fret then? God can take his time. He can wait.
Time is nothing to Him.

I have found that the superficial conscious will, jerked
about between breakfast and lunch, does not do much good
in expanding our spirit. But solitude and praying do. I am
embarrassed to use the word "prayer" because it has such
repulsive, cringing connotations from old-fashioned Sunday
school. Even the word "God" has been marred a little bit for
me. But I think prayer is a wonderful thing, because it is
the use of the Imagination, the Poetic Genius, which Blake
said was God in us. It is a kind of eloquent, free, improvising
let-go, so that we can see the new vision.

I do not believe in duty or "discipline" when it forces and
dries up people's true conscience, as it usually does. For so
much of this duty is living up to *other* people's consciences.
That is the reason for the cruelty and meagerness of the

Puritans, people who really wanted to drink and eat and make love, and needed to for their own development, but who, trying grimly and dutifully to live up to a conscience higher than their own, and making everybody else do likewise, injured their own souls very badly. A Shelley or a St. Francis, with a lofty sensitive conscience and life-conception, can be an ascetic and shed goodness, because he does not do so from duty but from his own lighted imagination and conscience.

I think God is a person and not a law. Because you cannot love a law. And anyway the personality of a mouse is greater than any law or abstraction or mathematic formula ever devised.

I believe in wonderful egotism, in being "kingy," as Inga says; that the malaise of the world is so-called modesty. I believe that we should all have a reckless, indomitable, arrogant, joyful blaze of self-esteem, self-trust, self-belief. You cannot have enough pride or egotism or energy or bravery, but it must be centrifugal (generous) and not centripetal (greedy).

I know that we live after death and again and again, not in the memory of our children, or as a mulch for trees and flowers, however poetic that may be, but looking passionately and egocentrically out of our eyes. And I know there is nothing to worry about on earth or in Heaven or in Hell. That is my belief.

Of course sometimes I have misgivings that I am like Uncle Fred. He was my mother's brother, a handsome, warm-hearted, brown-eyed man with thick hair and a brown mustache. He was so idealistic, so soaring, so full of beliefs and optimism. (Just like me.) When he had time he went to four improving lectures a week. (Like me.) And when his fortunes were shrinking, he was always sure that six months from now, by growing some apples or something, there would be plenty of money. Yes, about money he was an utter mysti-

cal pudding. . . . Like me. And as for my belief that everybody in the world is talented and great, if only we can take
the cover off them—I have just found a letter that he wrote to
Mother about his wife.

Aunt Katie was a tiny, plain little woman, wrenlike and
not particularly cultivated, a good, an adamant Christian and
church-goer. She was a Waterbury, whatever that was. But
she had not style or swing like my mother. Well, when Uncle
Fred's lumber business in Ada, Minnesota, dwindled to nothing, they went to Boston and lived in an apartment, a duplex
some place. And this is what Uncle Fred wrote:

Katie is in considerably better health than for some time past.
If finances were easier, it would not be long before she would be
well up in the best of Boston life. In one of the leading Congre-
gational churches, they are after her for advice and direction in
their numerous charities and well-doings. My respect and faith
in her powers grow with the advancing years. I doubt if there
are many her equal in leadership in great and good works found
anywhere. I have faith to believe that even yet she may find her
place in New England literature and influence.

Oh, dear, this is just like me, I think with a tiny shock.
But never mind. Uncle Fred and I are right. At least, what
we feel is right for us.

For when I have misgivings that I am nothing but a mystical pudding, and I go back to common sense and fine prac-
ticalness, saying to myself sternly: "You have a fine mental
instrument, and so use it, as other people say you should!"
And so I do: prudence, adding and subtracting. I even begin
to think of a budget and I try to plan and I say pettishly:
"I will give so-and-so fifteen minutes on Wednesday," etc.
But after about three days of this, I descend into Hell. I
cannot stand it and don't see why everybody who is this way,
including the U. S. Supreme Court and Owen D. Young, does
not commit suicide. And so again I believe in God and the
archangels and saints and talk to them all earnestly and
affectionately. Well, that is the way it is.

It is now February 9th, 1939, and Thursday, and it is now five minutes past two o'clock in the afternoon, by the clock on the shelf in the upstairs hall, which has such a pretty, bonging strike. It is twelve above zero outside, and there is a swift whirling snowstorm, so there is no horizon. Sky and earth and lake are white. The world is drained of color and sound, and there is just a prolonged flute note of wind on middle F, and the snow flies spasmodically and like clouds of white horses. You can see it against the black, patient, bare trees.

I sit here looking out the window. I have been working all night. I am wearing dark-blue flannel sailor pants, heavy brogues, a white cotton shirt, a red bow tie, a white sweatshirt washed so much that there are holes in it and the sleeves are frayed. I need a walk badly, for I have been working much too hard and steadily under pressure, for the last two months.

And it is queer, I have not a touch of resignation about the future, or nostalgia, or poetic mournfulness for the days that are gone. I seem to be entirely cheerful and full of anticipation. I seem to be always holding my breath with suspense, as though something wonderful were going to happen the next day and the next; and I wish everybody in the world could feel this way.

And now good-by.